DISCRETION AND WELFARE

DISCRETION AND WELFARE

Michael Adler and
Stewart Asquith

 Heinemann Educational Books · London

Heinemann Educational Books Ltd
22 Bedford Square, London WC1B 3HH

LONDON   EDINBURGH   MELBOURNE   AUCKLAND   HONG KONG
SINGAPORE   KUALA LUMPUR   NEW DELHI   IBADAN   NAIROBI
JOHANNESBURG   EXETER (NH)   KINGSTON   PORT OF SPAIN

British Library Cataloguing in Publication Data

Adler, Michael
   Discretion and welfare. – (Studies in social
   policy and welfare; 15)
   1. Social service – Great Britain – Administration
   I. Title   II. Asquith, Stewart   III. Series
   361.6′0941   HV248

   ISBN 0–435–82009–5

Printed in Great Britain by
Biddles Ltd, Guildford, Surrey

Contents

Acknowledgements

Many individuals and several institutions have contributed to the production of this book and we are grateful to all of them. We would, however, like to record our special thanks to Professor Raymond Illsley for his initial help and encouragement in planning the series of interdisciplinary workshops on 'Discretion and Social Policy' which gave rise to this book; to the Social Science Research Council for funding these workshops; and to everyone who attended the workshops and contributed to them. We should also like to thank Professor Robert Pinker, our series editor, for the care with which he assessed the papers prepared for the workshops and for his continued help and encouragement; David Hill of Heinemann Educational Books for his patience and general helpfulness; and all the contributors to this collection. Our thanks go both to those whose contributions were submitted punctually for their forbearance and to those whose contributions arrived somewhat later for eventually submitting to our persistent exhortations. Finally we would like to record our thanks to the University of Edinburgh for various kinds of assistance in the preparation of the manuscript, and in particular to the secretaries who re-typed several of the papers.

M.A.
S.A.
University of Edinburgh
September 1980

Introduction
Michael Adler and Stewart Asquith

This book contains a selection of papers which were originally presented at a series of workshops on 'Discretion and Social Policy' which the editors organised during the academic year 1978/79.[1] Although each of the papers has been revised for publication, the many developments in social policy that have taken place between the conclusion of the workshops and the publication of this book inevitably means that some of the references in the various chapters of this book are already somewhat out of date. However, this is not the case as far as the general themes of the individual chapters, or of the book as a whole, are concerned.

The establishment of the workshops was prompted by a number of developments in social policy that have taken place in recent years. The growth on the one hand, of bureaucracy and professionalism and, on the other, of the powers of the state have led to a situation in which the public are increasingly dependent on the decisions of administrators and professionals in the public services. Similarly, the growth of delegated legislation, administrative rule-making and departmental codes of practice and the (characteristically) weak forms of professional accountability have meant that many of these decisions are not prescribed by statute but are instead left to the exercise of official discretion. Whether or not these discretionary powers are greater than can be justified, the ways in which these powers are exercised are, or at least ought to be, a matter of considerable importance. Whether they are exercised by rule-making bodies or by individual administrators or professionals and whether they are concerned with the meeting of needs, the allocation of resources or the infliction of punishment their exercise raises important questions of welfare, justice and accountability. Such questions have, of course, been addressed by lawyers and social scientists but, by and large, their concerns have been governed by the dictates and interests of their respective academic disciplines.

In recognition of the general lack of communication between lawyers and social scientists, one object of the workshops was to provide a forum in which lawyers and social scientists could discuss the common theoretical and methodological problems raised by research on discretionary decision-making as well as their substantive conclusions. A second, and related, object was to identify those theoretical and methodological approaches which seemed most fruitful and those substantive issues which appeared most important and which together could serve as the basis of a programme of socio-legal research in this area. These two objects also provide the underlying rationale for this book.

In response to the growth of discretionary powers, there have been a number of appeals for a 'return to legality' whereby discretionary decision-making would be made subject to judicial review. Unfettered discretion, it is argued, leads to arbitrariness, unfairness, inconsistency and injustice, and it is only through judicial control that individual rights can be protected. However, in 'Discretion and Power', **Adler and Asquith** point out that the very existence of discretion reflects the powerful position of welfare institutions in society and suggest that attempts to control discretion which ignore the relationship between such institutions and broader social, political and economic forces may lead to the extension of *procedural* rights without in any way improving the *substantive* entitlements of those who are dependent on welfare. They criticise the theoretical sterility of much positivistic research on discretionary decision-making and argue that research from an interpretative or phenomenological perspective, which links the exercise of discretion with 'operational ideologies' has much greater potential. The theoretical significance of focusing on ideologies is that it points to the need to explain whence these ideologies are derived and how it is that, under certain conditions, particular ideological positions or forms of knowledge carry greater legitimacy than others. Such an approach requires a form of analysis in which discretion, knowledge and power are articulated in a framework in which micro and macro-sociological concerns can be reconciled.

In 'Discretion as an Implementation Problem' **Young** espouses an interpretative perspective and stresses the importance of subjective factors for understanding why agents and agencies act as they do. This is achieved by exploring the 'assumptive worlds' (which comprise the values, beliefs and perceptions individuals have of the world they act upon) of actors at the periphery of policy implementation. According to Young, the outcomes of a policy system are determined both by the degree of control over policy implementers and by the extent to which they share the policy-makers' 'definitions of the situation', that is by the degree to which they inhabit a common assumptive world. One advantage of Young's approach is that it transcends the restricted usage frequently advocated for 'implementation' and 'discretion' in which only evasion (but not conformity) is seen to call for an explanation.

In 'Discretionary Decision-making in Social Work' **Smith** attacks any attempt to define *a priori* the different possible meanings of discretion and any *a priori* assumption that discretion should be curtailed rather than expanded. He argues that the meaning of discretion can only be discovered by studying its use in specific contexts since the *language* of discretion can only be understood in relation to the *action* of discretion. It follows that discretion must be treated as a *topic* of research rather than a *resource* for research and that attention should be focused on the practical accomplishment of what the actors refer to as discretion. In the field of social work, Smith argues that the key question concerns the meaning of discretion for the various groups who are involved in the provision of personal social services and points to an apparent paradox in which professional social workers who are generally thought to exercise considerable discretion may not (because their decision-making is highly routinised), while clerical and administrative staff who occupy more mundane positions and are not generally thought of as exercising discretion may in fact determine the quality and quantity of service received.

Giller and Morris adopt a perspective similar to that advocated by Smith. In 'What Type of Case is This?' they present some results from their case study of social workers' decisions concerning children taken into care. They focus on the social workers 'operational philosophies' (defined as the means by which professional ideologies are mediated through the exigencies of practice) and argue that social workers locate cases on a care-delinquency continuum after ascertaining the moral status of the parties concerned. Decisions are not made but, rather, emerge as natural and logical responses to the way in which social workers interpret the case in the light of their practice-based ideologies. Thus, Giller and Morris are able to point to the implications of the social workers' operational philosophies for the routine accomplishment of their tasks.

Whereas the exercise of discretionary powers provides the point of departure for some papers, the existence of institutionalised discretion provides a starting point for others. Thus, in 'The Political Economy of Administrative Discretion' **Winkler** argues that the current concern with administrative discretion is but one manifestation of long-term structural changes in society. In the first part of his paper, Winkler argues that the exercise of discretion has become, at the same time, more frequent and more contentious. This is so, firstly because the role of the state in relation to the economy has shifted from being supportive to being directive; and secondly, because the retreat from the concept of a comprehensive welfare state has involved officials more in the exercise of 'negative discretion' – that is, in the denial of citizen's claims on the state. In the second part of his paper, Winkler analyses the implications for the provision of welfare and related services of two of the most important changes in the nature of state activity – controls over the primary distribution of real income and the 'off-loading' of welfare provision onto the community. His argument is that the issue is not one of more or less discretion but rather that the form in which administrative discretion manifests itself is being transformed in a number of ways. The changes in the exercise of discretion are thus qualitative ones.

Winkler's argument about the process of 'off-loading' the implementation of social policy onto voluntary bodies is considered by **Bradshaw** with specific reference to the creation of the Family Fund. In 'From Discretion to Rules', Bradshaw concedes that the establishment of the Family Fund (which was set up in the light of the thalidomide disaster in 1972 to allocate grants to severely disabled children) was an example of off-loading but argues that the government's reasons for setting up the Fund were very different from those postulated by Winkler. In so doing, he points to some of the dangers inherent in inferring motives from functions. The main part of his paper describes how the Family Fund developed from a flexible operation staffed by social workers (who all had considerable discretion) into a more rule-bound organisation staffed by clerical and administrative personnel. According to Bradshaw, the change took place in response to the pressure of work and the need to process applications rapidly, budgetary pressures and pressures on the Family Fund to maintain a degree of equity in its operations.

One of the major themes to emerge from the workshops was the need to analyse discretion in a broad social, economic and political context. In 'The Politics of Discretion', **Prosser** stresses the importance of understanding how discretion fits into the broader social structure and how its form and operation are determined by social, economic and political factors. Looking at the origins of unemployment assistance in 1934, Prosser argues that the existence of discretionary powers in the legislation was a crucial part of the government's attempt to disguise the fact that it intended to cut benefit levels. Prosser concludes that discretion (rather than rules) can provide the means by which government may avoid resolving difficult policy decisions by not stating clearly the policy being followed. Thus discretion may exist not just because rules are difficult to frame but because it performs the function of blurring political issues and disguising events likely to produce conflict. Turning to the Supplementary Benefits Review of 1978, Prosser argues that increases in the number and changes in the composition of claimants had made the supplementary benefit scheme virtually unworkable and generated considerable pressure for administrative rule-making. He maintains that a concern with individual needs is incompatible with the requirements of an organisation dispensing poor relief on a massive scale and that the main proposals were merely an attempt to improve the administrative efficiency of the supplementary benefit scheme. He concludes that pressure for more procedural rights can provide a basis for criticising policies and generating conflict but that procedural rights do not necessarily confer advantages on those affected by them since their existence can limit opportunities for exploiting the existence of discretion in advantageous ways.

Unlike Bradshaw, **Noble** argues that the Housing Corporation (which was set up under the 1974 Housing Act to promote the development of housing associations and to exercise some degree of control over them) exemplifies the processes of off-loading and co-optation described by Winkler. Moreover, he claims that the government's motivations in establishing the Housing Corporation were those that Winkler identified. In 'From Rules to Discretion' Noble describes how the Housing Corporation set about the task of registering housing associations. Rules and standards were laid down but unqualified associations were nevertheless registered. Noble attributes this failure to apply the rules to agency philosophy, the value systems of the field staff and the resource and time constraints under which the Housing Corporation operated. Thus the Housing Corporation and the Family Fund were pulled in exactly opposite directions. In his paper, Noble also refers to the very extensive and largely unchecked discretion of most housing associations e.g. in relation to house allocation, arguing (against Prosser and others) that the achievement of enhanced procedural rights is important, particularly at a time of public expenditure cuts in housing.

With specific reference to criminal justice, **McClintock** in 'Some Aspects of Discretion in Criminal Justice' argues that control over discretionary decision-making is particularly difficult to achieve where no one is responsible for the exercise of discretion within the system as a whole and where there is a lack of agreement about objectives and about the means of achieving them. He discusses de-criminalisation and the introduction of more face-to-face processes of social control (as advocated in the papers by Watson and by Bankowski and Nelken) as alternatives to greater control by the state over discretion in criminal justice but questions whether the criminal justice system would still be able to perform its present functions in society. Finally, he suggests that the demand for a return to legality could lead, as it has already done in Holland and in Sweden, to a 'separation of powers' in which the criminal justice system punishes offenders while helping agencies separately provide services, on a voluntary basis, to their clients (who would include those subject to criminal sanctions).

Extensive discretionary powers are often associated with powerful professions and welfare institutions. In 'Social Change and the Shifting Boundaries of Discretion in Medicine' **McGlew and Robertson** consider the implications of recent changes in the doctor–patient relationship for professional autonomy and for discretionary decision-making by doctors. They argue that, as the incidence of disease shifts from acute conditions (which doctors know how to manage) to chronic degenerative conditions (where medical knowledge is at best uncertain) so the doctor–patient relationship shifts from an authoritarian relationship (in which the doctor does things to the patient) to one of mutual participation (in which the doctor helps the patient to help himself). McGlew and Robertson also suggest that there is now a greater willingness to challenge the authority and judgements of doctors, and that changes in disease patterns are now leading to a renewed emphasis on preventative medicine. All these factors have considerable implications for professional autonomy and discretionary decision-making. The paper concludes by comparing peer-group review of doctors' decision-making in the USA (where it is very weak) and Britain (where it is somewhat stronger as a result of G.P. referrals to hospital consultants and the development of group practices with shared patient records); and by examining the implications of recent attempts to control resource allocation (in such a way that the outcomes of resource allocation do not necessarily reflect the values and priorities of the most powerful segments of the medical profession) for doctors' professional autonomy.

The last two papers reach rather similar conclusions from very different starting points. In 'Discretion, Moral Judgement and Integration' **Watson** makes a strong plea for discretion, in the strong sense in which Dworkin (1977) uses the concept to refer to people whose decisions are not constrained by standards set by those in authority. He puts forward a view of human society as comprising a network of roles constituted by a set of rules and argues that failure to follow the rules sustaining the roles can lead to social disintegration. He then distinguishes social policy from economic policy in terms of its concern to promote social integration and morally desirable social relations. According to Watson, discretion in the strong sense will be responsive to values in society and can thus provide the means of facilitating and legitimating changes in role structure and thus of achieving social integration. Using the example of the (Scottish) Children's Hearing System to support his case, Watson argues that participation in decision-making by children and parents helps them to grasp the rules to be followed and allows panel members to alter their role expectations in the light of changing values.

In the final paper, **Bankowski and Nelken** agree with Watson insofar as they also favour discretion in Dworkin's strong sense where it is exercised in the context of participatory democracy. In 'Discretion as a Social Problem' they regret the narrow conception of discretion as a problem caused by the absence of rules and argue that concern with discretion should instead be seen as an aspect of the general mistrust of power which is endemic in western capitalist societies. Because discretion is really about power, concern with discretion raises the very fundamental questions of how society should be organised justly and rationally. They consider, and reject, the possibility of legal and bureaucratic controls over power but favour control 'by the community' on the basis of shared values. But, in addition to raising these large questions of political theory and social organisation, and sketching one possible answer, Bankowski and Nelken also point to the need to develop a sociology of concern with discretion as a social problem.

Far from reaching agreement on the nature of discretion and how best to study it, there are some important and fundamental disagreements among the various contributors to this book. Nevertheless, there is a substantial measure of agreement that the 'problem' of discretion is not simply caused by the absence of rules or solved by a 'return to legality'. Likewise there is a broad measure of agreement that an adequate analysis of discretion calls for a framework which can accommodate broad social, economic and political forces. Thus, discretion should be studied in the context of power, knowledge, legitimacy, ideology, etc. Finally, there is also agreement that more research must attempt to link the hitherto somewhat disparate micro- and macro-sociological concerns.

One consequence of theorising about discretion as a research topic is that greater attention must be paid to the appropriateness of the methodologies employed in studying it. The papers in this book raise many important questions about the nature of discretion and its analysis, and raise numerous substantive issues of considerable importance. We hope that the publication of this book will stimulate a great deal more work in this area.

1 Discretion and Power
Michael Adler and Stewart Asquith

In this chapter, we adopt Davis's usage of the term 'discretion'. According to Davis (1974: p. 4):

> a public official has discretion whenever the effective limits of his power leave him free to make a choice among possible courses of action or inaction.

In recent years, considerable concern has been expressed at the extent of the discretionary powers granted under administrative law to officials, professionals and certain forms of tribunal in the area of criminal justice and in the social services. The exercise of discretion has been largely removed from the ambit of the courts and from legal and judicial scrutiny. As a result, there have been a number of appeals that, in the interests of justice, discretionary decision-making should be made subject to judicial review and other principles associated with the 'rule of law'. This call for a 'return to legality' has become a common theme among those who wish to limit what they see as the arbitrariness and unfairness of discretionary decision-making. It is, they argue, only through a return to legality that the functioning of welfare institutions can be improved and that greater protection can be offered to individuals against the vagaries of criminal justice and the official benevolence of the social services. Only in this way, Reich argued fifteen years ago (Reich 1963, 1964 and 1965), can individual rights be protected and dangers and threats to the freedom and dignity of the individual be avoided. These arguments have been repeated many times since then. However, it is important to stress that appeals for a return to the rule of law should not necessarily be taken as indicative of a desire to totally eliminate discretion. Thus Davis argues (p. 43):

> To fix as a goal the elimination of all discretion on all subjects would be utter insanity.

and advocates only (p. 3):

> in broad terms, that we should eliminate much unnecessary discretionary power and that we should do much more than we have been doing to confine, structure and check necessary discretion.

We have two major, and related, objectives in this chapter. First, we wish to show that claims for greater legal control over the exercise of discretionary powers, though ideologically attractive in offering further safeguards to individuals against the vagaries of welfare institutions, frequently ignore the relationship of those institutions to the wider social, political and economic order. Second, we want to argue that an adequate analysis of the actual exercise of discretion at the 'face-to-face' level, i.e. between the providers and the recipients of particular social services, must be informed by an understanding of the structural position of welfare institutions and their relationship to the broader social, political and economic framework of society. Our position is that much research on the exercise of discretion

> is primarily concerned with the rational and efficient functioning of [welfare] systems as relatively self-contained entities and not, for example, with the structural basis of such systems, with their relation to any of the other systems that go to make up the complex of social institutions that is society or with any other questions that have traditionally pre-occupied mainstream sociology.
>
> (Low 1978: p. 14)

Studies of discretion have tended to focus either on the exercise of discretionary decision making at a micro-sociological level or on the growth of discretionary powers and their relationship to particular configurations of social, political and economic arrangements at a macro-sociological level. There have rarely been any articulations between these micro- and macro-sociological concerns.

In this chapter our main focus will be on what McBarnett (1978) has referred to as the 'false dichotomy between macro and micro-studies, between abstract theorising and empiricism'. By considering the relationship between power and knowledge which, we argue, results in the domination of certain conceptions of social reality and thereby contributes to the maintenance of particular forms of social order, we identify the concept of ideology as a significant medium through which to analyse the exercise of discretionary powers. The theoretical and methodological relevance of ideology is premised upon the claim that the assumptions which inform discretionary decisions have of necessity to be located within much broader social–structural concerns.

Discretion as a Macro Problem

Much recent writing and research on discretionary decision-making has been motivated by a (quite legitimate) moral concern with the outcomes of decisions for those who are affected by them. Particularly in the context of administrative decision-making, excessive discretion has been seen as leading to arbitrariness, inequality and dependency and failing to meet the most basic requirements of justice (Davies 1971, Thomas 1974). On the other hand, too rigid an adherence to rules and rule-guided procedures has been criticised for giving rise to inflexibility, insensitivity to differing needs and circumstances and impersonal treatment (Titmuss 1971). Critics have not hesitated to propose changes in the ways in which decisions are taken so as to enhance either 'proportional' or 'creative' justice (Stevenson 1973). Most of them, in particular those who have championed a return to legality and the rule of law, have sought to emphasise proportional justice at the expense of creative justice by arguing that discretion should be restricted and rights created wherever possible.

We do not wish to take issue with the merits of these proposals (indeed we are broadly in agreement with them), but we do, nevertheless, criticise many of the critics and their proposals for failing to question who benefits (and why they do so) from the existing mode of decision-making and not merely who loses out, and for failing to consider the political obstacles involved in moving away from a prevailing mode of decision-making. Social reform generally calls for a transfer of power and this is particularly true in relation to discretionary decision-making. Discretionary powers are not exercised in a vacuum – they are exercised over individuals whose only protection may be their possession of certain rights. (By a right is meant simply an enforcible claim. Here we are not particularly concerned with moral rights, i.e. with those claims which can only be enforced by an appeal to morality. Rather, we are more concerned with legal rights, i.e. with those claims which can be enforced through the law since it is widely believed that strengthening such rights is an effective means of limiting the discretion of public officials.) Marshall (1963) distinguished three categories of legal rights – civil rights, political rights and social rights – which together comprised what he called citizenship and it is with what he referred to as social rights (which include the right to a substitute income during periods of interruption or cessation of earnings, the right to health care in periods of sickness, to housing, education, social work, etc.) that we shall be largely concerned.

The three categories of rights include both 'positive' and 'negative' rights. Positive rights refer to rights of access to public welfare, i.e. as consumers of social services, to private welfare, e.g. by spouses to a share in matrimonial property and to the law, i.e. to lawyers and the courts as a means of securing legal redress; while negative rights refer to protection from public authorities, private individuals and the criminal law. A public official's discretion may be limited in a number of ways, e.g. statutorily, administratively, professionally, politically or judicially, but the stronger the claim an individual has the greater is his power to make and enforce demands on officials. Conversely, the weaker the rights an individual has, the more he will be at the mercy of their discretion. These statements apply equally in the case of positive and negative rights. Of course, in order to limit effectively the powers of public officials in this way, the individual must both be aware of his rights and able to enforce them. In relation both to criminal justice and to the social services, even where rights do exist in theory these two conditions are frequently not met.

It follows, both from our introductory remarks and from the above, that the public official's discretion and the rights of those who are subject to it are aspects of a relationship of power between them. Moreover since discretion is conferred (or legitimated) and rights are granted by the state, the power relationships between these officials and the public must also be seen as reflections of structured power relationships in society. Thus, attempts to modify the nature of these relationships must acknowledge the social and political forces sustaining forms of decision-making which have to be overcome for the achievement of meaningful social reform. Many of the best known writers on discretion can be faulted for not doing so.

Davis is clearly doubly guilty. Likewise, in advocating greater procedural safeguards for the 'new property' rights inherent in modern welfare provision, Reich is equally guilty of failing to ask who benefits from the absence of procedural protection for the rights in question and to question what political obstacles might stand in the way of the reforms he proposes (Reich 1963, 1964 and 1965). Of course both authors (and Reich in particular) could claim merely to be clarifying the objectives and thus influencing the strategies of movements for social reform which were already in existence (in Reich's case the American Welfare Rights Movement) but, by confining themselves to advocating change on moral grounds, they can be criticised for engaging in 'utopian' social engineering. By no means everyone has fallen into this trap. To give just one example, Macpherson has recently argued (like Reich) for the need to create new rights in common property but at the same time has identified those political forces which would be required to bring about such changes (Macpherson 1975).

Professional Discretion

In many of the social services (most noticeably in health, education and social work) where the service providers are mainly professionals, decision-making is of an extremely discretionary kind. Although it is common to think of professional decision-making as calling for the exercise of judgement rather than discretion, except for the fact that the persons concerned are not strictly speaking public officials, professional decision-making clearly involves the exercise of discretion in Davis's sense. Professional decision-making is also subject to particularly weak forms of public accountability and control. Individuals have positive rights only in the most general sense that they have rights of access to the services concerned, e.g. to consult a doctor, go to school or college (for children between the ages of 5 and 16 this is, of course, a duty) or seek the advice of a social worker. They do not have rights to any particular forms of treatment, tuition or help nor do they have rights to any particular standard of health, education and welfare.

The growth of discretion has gone hand in hand with the growth of powerful professions which lay claim to esoteric professional knowledge and are able to support these claims through the development of powerful forms of occupational control (Johnson 1972). As government became increasingly involved in the direct provision of health, education and welfare so it has been able to enlist the support of the professions concerned. Although fearful of 'political interference' the power of the professions has been sufficient to protect them from public accountability and control. Thus, although the government is the main source of employment and remuneration for doctors, teachers and social workers, the doctors' clinical freedom, the teachers' control over what is taught in the schools and how it is taught, and the social workers' decisions about what kind of help, if any, should be given are largely immune from any form of democratic accountability and control. Partly because they are such powerful groups, partly because of their symbolic significance (public support for their activities symbolises a commitment to the enhancement of welfare for which government takes credit) and partly, as we shall see later, because of the ways in which they sustain particular conceptions of social reality which contribute to the maintenance of social order, they have been able to retain their very considerable discretionary powers.

Administrative Discretion

Although the professions are probably the main carriers of welfare ideologies and are a very important means of delivering the social services, they are not the only means of so doing. Many social services, e.g. housing and social security, are made available through large bureaucracies staffed by administrators. The distinction between welfare services that are staffed by professionals and those that are staffed by administrators would seem to reflect a difference between those services which attempt to do things to people and those that mainly attempt to provide things for them. (We realise of course that the rather neat distinction between professional and administrative decision-making is a gross over-simplification and recognise that, theoretically, such a distinction is difficult to maintain. In organisational terms 'administrators' may often be required to make decisions akin to those we have associated with 'professionals' and vice versa. However, the ideal-typical designations we employ at least have the merit of identifying some of the more important characteristics of the exercise of discretion in different contexts.) In comparison with a professional, who is a member of a powerful occupational group and is socialised into the professional ideology through long periods of training and apprenticeship, an administrator is often an official who has simply been assigned to a particular administrative task. Thus, we would expect a professional to have a considerably greater personal commitment to an ideology of welfare than an administrator. As we have already pointed out, professionals have largely unfettered discretion and make their decisions by reference to a body of esoteric professional knowledge. By contrast, administrative discretion is characteristically constrained by rules. Administrators make their decisions by reference not only to rules but also to guidelines which are intended to shape their decisions in circumstances which are not covered by the rules. Although the professions have extremely wide discretion, the power and status of the professional groups concerned and the esoteric nature of their professional knowledge have, on the whole, ensured that professional prerogatives have gone unquestioned. There have, of course, been some powerful and popular attacks on the welfare professions (see, for example, Illich 1971 and 1975; Platt 1975) but, on the whole, professional discretion has been questioned less than administrative discretion. Although administrators characteristically have less discretion than professionals, they have fewer sources of institutional power (since they can be replaced far more easily than their professional counterparts) and lower status. Moreover, the more mundane nature of the imposed welfare philosophies means that they are more easily called into question both by administrators and the public. Administrative discretion is thus not only more open to distortion by officials when it conflicts with their own value assumptions, it is also more readily criticised by the public. Public criticism has been directed both at the official welfare philosophies and at their distortions in practice. Hence the calls for more rules and further controls on the exercise of administrative discretion. Administrative discretion is the 'soft under-belly' of welfare.

Rules and Discretion

Rules and discretion can be seen as providing alternative modes of decision-making and of allocating scarce resources. Rule-guided procedures can be more visible, are more explicit and may be preferred where they can be formulated and where the major concern is to ensure 'fair shares' for all. By comparison, discretion is inevitably less visible and more implicit but will be favoured where considerations of individual welfare are paramount. In general, rules will be introduced where the decision-makers are officials, where they have low status and/or little power, where there is dissatisfaction with the exercise of discretion by those who make the decision and/or by those for and against whom it is exercised, where there is outside political support for groups who are critical of the exercise of discretion and where it is, in principle, feasible to formulate a set of rules. Discretion, on the other hand, will be favoured where the decision-makers are professionals with high status and/or considerable power, where there is dissatisfaction with the operation of rules by those who make the rules or are subject to the rules, where there is outside political support for groups critical of the operation of rules or where it is not, even in principle, possible to formulate an acceptable set of rules.

A shift in one direction or another will thus take place in response to political pressure for change. At the present time, and especially in the context of cut-backs in public expenditure, there is considerable pressure for change directed towards the curtailment of discretion and the introduction of more rule-guided procedures. As we have seen, much of this pressure is directed at administrative rather than professional discretion. Although such moves are championed by those who argue for a return to legality, the introduction of rules is not sufficient in itself to enhance the rights of those affected by the decisions. In order to enhance the rights of those affected by the decision, the rules must be made public and those affected by them must be able to enforce those rules through the use of legal procedures. As Nonet (1969) has pointed out, this demands a level of 'legal competence'. Because legal competence, i.e. the ability to take advantage of such legal procedures as are available, is not equally distributed throughout the population, it does not follow that even legally enforcible rules will be equitably enforced.

Procedural and Substantive Rights
In order to ascertain whether a return to legality will enhance individual rights, a distinction has to be drawn between 'procedural'

and 'substantive' rights. Procedural rights refer to process – to a 'fair' trial, to having one's claims dealt with according to the rules or, in the absence of explicitly formulated rules, according to generally accepted conventions of natural justice. Substantive rights refer to outcomes – to the receipt of redundancy pay, or unemployment benefit at a given level for the unemployed, to the allocation of tenancies to homeless families or to medical (or social work) help of a certain kind to a sick person or someone with social or personal probems, etc. Most of those who have wished to limit discretion have wished to strengthen the procedural rights of those who are subject to it. Of course, it does not follow that, by so doing, the substantive rights of those who are subject to these powers will be enhanced in any significant way. This was the point made by Handler in his critique of Reich's advocacy of procedural safeguards for the 'new property' (Handler 1966). Handler argued that changes in welfare policy and administration which would improve the substantive rights of welfare claimants would bring far more benefits to them than granting them greater procedural rights, e.g. to a fair hearing under the existing welfare system. The same point was made more recently by Prosser in relation to supplementary benefit appeal tribunals (Prosser 1977) and the same argument can be used against the proposals contained in the recent Supplementary Benefits Review (DHSS 1978) and in subsequent legislation. Simplification of the supplementary benefits system and an attempt to place the scheme on a firmer legal footing will entail a reduction in the discretion currently exercised by officials and a corresponding increase in the rights of claimants. However, it is only their procedural rights which can be enhanced in this way. Since it was neither proposed that fewer people would be dependent on Supplementary Benefits nor, with the possible exception of the long-term unemployed, that recipients of Supplementary Benefit should receive more cash, the substantive rights of claimants will be affected hardly at all. One can, of course, go even further by arguing, as Prosser and others have done, that such proposals will make fundamental change to the system of poor relief less likely and more difficult to achieve by conferring the 'symbolic appearance of legality' upon the Supplementary Benefits scheme. As Prosser (1977: p. 60) has argued:

> If legality is seen in isolation from the social and economic conditions on which it is based it can be merely an 'empty procedural device' serving to legitimate social organisation by giving an appearance of formal equality without providing substantive rights.

We shall develop this argument later in the chapter.

Public Expenditure Cuts

In a period of low economic growth, high unemployment and incipient inflation, many powerful demands for resources are made on the state. It does not follow, as Klein (1975) and others have argued, that expenditure on the social services cannot grow, only that there will be strong pressures on it not to do so as private consumption and investment in public and private industries (particularly exports, defence, etc.) compete with the social services for scarce resources (see Gough 1975 and 1979). In these circumstances, the prospect of further enhancement to the substantive rights of welfare recipients in the near future is rather slim. However, the prospect of enhancing procedural rights, particularly if these do not confer additional substantive rights which would entail additional public expenditure, may be very attractive. The gains to the state from such a strategy may be quite considerable – it may increase the legitimacy of government, inhibit potentially less acceptable demands for increased substantive rights and entitlements and satisfy the recipients of welfare without significantly altering the distribution of power in society. Thus, as we have already mentioned, government can proceed to codify supplementary benefits law, reduce the discretion of officials and thus increase the procedural rights of claimants in the context of a set of no-cost proposals which neither reduces dependence on supplementary benefits nor increases levels of benefit for those who are dependent on it. Likewise, government could introduce legislation which imposed a duty on local housing authorities to house homeless families since this entailed no extra resources and has merely led at best (given the very restrictive ways in which many local authorities have interpreted their discretionary powers) to a very marginal redistribution of existing tenancies. Similarly, government can contemplate with equanimity granting to parents a limited choice of schools for children since there are no plans to provide extra resources to improve the quality of unpopular (and presumably less satisfactory) schools.

Through reforms of the kind mentioned above, by extending the powers of the Parliamentary Commissioner for Administration and establishing Commissioners for Local Administration, by the possible introduction of a 'tenants' charter', etc., the state appears to be concerned to enhance the procedural rights of welfare recipients. Likewise, through lay participation and community involvement in the form of Community Councils (in Scotland), Community and District Health Councils, Schools Councils, etc., albeit with rather limited powers, the state might appear to be concerned with making services more responsive to their consumers. Although we do not wish to dismiss innovations such as these, we do stress that they have all been introduced or are being mooted when resources are at best being held steady and in some cases are being cut back and that they are unlikely to curb effectively the decision-making powers of those who provide the services particularly where these are professionals, or increase the substantive rights of recipients collectively. Lynes (1975) has described how Unemployment Appeal Tribunals were introduced in 1934, not in order to strengthen the rights of the unemployed but rather as a means of defusing opposition to an inherently unpopular reform which entailed cuts in benefit rates and to protect the government from parliamentary and public criticism. The wide-ranging reforms described above may likewise be less an effort to promote the rights of consumers or the accountability of services and more an attempt to mask the effects of public expenditure cuts and the perceived shortcomings of the services, and to protect the government by deflecting or co-opting its critics.

The Crisis in Law

The roots of the problem of controlling discretionary decision-making in the provision of welfare are to be found not just in our present economic difficulties. Tay and Kamenka (1975) suggest that they have their origins in a crisis in law and legal ideology which itself reflects structural changes in society. They identify three competing legal and administrative traditions.

In *'gemeinschaft* law' justice is substantive and directed to a particular case and a particular social context. In general, the law

expresses the norms and conventions of an organic community –
distinctions between the public and the private, between civil
wrongs and criminal offences or between political, legal and moral
issues do not exist and the community is paramount. This type of
law is best expressed in feudal society.

In '*gesellschaft* law', on the other hand, the opposite is generally the
case. This type of law arises out of, and is based on, atomic
individualism and private interests. Each person stands before the
law as a holder of rights and duties, as a legal person and not
someone trailing status and history after him. The emphasis is on
formal procedure, impartiality and adjudicative justice. The model
for all law is contract and the *quid pro quo*: this is achieved by the fact
that all persons are regarded as equal before the law. A distinction is
made between law and administration, and between the legal, the
political and the moral. This type of law is most clearly expressed in
individualistic *laissez-faire* society where there is a sharp distinction
between the public and the private but where the public or state
interest is defined as just another, sometimes overriding private
interest.

In 'bureaucratic–administrative law' the concern is not with the
organic community or with a *laissez-faire* society composed of private
individuals but rather with the pursuit of public policy in which
individuals are seen as agents rather than holders of rights and
duties as they were under *gesellschaft* law. The point of this type of
law is to provide for the regulation of an activity rather than
adjudicate disputes between individuals. It predominates in a
managerial directive type of society. Tay and Kamenka see it as
most fully developed in Eastern European socialist states but it
clearly exists wherever the state assumes a regulatory role over the
economy and within society and a concern with promoting the
'public interest' and the 'general good'. Bureaucratic–administrative
law, they claim, elevates the socio-technical norm against the
private right of the *gesellschaft* and the organic community of the
gemeinschaft.

The real crisis that we are witnessing today is, according to Tay
and Kamenka, a crisis in *gesellschaft*-type law. As the state has
assumed a greater regulatory role in society, so bureaucratic
administrative law has grown up to cater for it. The concern of the
state is with the achievement of public policies in which individuals

are often a means to an end rather than an end in themselves. Examples might include the pursuit of income redistribution, the equalisation of educational opportunity through positive discrimination and, more generally, the provision of welfare services by the state. For lawyers and others who are trained in the traditions of *gesellschaft* law, such developments are a threat to all that they have been taught to believe in. Hence the call for a return to legality and the rule of law.

According to Winkler (1975 and Chapter 5 in this volume), we are now moving into a new phase. In the 'corporate state', defined in terms of public control over the largely private ownership of the means of production, the state assumes powers of economic regulation and control through the use of discretionary powers not necessarily made explicit in law. The crisis is precisely that *gesellschaft* law cannot provide a means of controlling these discretionary powers. By the same token, a return to legality cannot effectively control discretionary decision-making in welfare precisely because the ideologies of welfare and legality do not articulate with each other. Dworkin (1977) has argued that, at least in what he calls 'hard cases', public law can be checked by the courts where the policies it advances conflict with accepted legal principles or with the moral rights of those who are subject to the law. However, in general, the pursuit of welfare, like the pursuit of other policy goals under bureaucratic administrative law, is simply not amenable to judicial control. Judical control of discretionary decision-making in welfare can mean, at best, that the procedural rights of the individuals concerned are offered greater protection, but it cannot lead to any significant improvement in the conditions and circumstances in which they find themselves. The dangers of a return to legality are that, by focusing on the procedural aspects of decision-making more subtle forms of control are left unexamined, and by introducing an ideological veneer of equality, equity, fairness and justice, attention may be deflected away from basic social and structural inequalities.

Discretion as a Micro Problem

We now turn our attention to the actual exercise of discretionary decision-making at the point of contact between the decision-maker and the person who is subject to his decisions. We have already argued that discretion is exercised within a context which is imbued with power and now wish to point out that it results in the domination of particular modes of thought over others. The point we wish to emphasise is that with the development of bureaucratic administrative forms of law, the professions have emerged as the main means of implementing welfare policies. The professions play a crucial role as the carriers of a welfare ideology and are a very important means by which certain conceptions of social reality are sustained and by which particular forms of social order are maintained. We are concerned here with what Foucault (1977) has called the microphysics of power'.

Many criticisms of discretionary decision-making have been prompted by evidence derived from empirical research. Reflecting the dominant schools of thought within the social sciences, empirical research on the exercise of discretion at the 'point of contact', i.e. at the 'face to face' level, has either been positivistic in its approach or been carried out from an interpretative or phenomenological perspective. Of these two methodological approaches, we believe the latter has much greater potential for analysing the exercise of discretion at the point of contact and for linking micro-social problems with macro-social issues.

Positivistic Research

In criminology and penology, perhaps more than in any other area, empirical research has been overwhelmingly positivistic in its methodological orientation (see Hood 1962; Hogarth 1971; Bottomley 1973). Much of this research has recently been criticised for its theoretical sterility. Thus, in his critique of strategies involved in research on inconsistencies and disparities in sentencing, Hogarth criticised much sentencing research as 'black box' or 'input-output' research. Just as criminological positivism had fostered an approach to the study of crime and delinquency which attempted to 'explain' criminality in terms of particular antecedents or causal factors, so it fostered a similar approach to sentencing research. Thus attempts were made to explain apparent inconsistencies in sentences by looking for associations between sentences and factors in the background of the offender, the sentencer or a combination of the two.

There was no attempt to elicit the penal philosophies or the working ideologies employed in the course of sentencing or to appreciate the 'logic in use' employed by key personnel such as judges and magistrates, just as there had been no attempt to understand the significance of committing offences for the individual offender (Matza 1964).

Positivistic research is, of course, not confined to the fields of criminology and penology. Nor is it all as theoretically sterile as the research just described. Thus Davies has developed some very sophisticated statistical techniques for analysing area variations in the provision of personal social services (Davies 1968; Davies et al. 1971). Davies's deterministic models show which factors are associated with various levels of serive provision but, although they can be a fruitful source of hypotheses, they tell us nothing directly about how resources are actually allocated. At their best, positivistic studies of discretionary decision-making have only succeeded in describing what kinds of antecedent factors are associated with given outcomes: they have been unable to describe how people exercise discretionary powers and any conclusions that are drawn about human involvement are only at the level of inference (see again Hogarth 1971). As McBarnett (1978) points out there have been few attempts, perhaps because of what she refers to as the 'inherent myopia' of positivism, to articulate any relationship between decision-making at the micro-level and broader (macro-level) social concerns.

Interpretative or Phenomenological Research

It is perhaps not a coincidence that, at a time when the rights of individuals are being championed, the legitimacy and authority of professional expertise and knowledge is being challenged and increasing recognition is being given to the providers and to the recipients of services and to the fact that both may have something valid to say about decision-making. In reference to juvenile delinquency, Platt (1975) has suggested that the definitions of delinquency espoused by public officials and the ways in which they contribute to and sustain the subordinate status of powerless groups is an important area of concern, and a number of studies have recently examined the 'operational ideologies' (Smith 1977) and 'frames of relevance' (Asquith 1977) of those responsible for implementing welfare policies. In our view, a major advance made by interpretative or phenomenological sociology has been the linking of the exercise of discretion with the operational ideologies of those involved. We consider first professional ideologies and second, because of increasing attempts to involve lay people in the administration of the social services, lay ideologies.

Professional ideologies

Perhaps in recognition of the fact that the objectives and aims of social policies may be distorted and modified in the course of implementation, a number of studies have recently been published which have examined the operational philosophies employed by members of particular professions. Thus we find studies of the ideologies of magistrates (Hogarth 1971; Lemon 1974), probation officers (Cicourel 1977; Hardiker 1977), social workers (Smith 1977) and psychiatric hospital staff (Strauss et al. 1964). Although their empirical object is different, all these studies assert the theoretical primacy of the actors' construction of social reality with special reference to their professional activity, the possible (indeed probable) modification of the formal goals and practices of an institution or policy in the course of the day-to-day accomplishment of the professional task, and the importance of the individuals' tacit assumptions and knowledge for the exercise of discretionary powers granted to them under the auspices of their particular profession. The probability of goal displacement and the possible conflict between an official philosophy of welfare and the values and assumptions of those who implement welfare policy are, if anything, even more important in respect of administrative discretion (see Hill 1972).

Lay ideologies

There have been two separate empirical concerns in research which has considered lay or public as opposed to professional ideologies. First there have been a number of studies which have sought to examine the working philosophies of lay persons responsible for the operation or administration of welfare institutions. Thus, for example, Herman (1972) and Lister (1975) have examined Supplementary Benefit Appeal Tribunals in this way, while Watson (1977) has studied the exercise of discretion by lay persons involved in the administration of juvenile justice. Juvenile justice studies have questioned the possibility of conflict between lay and professional ideologies, because the particularly powerful position of the professions under a bureaucratic administrative form of law means that lay knowledge has considerably less authority than professional knowledge, and have explored the implications this may have for the administration of the institutions concerned. Second, increasingly more work is being done from a welfare recipient or consumer perspective. In the field of social work, for example, Mayer and Timms (1970), Sainsbury (1975) and Rees (1978) have all sought to elicit the client's point of view and, in the field of juvenile justice, Morris and Giller (1977) and Petch (1977) have examined parents' and children's perceptions of their involvement in the formal processes of social control. Rose (1973) examined alternative strategies for representation at Supplementary Benefit Appeal Tribunals and concluded that a 'successful' strategy, i.e. one that leads to a beneficial outcome for the appellant, was likely to be one that tacitly accepted the operational ideology of the tribunal members. If lay decision-makers are unable to challenge effectively dominant professional ideologies, it is perhaps not surprising that the ideologies of other lay participants (in this case appellants and their representatives) should likewise be subordinated to the dominant ideologies of those who exercise power. The same point can be made with even greater force about the lay public as recipients of welfare.

As McBarnett (1978) rightly claims, phenomenological sociology has been a powerful medium of de-mystification in that it has pointed to important differences between the rhetoric and the reality of many welfare institutions. This is the basis of the appeal it holds for those who advocate the strengthening of legal safeguards against the use of excessive discretion by welfare agencies whose practice differs from their official philosophy. However, as McBarnett also points out, studies of discretionary decision-making frequently 'get lost in micro-sociological description and indignant de-mystification'. The main danger of a phenomenological approach is, we suggest, that it can be construed as a form of ideological relativism. Thus, for example, both Smith (1977) and Asquith (1977) have pointed to the differing interpretations and objectives placed on delinquency control by different persons within the social control network. However, they largely ignore the question of why some particular conceptions of delinquency and certain world views are considered more legitimate than others. The basic criticism we wish to make of such studies is that they usually operate at a level of analysis which is divorced from any notion of power in social relations. By ignoring the social derivations of differing ideologies, insufficient consideration is given to the fact that the powerful and authoritative position of the professions in the wider social and political arena renders the relationship between the decision-maker and the person who is subject to the decision a hierarchical one and one which is imbued with power.

Professional Knowledge and Discretionary Powers

The possession of particular forms of knowledge is especially important in deciding who has the right to exercise discretion since, to cite Giddens (1976: p. 113):

> [The] significance of frames of meaning is characteristically unbalanced in relation to the possession of power, whether this be a result of the superior linguistic or dialectical skills of one person in conversation with another, [or] the possession of relevant types of 'technical knowledge'.

Moreover, Giddens continues, what stands for social reality is closely connected to the possession of knowledge and thereby of power. The significance of this is that it is through the possession of power that professionals, and to a lesser extent other welfare personnel, can, in the process of exercising discretion, impose particular constructions of social reality and exert subtle forms of social control. As Schutz (1971: p. 239) recognised:

> We are less and less masters in our own right to define what is and what is not relevant to us. Politically, economically and socially imposed relevances beyond our control have to be taken into account.

And, recognising that socialisation into forms of knowledge provides not only a means of communication among members of particular professions but also a means of excluding others who are not in possession of the relevant (professional) knowledge, he argued that (p. 240):

The expert knows very well that only a fellow expert will understand all the technicalities and implications of a problem in his field and he will never accept a layman or dilettante as a competent judge of his performance.

Thus socialisation into particular types of professional knowledge, e.g. through training, 'apprenticeship' and professional acculturation makes the already powerful social and political position of welfare agencies and institutions relatively unassailable from criticism by the body politic. Through the exercise of discretionary powers, professions and aspiring professions are thereby able to foster and sustain their own versions of social reality and their own conceptions of social order. The problem with the strategy which seeks to subject their discretionary powers to a greater measure of legal control is that it leaves unquestioned those inequalities in society upon which they depend and to which they actually contribute. With specific reference to crime, Platt (1975: p. 101) put it precisely when he wrote that:

> The 'diluted liberalism', to use C. Wright Mills' apt term, of most research on juvenile delinquency, for example, results from the fact that researchers are typically prepared to accept prevailing, i.e. state definitions of crime, to work within the premises of criminal law and to concur, at least implicitly, with those who make and enforce laws as to the nature and distribution of the criminal population.

In relation to the failure of the 'welfare state' to fulfil its promises, George and Wilding (1976) have suggested that the gradualist and incrementalist programmes which have been characteristic of social policy since the Second World War reflect a basic tension between the ethic of capitalism and the ethic of welfare which has resulted in the uneasy compromise of welfare state capitalism. That is, the development of welfare policies in the guise of liberal reformism has taken place within a configuration of economic and social relations which characterise capitalism. Although George and Wilding recognise the philosophical incompatibility of capitalism and welfare, we believe that they have underestimated the potential for functional interdependence between the two. The functional attribute of welfare is that it serves to direct attention away from social, political and economic inequalities. The case for extending judicial and legal principles in relation to the provision of welfare can be criticised on the grounds that these principles mask the underlying structural inequalities with a thin ideological and moral veneer of equality. Thus, as we have already argued, the danger of a return to legality in an effort to control the worst excesses of discretionary decision-making is that, by simply focusing on the enhancement of procedural rights, the substantive rights of those who are dependent on welfare will remain unaltered. The achievement of procedural equality which might confer increased legitimacy on welfare institutions would thus draw attention away from continuing substantive inequalities. As Prosser (1977: p. 39) has argued

> One cannot simply take legality and see it in isolation from the other social factors on which it is founded; its usefulness as a concept to any group depends on the context in which it operates.

Moreover, it is significant that the exercise of discretionary powers in the context of welfare takes place on a face-to-face level between individuals. The individual's problems are seen as 'personal' problems in abstraction from the context in which they arise. They are certainly not seen as problems of the wider political or economic framework. Indeed, the political and economic framework acquire the status of the taken-for-granted and become reified as part of the natural order of things. But, as Pearson (1975: p. 9) points out,

> These are practical questions. Social order is taken for granted; one does not need to know why men conform, only why men fail to fulfil their place in the natural order of things.

As a corollary of this, only those who have appropriate knowledge can be allowed to exercise discretion in the provision of welfare. Only experts can claim to possess this knowledge and thus the right to intervene. Whether the experts are professionals or merely officials, their expertise frequently results in what Pearson, following Wright Mills, has called 'privatised solutions of public ills' and the attribution to individuals of responsibility for social problems. In the case of welfare professionals, their expertise is not seriously assailed. Their powers, based on their special expertise and their superior grasp of the problem, are not only legitimated by the state but are also largely accepted as legitimate by the public. The situation of many non-professionals in welfare is, as we have already pointed out, frequently very different. The powers which have been conferred on them are not necessarily accepted as legitimate by the public or, even, by the officials themselves. This is in part because their expertise is typically seen as being less esoteric and more partisan, and therefore more likely to be in conflict with the values of the public and possibly the officials themselves; in part because officials constitute much less powerful occupational groups with considerably lower status. A welfare ideology which is imposed by government inevitably creates greater problems of enforcement than a welfare ideology sustained by a professional group and legitimated by government.

Arguing thus is not to argue that the ideologies of welfare personnel are necessarily to be regarded as 'pure' welfare ideologies. Under welfare state capitalism, the ideology of welfare at best coexists with the ideology of capitalism. Although they are separable in theory, they are not always so in practice. It is by identifying the functional interdependence of welfare and capitalism, at an ideological as well as an institutional level, that the legitimacy of state activities in the name of welfare can be called into question. As Gillis (1973: p. 131) has written, it is in the functional interdependence of welfare and capitalism that the state

> manages to produce the social ills it claims to abhor but which it must have to sustain the ideologies and institutions that are based upon it.

We believe that the exercise of discretion by those responsible for the realisation of welfare policies is, at the face-to-face level imbued with power and authority that derive from a particular social order and that the control and domination displayed in the 'micro-physics of power' by welfare personnel (professionals or officials) can only be understood in reference to specific configurations of economic forces and social relations. Giddens (1976) has pointed in general terms to the significance of the association between the legitimation of knowledge and the social distribution of power. We believe that the relationships of power and domination between individuals at a face-to-face level and the relationships of power between institutions at a structural level require further articulation and, in a very real sense, provide the key to the study of discretionary decision-making in the social services and the law.

Lay Knowledge and Discretionary Powers

So far we have referred mainly to the exercise of discretion by professionals and other officials. However, there are many contexts in which discretion is exercised by lay members of the community, e.g. in magistrates' courts, juvenile justice and various forms of administrative tribunals. Though some people (e.g. Morris 1974) have argued that lay participation in decision-making provides a populist check on professional or administrative discretion, this should not be seen as implying that 'professional' and 'lay' are clear-cut categories. Indeed, one of us has argued (Asquith 1977) that, far from being diametrically opposed categories, 'professional' and 'lay' should be conceived as points on a continuum. After all, professionals (and other officials) are, at the same time, individuals with their own values, ideologies and ways of ordering social reality. Likewise lay participants in decision-making must subscribe, at least in part, to the professional or other official ideology of welfare. Nevertheless, the notion that professional power can be controlled by the activity of lay persons is an attractive one, particularly to adherents of a more participatory form of democracy. The idea of community involvement is attractive for the same reason.

Bankowski and Mungham (1978) have argued that lay participation and community involvement, e.g. in administrative tribunals, are ideologically attractive precisely because they promise to rid us of the element of control and domination associated with the exercise of discretionary powers by public officials. However, they go on to question whether lay participation and community involvement really result in a challenge to the professionals' monopoly of knowledge and thus in an actual transfer of power. We have argued in this chapter that the establishment of particular modes of thought as legitimate ways of viewing the world involves a conflict of interests between proponents of the legitimate and of alternative ways of viewing the world and provides the structural means for mediating power in even the most transient of social relationships. We have earlier criticised studies that examined the implications for the exercise of discretion of the different ideologies available to and employed by the individuals concerned for ignoring questions of power and control which result from the imposition of a dominant welfare ideology. Although lay persons may be involved in the exercise of discretionary decision-making, their involvement rarely poses much of a threat to professional or official domination or control. That this is so is in part a result of the means of selection and training, which is often left in the hands of officials and professionals who can thus ensure the involvement of appropriate people and the development of appropriate attitudes, and in part to the deliberate promotion of certain individuals and the deliberate containment and exclusion of others. Thus, to take just two examples, Asquith (1977) has described the ways in which social work stereotypes of delinquency and delinquency control are influential in determining selection and training in the Children's Hearing system, while Lister (1975) has described how the Chairmen of Supplementary Benefit Appeal Tribunals are selected from members who are acceptable to the DHSS (these are rarely trade unionists), while unacceptable members (almost always trade unionists) are called less often and can, in any case, be isolated on a tribunal of three members. In addition, in relation to community involvement, the terms themselves ('community', 'representative-ness', etc.) are, as Mungham and Bankowski (1976) point out, extremely problematic. Thus, a commitment to lay participation and community involvement may help to impart a spurious legitimacy to the institutions concerned without seriously challenging the powers of the professionals or the experts or the domination of certain modes of thought, constructions of social reality and conceptions of social order.

Conclusion

Our chief concern is that a shift to legality would merely entail the grafting on of elements of a form of *gesellschaft* law to social relationships which can be characterised by the domination of certain forms of knowledge over others. The resulting ideological and moral veneer of equality and the concern for procedural rights would effect little change in the circumstances of the recipients of many of our social services. While the concept of the juridic person fits in well with notions of democracy, it conceals the subtle and covert expression of power associated with the exercise of discretion. The paradox is that a form of legality that promotes equality and individual rights would function to conceal what Foucault (1977) presumably means by the 'dark side of democracy'. Equally the involvement of lay persons in the exercise of discretion (in juvenile justice, in various forms of tribunal, on parole boards, etc.) does little to challenge the powerful position of the professionals and administrators in welfare or the legitimacy of professional or expert knowledge which provides subtler forms of domination than overt displays of power.

Earlier we argued that one of the dangers of the phenomenological approach to the analysis of decision-making is that of ideological relativism – i.e. that of merely showing that different people may operate according to different 'working' or 'operational' ideologies. However, we believe that the *theoretical* significance of focusing on 'ideologies' as we propose is that it points to a need to explain first, whence ideologies are derived and secondly, how it is that at certain points in time certain ideological positions come to be seen to be more legitimate than others. (The conception of ideologies as 'systems of interacting symbols and patterns of interwoven meanings' developed by Geertz (1973) fits our purpose admirably.) *Methodologically*, this emphasis requires that an analysis of the exercise of discretionary powers has to be couched in a framework in which micro-sociological and macro-sociological concerns can be reconciled. An adequate analysis of discretionary decision-making by members of welfare (and other social) institutions will necessarily involve an explication of the relationship between power and knowledge and of the process by which particular structures of domination are produced and reproduced. In this respect, moral concern at the lack of procedural safeguards afforded by discretionary decision-making within welfare institutions cannot readily be divorced from a consideration of the relationship of such institutions to broader political, social and economic concerns. It is, we suggest, through the empirical study of ideologies informed by the kind of theoretical considerations recently put forward by Giddens (1979) that such relationships can best be articulated and that studies of the exercise of discretion can most fruitfully move forward.

2   Discretion as an Implementation Problem: a framework for interpretation
Ken Young

This chapter is addressed to the issue of discretion as a source of 'implementation problems'. Such problems have traditionally been viewed as arising from control loss, a phenomenon which, some will argue, is a consequence of increasing societal complexity (La Porte 1975). On the other hand, increased discretion and its associated decentralisation of power may be seen as an appropriate response to complexity by enhancing the responsiveness and adaptability of private and public bureaucracies (Thompson 1967). Such a concern with issues of power and control, while clearly relevant to the understanding of discretion, is however excessively formal. Discretion involves both power and choice (Davies 1971: p. 4) and we must consider not only the rules that define actors' power but also the purpose and preferences that shape the choices made in its name.

As Thompson pointed out, an individual's propensity to make discretionary choices is rooted in his ability to tolerate the ambiguities that his role confers. Moreover, discretion is rooted both in the explicit rules of formal autonomy and in the informal guidelines by which decision-makers operate. The interpretation of formal rules, the creation of informal guidelines and the exercise of preferences within them comprise a set of subjective factors which enable discretionary decision-makers to make sense of and operate upon their everyday world. Yet the ways in which they 'make sense of their situation' pose a challenge both to policy-makers and to policy analysts. This chapter seeks to establish the precise nature of that challenge.

In the first section I attempt to define the sphere of activity with which we are concerned: the propensity of subordinate or peripheral actors within the policy system to make choices which are incongruent with those of the formal 'policy-makers'. The analysis is one which highlights the importance of subjective factors in shaping 'the definition of the situation', to use McHugh's (1968) term. The second part of the paper proposes a particular conceptualisation of these subjective factors as 'the assumptive world of the actor' and some problems in the explanatory status of such a formulation are discussed. In the concluding part of the paper the two distinct arguments are drawn together to interpret 'implementation problems' in the light of these concepts.

Discretion as an 'Implementation Problem'

Public and intellectual concern with problems of 'policy implementa-tion' has increased in recent years (Pressman and Wildavsky 1973; van Meter and van Horn 1975; Lewis and Flynn 1979; Dunsire 1978; Hill 1979). It is possible to relate this concern to a broader and pervasive anxiety about the diminishing efficacy of public policy and indeed of government generally. This anxiety is crystallised in a number of slogans to which recent commentators have addressed themselves: the 'failure of the state' (Cornford 1975), 'governmental overload' and 'the ungovernability thesis' (King 1975; Rose 1979). The gap between government's reach and government's grasp is held to be increasing and a number of writers have put forward accounts of why this might be so. In the first place there are the arguments that the scope of government has increased so rapidly as to produce diminishing marginal returns and actual policy failures; the material and political resources available to government are insufficient for the tasks which, in a competitive electoral situation, it chooses to assume (Brittan 1975). In the second place there are the arguments to the effect that contemporary advanced industrial societies are becoming harder to govern; increasing social and economic complexity and the increasing interdependence of activities render the effect of policies uncertain. On this analysis, the con-sequences of policy may often be unintended or counter-intentional (La Porte 1975; Forrester 1969).

This debate about the problems of governing advanced societies underlies the fashionable concern with implementation. The problem facing policy-makers is to effect 'real world change' in intended directions. The degree to which they succeed in doing so is a measure of policy impact. Yet policy is rarely applied directly to the external world. Characteristically, it is mediated through other institutions or actors. Thus the impact of policies is affected as much by the mediation of other key actors – the 'implementers' – as by the intrinsic merits or feasibility of the policy itself. To recognise the crucial role of policy mediators is to redefine the policy process as the centre's manipulation of the external world via the manipulation of the actions of the periphery. The problem for central policy-makers becomes one of deploying instruments and influence to achieve desired ends.

It is platitudinous to point out that the desired ends of central policy-makers often diverge from those of the mediators of policy in the peripheral agencies. Where divergence is recognised, it has usually been attributed to crude clashes of organisational interest, as in the perceived tension between 'central control' and 'local autonomy'. Similarly, to speak of policy shortfalls as 'implementation problems' or to debate the need to further regulate or enhance 'discretion' in a range of policy areas is to over-emphasise the significance of direction and control in the achievement of social purposes.

A more subtle, but I think more valuable perspective, is to see 'problems of implementation' as referring to the centre's failure to comprehend the values, perceptions, motivations and 'definitions of the situation' held by peripheral actors. In these terms, feasible policies are those which are constructed or negotiated in relation to such subjective factors, while radical policies would be so constructed as to change them. In either case, because those subjective appreciations are embedded in the everyday situation of the mediating actor, the expression of policy has to be seen as a persuasive or political, rather than a directive activity. Similarly, practical policy analysis must be informed by an understanding of these subjective factors and their situational determinants (Gordon, Lewis and Young 1977).

Understanding the actions of mediating agencies is then a prerequisite of effective political action. Such understanding is necessarily interpretative, in Becker's (1968) sense of understanding 'from within' the world of the agent. Naturally enough, central policy-makers attach great significance to the statutory requirements, rules, guidelines and advice which they press upon the mediators. But from within the world of the mediating agents, such communications are seen as events to be assessed in the context of their own organisational 'life world'. Peripheral agents place their own construction upon central advice or directives. Within their 'interpretive space' central intentions may be assimilated, ignored or inverted; response to them is essentially discretionary.

Consider the situation of the individual agent operating 'in the field', at the interface between the agency and the public. At this point, where power and policy is exercised and challenged face-to-face, the 'street level bureaucrat' – teacher, social worker, policeman – is the mediator par excellence (Lipsky 1976). The 'street level bureaucrat' operates in an unenviable environment. His job is characterised by inadequate resources for the task, by variable and often low public support for the role, and by ambiguous and often unrealisable expectations of performance. His concerns are with the actual effect of policies upon his relationship with specific individuals; these may lead him to disregard or fail to assimilate the wider policy issues which concern those 'higher up' in his agency.

The 'street level bureaucrat' as a scapegoat for policy failure is a familiar figure. Moreover, his role is necessarily uncertain. A modicum of semi-professional training defines the role as the actualisation of a set of ideals inculcated in that training. Yet the street level bureaucrat is also the representative of a governmental agency, one which is itself subject to conflicting pressures. Finally, the street level bureaucrat, in day-to-day contact with clients and with the community at large, becomes to some degree locked into the support of individuals and groups who may be antipathetic to his employing agency. In this situation of role confusion and role strain, the person at the end of the line is not disposed to react to new policy initiatives from above as if he or she were a mere functionary; they are but factors in a whole web of demands which peripheral actors have to manage. Those demands, response to which engenders the role strain, are the dynamic factors operating within the interpretative space which their very situation grants to actors at the state/citizen interface.

Analogous strains are experienced by all mediating actors and most acutely by those who operate at the boundaries of organisations. The everyday worlds of local authority chief officers, SBC office managers, or street level bureaucrats of course differ; but what they have in common is marginality and its attendant role strains. As 'implementers' or as 'discretionary officials' they are simply a special case of the general category of organisational actor. Like any other social being mediating actors seek to impose order on this uncomfortable experience. They strive to resolve their role strains and the competition of demands into coherent 'definitions of the situation' which will enable them to interpret their experience and to predict and manage their everyday world.

What the outside observer then sees is the mediator 'behaving' more or less consistently in accordance with an ideology or set of values which make situational sense (Smith 1977). While academic policy analysts are eager to agree that these subjective factors should be somehow mobilised in explanation, they have paid little attention to conceptualisation. The next section of this paper is, therefore, devoted to outlining an approach to the interpretation of this distinct form of social action. Such an appraisal must deal both with the relationship between subjective factors and behaviour, and with conceptualising subjective experience itself.

Interpreting Discretionary Action

In this section of the chapter I look first at the contention that subjective attributes explain behaviour. For the sake of simplicity the argument is centred upon 'values' as a widely used surrogate for a range of subjective factors. I then discuss some problems in the conceptualisation of values and argue the case for the concept of 'the assumptive world' as encompassing the wide range of subjective attributes with which we are concerned.

'Values' as explanations of outcomes

The contention that 'values' operate within the policy process is hardly a matter for dispute. Nevertheless, a host of problems stand in the way of any advance on this statement. One such problem is the level of analysis at which 'values' have explanatory status. In some cases we refer to variables at the level of the individual actor (tolerance of uncertainty or ambiguity for example), in some cases values attach to a role (of local respresentative), in other cases values are specific to a group (working class Labour councillors' intolerance of social or sexual deviance), in yet others to the organisation (a set of shared and transmitted assumptions or 'deep structures' about 'how things are'), in still others to the dominant orientations of discrete and perhaps relatively homogenous social areas (the East End, the coastal town, the growing suburb), while in cross-national research we may be concerned with the effect of cultural values on domestic and foreign policy.

A second problem arises when we recognise that values may be in conflict within the policy process. Such conflicts may occur between individuals, between individuals in their roles, or between personal and organisational values. Conceptualising conflict resolution in the policy process is a separate question (see Young and Mills 1981). I propose to bypass it here by means of the simplifying assumption of a single agent or unified agencies.

A third problem is captured in the argument that values 'explain' only at an unacceptable level of triviality. This is the general position adopted by Brian Barry in his *Sociologists, Economists and Democracy* (1970). I am not concerned here to defend political sociologists from Barry's barbed wit, although there is certainly a very powerful case to be made for the defence, even on grounds of Barry's own choosing. What is of immediate concern here is Barry's general dismissal of the study of values as unscientific and as excessively complicating his preferred logico-deductive model of political behaviour.

Barry attacks value analysis at the level of culture and ignores volumes of research carried out in more limited contexts. He skips easily from fairly satirising the confused circularity of certain cultural determinists to the contention at lower levels of generality that 'by definition, the evidence for a "value" is simply a description of the behaviour it is then used to explain' (1970: p. 89). Barry quotes a number of examples of this flawed logic in value analysis, and his warning against circularity in the inference of values from behaviour and subsequent explanations of that behaviour by reference to those values is salutary. Nevertheless, he overstates his case when he develops an extraordinary argument about causal explanation from the example of his arriving late at an appointment through missing a train, an example which though trivial will serve well enough to refute his own argument that values are necessarily descriptions of the behaviour they are intended to explain.

In the case of Professor Barry and the missed train, we might have a number of explanatory goals. We might be interested in his values, in which case his consistent missing of trains (but not an isolated incident) taken with other supporting evidence (consistent lateness for meetings and perhaps behaviour within meetings) would enable us to make inferences about one dimension of Professor Barry's values: his orientations-to-meetings. The behaviour would be evidence for the values and, if it were considerable, would enable us to explain or even predict his behaviour in quite other situations by reference to these values. On the other hand we might be concerned to explain his behaviour, in this case 'travel behaviour'. Here we would need a body of evidence as to his values (independent of his travel behaviour) derived perhaps from life history, projective tests, depth interviews, semantic differentials or a battery of other techniques in order to say that in certain situations, Professor Barry is likely to 'decide', arrange, or unconsciously manage to miss his train.

The (presumed) problem of Professor Barry and his trains is directly analogous to the task of explaining policy outcomes by non-tautological recourse to 'values'. Moreover it points to the need to examine the subjective processes through which situational factors are mediated; we would not for example accept distance from the station as an 'explanation' of Professor Barry repeatedly missing his trains.

The final problem in 'value analysis' is the range of meanings attributable to the term. This is often obscured by the practice of asserting in some highly general and platitudinous fashion that values are 'important' or 'crucial' for understanding behaviour. The intellectual disservice performed by such uncritical generalities can be seen in the following passage taken from an undergraduate text in political sociology:

> We defined political sociology as the examination of the links between politics and society, between social structures and political structures and between social behaviour and political behaviour; and in discussing its development and the approaches and methods appropriate to its study, we touched upon the problems of objectivity and the study of values and ideas in political behaviour. These are of course problems common to the whole of social science – the extent to which its practitioners can be objective in their studies and whether values are of legitimate concern to them. The behavioural approach in particular stresses the need to separate facts from values, though it does not necessarily hold that the latter should be ignored. No-one acts in complete isolation of values.
>
> The political sociologist is therefore deeply concerned with the values

held by individuals, with the ways they are acquired and the way in which they change, since values hold the key to political behaviour.

(Althoff and Rush 1972: pp. 185–6)

In order to go beyond statements of this sort we must be more precise in saying what we think values are. The first problem we encounter is one of identifying values, and the second one of agreeing on terminology that is less ambiguous than that which led the authors cited above into such an intellectual quagmire. The term 'value' is clearly used to denote a wide variety of meanings. Its use by economists to represent a utility generating property or as the valuation revealed in a preferential choice serves to confuse the issue by the use of a term which is common also to psychology and anthropology (Jacob and Flink 1962). Indeed the multi-disciplinary parentage of words compounds the confusions that arise from uncertainty as to whether political scientists are 'really' economists, historians, sociologists, psychologists or anthropologists *manqué*. For example, the 'economic' usage – and I use the term according to Barry's criterion – is not without influence in political science. Lasswell and Kaplan speak of values as 'desired' or 'goal' events. As they explain:

> X values y means that x acts so as to bring about the consummation of y. The act of valuing we call 'valuation' and we speak of the object or situation desired as value.
>
> (1952: p. 16)

A distinct yet related usage occurs in Easton's (1965) conception of the political process as 'the authoritative allocation of values'.

A good deal of interdisciplinary confusion arises if these understandings of value, valuations, and values are not properly distinguished from those concepts of value which are intended to denote broader characteristics of the actor, characteristics which this paper sets out to discuss. Indeed, if it were not for the economists' unrecognised penetration of political science, the very centrality of the value concept in economics would constitute a strong case for relinquishing our claim to the similar term. But values also have a long record of usage within psychology, anthropology, sociology and political science, and it is important to clarify just what it is that we are trying to express and how it differs from the economists' usages.

In their broad survey of values in the policy process, Jacob and Flink reviewed a whole spectrum of meanings before settling for a working definition of values as 'the normative standards by which human beings are influenced in their choice among alternative courses of action which they perceive' (Jacob and Flink 1962: p. 10). This definition, which points to the policy analyst's interest in the criteria governing evaluation rather than the economist's concern with valuations themselves, is closely in line with the way in which sociologists have handled the concept. But an obvious problem remains. In the business of making policy judgements, the perception of alternatives – indeed, the perception of the field of action – is clearly as vital to outcomes as the normative standards by which choices are made. And policy-makers, like anyone else, define situations in terms of prevailing 'realities' as well as in terms of the normative currents that flow within them.

These considerations lead, I think, to an inescapable conclusion. If we are to understand the role of 'values' in public policy-making, we must either define the term in a very precise manner, narrow enough to exclude valuation but broad enough to include perception and belief; or we must abandon it altogether for something less ambiguous. The fact that we all think we know what we mean by values – worse, that we know what the other fellow means – is the root of our confusion.

As soon as we look beyond the term 'values', we find that the conceptual field is drastically overpopulated. Consider just some of the more important works that have focused on the phenomenon of normative–cognitive bases for action. We are all familiar with Vickers's (1965) concept of the 'appreciative system' which denotes the actor's representation of the world in which he acts. There is also Boulding's (1956) seminal essay, *The Image*, in which he is concerned in particular with the structuring of the actor's subjective knowledge of his world. There is Miller, Galanter and Pribram's (1960) more ambitious notion of 'Image-and-Plans' which captures both perceptual and active aspects of human life. There is Robert Lane's (1972, 1973) work on 'core belief systems', where he is concerned with 'how a person thinks of himself in society'. There is Geertz's (1973) rather specific notion of ideology as actors' 'maps of problematic social reality'. And there is the notion of 'value orientations', a blend of existential and normative propositions, employed by Kluckhohn

(1951) and Kluckhohn and Strodtbeck (1961). There are of course very many other terms possessing an approximately similar function (Lane lists forty, and his listing is by no means exhaustive) as well as alternative meanings to be attached to such dangerously familiar terms as 'ideology'.

To sum up, the attempt to 'explain' behaviour through 'values' has little chance of success until the underlying conceptual confusion has been tackled. The adoption of conventional terminology is not in itself sufficient to the success of the enterprise, although it is perhaps a necessary first step. The next part of this section is therefore addressed to formalising a concept for this purpose.

The assumptive world of the actor

On the argument above, any acceptable term for the subjective attributes which actors bring to the policy implementation process must necessarily cover a wider range of meaning than the familiar 'values', 'perception', or 'belief'. In a series of earlier papers I proposed a framework for conceptualising a person's total subjective experience as his 'assumptive world' (Young 1977; Young and Mills 1980; Young, Mason and Mills 1980). Within this are integrated the values, beliefs and perceptions the individual has of the world he acts upon. At any level of generality four elements are distinguishable, although interdependent and inseparable.

First there is the cognitive element, a man's ability to recognise the facticity of his world. Second there is the affective element; a man's valuation of aspects of the world as he apprehends it. Third there is the cathectic element, which refers to a man's sense of relatedness to the world he both creates and experiences. Fourth there is the directive element, wherein a man is moved to act upon the world. The interdependence of these elements is discussed at length in Young (1977).

The assumptive world may also be thought of as hierarchically organised. Lower level opinion, beliefs or precepts derive in part from and may be validated by appeal to the more fundamental aspects of culture or personality. These will include the middle-range constructs with which we manage the world as it is presented to us. At a still higher level of generality are the generalised, symbolic, taken for granted and untestable representations of the world.

The formal, or structural, properties of assumptive worlds are however a secondary issue here. The primary issue is their explanatory utility. Much of the discussion of 'values' and 'ideology' assumes a distinction between these subjective properties on the one hand, and 'behaviour' on the other. Whether one seeks to associate such variables for the purposes of description, *post hoc* explanation, or the prediction of future outcomes is immaterial. The dichotomy itself is a false one, and the weak empirical links between attitudes and behaviour (Fishbein 1967; Tittle and Hill 1967), far from supporting the extreme positivist case, merely reflect the inadequate conceptualisations of 'attitude studies'. On the present analysis, aspects of the assumptive world infuse behaviour with meaning compelling us to speak of action (a category which embodies significance for the actor) rather than of behaviour (a category which embodies significance only for the observer). This conception of the phenomenon of meaningful human action forgoes 'objective, explicit explanation' *(Erklären)* in favour of the interpretation of the actor's subjective meanings *(Verstehen)* (Ermath 1978; Baldwin and Baldwin 1978; Dallmayer and McCarthy 1977). The relationship between 'values' and behaviour need not then be argued in Professor Barry's terms; he presents us with a pseudo-problem.

The term 'assumptive world' is deliberately chosen to reflect the analytical significance of the actor-in-his-world, and embodies a notion of man as an active creature within a world which is subjectively and intersubjectively constructed (Berger and Luckman 1966; Schutz 1967). The actor then interprets the world as he acts within and upon it. Such interpretations have the status of 'imaginative simplifications' and so function as to bring order to the chaos and flux of everyday experience (Neisser 1967; Abler, Adams and Gould 1977). In 'endlessly simplifying, organising and generalising his own view of his own environment' the actor necessarily 'imposes on this environment his own constructions and meanings' (Bateson 1944) and 'by learning to recognise and act appropriately within his expectable environment a man makes a lifespace his own' (Parkes 1971).

Much as all social actors operate within an expectable lifespace (Lewin 1948, 1952; Mey 1972) so too do governmental actors, from the policy-maker to the street level bureaucrat, come to define and operate within a bounded domain or 'action space' (Thompson

1967; Randall 1973). The dimensions of the assumptive world of the governmental actor that are relevant to our purposes are therefore those that pertain to his policy-system role (as prison governor, Under Secretary, Chief Executive or health visitor) rather than those that pertain to his other social roles (as paterfamilias, bridge player or prize marrow-exhibitor).

Finally, it may be objected that this portrayal is of a passively adapting 'actor'. Recall, however, the formal structure of the assumptive world as an interplay of not just cognitive and affective but also cathectic and directive elements. The actor creates a model of the world as it is, as well as preferred and dreaded scenarios for its future development. While these models enable him to 'make sense of experience' they also place the actor firmly within that experience and compel him to respond to it. The mismatch between image and experience may lead to passive adaptation of the 'world in the mind' or, if the foregoing analysis of the structure and functioning of the assumptive world holds, to manipulative intervention within the experienced world (Young 1979). Unlike 'lay' mortals, governmental actors demonstrably intervene in pursuit of purposes in the 'real world'. Because such purposes reflect the mismatch between imagination and experience, purposive action – as distinct from routine or compliant action – can only be understood in the context of the assumptive world of the situationally embedded actor. And our interest in the exercise of discretion as a 'problem' of implementation attaches to the point where mundane action ends and purposive action begins.

Conclusions

The view of discretion as an implementation problem accords a central place to the analysis of the peripheral actor's situation and meaning-structures. I have argued that the actions of 'implementers' can only be understood in terms of their own 'definitions of the situation'. Given their subordinate position within the policy system, these definitions will often fail to match those of the policy-makers; not only will they have divergent appreciations of problems but they will often attribute problematic status to rather different phenomena.

Such subjective factors, while central, are not of course the sole dimension of the issue of discretion. Davis (1971) provides a starting

point for several of the contributions to this volume in calling attention to two issues: the extent of an actor's power and his propensity
to make choices. While I have suggested elsewhere that 'power' is
itself subjectively defined (Young, Mason and Mills 1980) we can,
for the purposes of the present argument, treat power (control) and
choice (definitions) as independent dimensions of discretion.
Thus, while discretionary action is a general issue in the study of
social action, 'implementation' is a relatively limited concept which
should be taken to refer to a particular configuration of control and
choice.

The argument may be put as follows: the outcomes of the policy
system are determined *both* by the degree of control over discretionary
officials *and* by the extent to which they share the policy-makers'
definitions of the situation, that is the degree to which they inhabit a
common assumptive world. Where control is direct and the situation
evokes a common appreciation on the part of both centre and
periphery, then 'policy implementation' may be said to occur.
Where control is direct and there is no common appreciation, then
'policy evasion' (the classic 'implementation problem') may be the
response of the periphery. Where control is diffuse and there is no
common appreciation, the pattern of outcomes will display 'policy
variation'. Where control is diffuse but centre and periphery share a
common definition of the situation, then 'policy assimilation' has
taken place (whether this is from centre to periphery or from
periphery to centre). In neither of these latter cases is it helpful to
speak of implementation or 'implementation problems'.

Dimensions of discretion

| | | Definitions of the situation | |
		Discordant	Concurrent
Degree of control	Direct	Evasion	Implementation
	Diffuse	Variation	Assimilation

It may be left to the reader to exemplify the categories with
examples of policy issues in each type of situation and to speculate as
to the relative efficacy for central policy-makers of control shifts and
persuasive efforts. The value of this perspective is not that it

illuminates the nature and limits of discretion *per se*, for the other contributors to this volume have accomplished that task in a distinct and plausible fashion. Rather, its value lies in the restricted usage advocated for 'implementation', in which only evasion is seen as an 'implementation problem'. Moreover, it draws attention to the centrality of the subjective dimension in the transmission of policy intentions and in the exercise of *de facto* discretion. That subjective dimension, apparent in the 'appreciative gaps' or conflicting 'definitions of the situation' that characterise inter and intra-agency relations, demands the systematic exploration of the assumptive worlds of 'policy-makers' and 'policy implementers'.

3 Discretionary Decision-making in Social Work
Gilbert Smith

This chapter is about discretionary decision-making in social work but addresses in particular the question of how useful this notion might be as a focus for empirical research into the structure and functioning of the personal social services. I shall begin with an observation, suggesting that the way in which the issues of discretion have been framed in some other fields of research may require some modification before transfer to the social work scene. I shall expand on this point by reviewing briefly, and in the light of social work, some of the main questions raised throughout this book and I shall draw some parallels with the medical profession. I shall comment on some existing research into the practice of social work and conclude with some suggestions for future research.

The main thrust of the paper will be to argue, first, that any extended *a priori* definitional debate about the term 'discretionary decision' is not a good investment and that the merits of research converging on specifically 'discretionary' decision-making are dubious. In summary, my reasons for holding these views are as follows. Presumably the idea of a 'discretionary decision' implies the idea of a 'non-discretionary decision'. I take it that a decision of this latter kind would in principle be totally predictable, programmable, and thus in an important sense, hardly a decision at all. Some notable developments have recently been reported in programming the process of medical diagnosis and certainly most scenarios for the future in a high technology society envisage redundancy for the general practitioner as a diagnostician. Similarly, concern in the field of social security or housing provision about the discretion exercised by low level officials reflects the view, not so much that discretion is abused, but rather that a set of operational rules and clear client rights should eliminate decision-making itself from the system at the point of service provision. We then regress to the problem of defining 'decision'. I am arguing that this line of discussion does not auger well. The uncomfortable process of moving from theory to data (and back again) is more promising. This is not to say that the idea of discretion has *no* place in research on social work. It has. But insofar as the notion does feature in a programme of investigation it should constitute a topic rather than a resource for social scientific enquiry. For the most interesting thing about the idea of 'discretion' is not how it is defined but how it is used.

An Observation

The argument begins with an observation. On the one hand there are, within social work organisations, groups of people who are not generally credited with exercising any significant impact upon the quality of service provision to clients and who would not typically describe themselves as wielding any substantial discretionary powers. Indeed some of them, at least, would repudiate such a designation of their activities. These people are the secretaries, telephonists, receptionists, typists, filing clerks and junior administrative staff who are so immediately apparent on entering a social work office but who are so rarely mentioned in the textbook accounts of social work. Yet a growing body of evidence indicates that, in practice, the impact of the decisions which these people make is substantially more than is often recognised. Hall (1974), for example, has described the activities of receptionists in the child-care service within the framework of Blau's classic study (1960, 1963). He quotes Blau's general conclusion that receptionists exercised considerable discretion in interpreting agency procedures for screening applicants for job interviews. In certain respects this meant that the service was offered inequitably, but that was of no great concern to the professional interviewers because the receptionists' activities ensured that on a day-to-day basis the agency operated smoothly with a regular flow of applicants and interviewees. Hall's own conclusions (p. 127) are similar:

> Some social workers delegated tasks to the reception staff which they themselves were unwilling or unable to perform. However, this practice was also functional for the receptionists, despite their criticism of the practice. This informal delegation of additional powers helped to increase

their own job satisfaction whilst at the same time making it easier for them to deal with difficult situations when they arose. In the process *receptionists were drawn even further into the social work activities of the agency.* (emphasis added)

In another study on the same theme Zimmerman (1971) has described how intake workers in an American welfare agency exercise discretion in order to convey the appearance of behaving in accordance with 'the rules'. He comments (p. 232):

By suspending the rule in light of the exceptional character of the situation, the intent of the rule might be said to be honoured – its intent being formulable on a particular occasion by situationally relevant reference to the 'usual' course of affairs its routine or precedented use typically reproduces. Through the situated judgmental modification of the routine application of the rule, the 'same' business as usual course of affairs may be – for all intents and purposes – reliably reproduced. In other words, *what the rule is intended to provide for is discovered in the course of employing it over a series of actual situations.* (emphasis added)

That is why professional supervisors do not always understand (or acknowledge) the level of discretion that their so called subordinates are effecting and that is why research workers who only talk to professionals may not learn about it either. Certainly when doing research it is easy to make the mistake of neglecting the activities of people who are not held to be important by others. In conducting the fieldwork for a study of intake and allocation routines in social work (Smith 1980) it took me some time to learn that the behaviour of the professional social workers was, in some respects, rather predictable and that in seeking answers to my questions I was to have to spend more and more time observing the variable and complex events in the reception offices, typing pools and filing rooms.

Thus we can advance the generalisation that clerical and administrative staff in social work agencies, who would not normally be so described by others, are nevertheless making decisions which affect services to clients and which are not programmable so as to be totally predictable.

On the other hand, for professional social workers the position is the reverse. For them the idea of programmed decision-making is an anathema and the notion of discretionary decisions, rooted in the worker's own knowledge and skills, is a crucial part of the collective self image of social work as a profession. Adler and Asquith (chapter 1 in this volume) are correct in observing that it is an important part of the ideal account of professionalism that 'professionals have largely unfettered discretion and make their decisions by reference to a body of esoteric knowledge'. Likewise, most professionals seek to maintain the distinction between 'administrative' and 'professional' discretion, for it is helpful in establishing and defending a domain of privilege. Although it is beyond the scope of this chapter to enter a broad discussion of the role of professionals in modern society, it is clear that social workers are no exception in seeing that, if they can 'pull off' a professional image in respect of their freedom to make decisions, major advantages accrue both organisationally and more generally. As observers, however, it is important to avoid the error, which Adler and Asquith subsequently make, of believing an ideal to be an accurate account of situated decision-making behaviour. The explanatory utility of linking the ideas of 'profession' and 'discretion' must remain an empirical question.

Nevertheless the link is made and in social work this stance is accentuated by the way in which casework is so highly individualised. In spite of some superficial impact of sociology and social policy within social work education, and in spite of courtesy references to social work with 'families', 'groups' and 'communities', social work in practice remains largely wedded to the idea of idiosyncratic treatment programmes for clients. This is accompanied by notions of the peculiarity of each professional decision, and this in turn accounts, in part, for the importance attached to the existence of professional autonomy in decision-making: all of which is encapsulated in the notion of 'the one-to-one relationship' so frequently encountered in social work.

This theme is well illustrated by the rich data in Stevenson and Parsloe (1978). This collection of research reports is a particularly good source of ideological material as it is heavily dependent upon interviews with social workers and, overall, presents 'the practitioner's view'. As I shall go on to argue, the study of discretion must rest heavily upon triangulated methods, including substantially more observational research than is currently available, but 'method bound' studies are nevertheless useful, provided we are clear about which particular aspect of the phenomenon of discretion is being tapped. Browne (1978: p. 134) concludes that 'A feature of all the studies was the wide ranging freedom which social workers had to choose the style and content of their direct work with clients.' And, in reference to the way in which their work was organised, social workers are quoted as saying:

> 'It is left very much up to me.'
> 'I do it myself – [I have] quite a lot of discretion.'
> 'Cases are reviewed by my concern about them.'

A team leader adds (p. 81): 'I like to regard my colleagues as professionals in this respect.' In the same study Parsloe and Hill (1978: p. 222), discussing 'supervision and accountability' quoted a social worker, whom they describe as 'unusually clear about the issue', as saying that it was:

> difficult to know the line where advice stops and direction begins, where professional responsibility ends and managerial responsibility begins. In supervision it is not at all clear what happens if I am told to do X and I say 'No'. Nobody has told me I have to say 'OK' and nobody has told my senior she has the right to do such and such. What happens? It's a mess.

Parsloe and Hill themselves conclude (p. 223) that the arrangements for supervision, as the social workers described them, placed a heavy responsibility on team members to keep their team leaders informed and to know what they would be informed about 'for it is a mark of professionalism in social workers to know their own strengths and weaknesses and to be able to identify when they need help with their work'.

Yet in spite of the central position of 'discretion' in the imagery of professional social work, a growing body of evidence indicates that social workers are probably behaving in ways which are very much more highly routinised than is generally acknowledged, certainly by social workers themselves. There are several grounds for believing that this may well be so.

Firstly, the problematic relationship between professional ideologies and organisational practice is well established in research on health and welfare agencies, much of which follows the original investigations of Strauss et al. (1964) into the functioning of psychiatric institutions. Rees (1978: p. 53) has made the general point in the context of British social work:

The almost mystical reverence given to the importance of 'the casework relationship' can be maintained if it does not depend on empirical evidence of what social workers actually do and if the goals of casework appear sufficiently high minded. But theories and hopes are not practice.

Secondly, as Zimmerman (1971) has pointed out, welfare organisations typically claim that (at least most of the time) they handle their affairs in a rational and responsible manner. It may be easier to make that claim if decisions are taken in a routine fashion. For while a professional may have vested interests in claiming the knowledge and skills to exercise discretion in *general*, in any *particular* cases of dispute the firmer ground is to be able to demonstrate that the decision was made in ways which were entirely 'normal' or 'usual'. Indeed, when apparently bizarre or discretionary decisions on the part of officials are contested by patients or clients affronted by them, they are often justified as 'only a matter of routine'. For discretion is a two-edged weapon and a discretionary decision may equally be cast as an 'arbitrary' one.

Thus social work and social services departments accused of irresponsibility, in releasing a child from their care or making excessive cash payments under section 12 of the Social Work (Scotland) Act 1968, typically react by 'tightening up on their procedures'. It is a regular defence against charges of incompetence for a health or welfare organisation to demonstrate that there was strict adherence to standard guidelines. A regional policy and procedures handbook for internal use on sections 10 and 12 of the Social Work (Scotland) Act 1968 may run to 100 pages or so and the Chairman of an English Social Services Committee facing press criticism recently said in interview that he was now confident that the departmental procedures for returning children in care to their parents were 'watertight'. Certainly social workers seldom refer, in specific cases, to the precise skills or pieces of knowledge which justify a decision. Indeed Browne (1978) has noted this feature of social work as posing a particular problem for the profession (p. 135):

There was evidence that social workers used concepts from sociology, social and individual psychology to understand clients and their difficulties. But there was less evidence that those concepts had been assimilated into an integral system to guide practice.

As a result, decisions that are not routinised may provoke high levels of anxiety as social workers seek to avoid taking responsibility for the consequences of their discretion. Browne refers to the decision to close cases and quotes a respondent (p. 86); 'I think *we* can't close them, it isn't that the cases are not closable'. (emphasis original). This is a particularly good example of the general point that I am making here for many social work agencies have minimal established regular procedures for case closure (as compared with the complex routines for reception, intake and allocation). Social workers are apparently rather free to make this decision but often cases merely pile up 'on the books' (and continue to feature in official statistics) while in practice they are organisationally 'dead'.

A third pointer to the likely routinisation of professional decisions lies in the role of files and records within social work. Many social work texts discuss professional–client interaction as if it were invariably 'face-to-face'. Often it is not. Many of the most crucial decisions in a clients' 'organisational career' may be taken when the client is not present, and with heavy reference to recorded material. Examples include the decisions of allocation, case closure (when it is made) and any action taken on the basis of a case conference. Certainly in many medical contexts case conferences are dominated by the case files and nursing 'Kardex'. Insufficient empirical data is available on the construction and use of welfare records to draw any definite conclusions (but see Zimmerman 1969b), although references are to be found to the role of files and records in comparable contents within the health, educational and juvenile justice systems. Cicourel and Kitsuse (1963) note in passing the part played by counselling records in identifying a child and parents as 'problems' in the educational system. Macintyre (1978: pp. 607–9) concludes a discussion of record-taking and making in an antenatal clinic with these comments:

> The patient already, to some extent, *is* what the records say she is. In some sense, therefore, record-makers find what they expect to find. Their investigative procedures are mooted in particular conceptions of the social world and these conceptions are then reinforced by the results of such investigative procedures. Everything I have said above about the relationship between cultural assumptions and investigative procedures points to the conclusion that there is not a randomisation of responses but rather systematic trends.   (emphasis original)

Within the organisation of juvenile justice (Cicourel 1977), the systematic impact of professional ideologies upon social enquiry reports in particular, has been noted (Hardiker and Webb 1979). Carlen (1976: p. 23) paints a picture of the impact of paperwork on court procedures from the defendant's point of view:

> The defendant, bereft of any relevant rubric giving guidance on how to elude the judicial objectivation processes which engulf him, struggles to tell each new and overtly sympathetic report-writer, form-filler and record-keeper how *he* defines himself and his situation. On each occasion he finds that his court records, prison records, medical records, employment records, school records and those of any other agency of which he has been client, patient, worker or prisoner have preceded him. The living obituaries actualise a social structure in which the defendants in magistrates' courts have lost the information game before it even starts. Most of them know all along that it isn't a game anyway.   (emphasis original)

The point of relevance to the discussion in this chapter is the overriding impression to be gained from these comparisons of the way in which records reduce cases and decisions to a rather limited number of standard forms. On the one hand, the record provides the framework in terms of which the people and events shall be construed. For example, an intake interview must be no more than twenty lines long. A distinction is drawn between 'action', 'assessment' and 'problem'. A client's 'problem' is reduced to six words for the central card index – and so on. At the very least a social worker must see the infinite variety of clients as potentially recordable. In practice most social work agencies get by on about seven or eight major categories of 'problems' or 'needs'; for example, 'homeless', 'financial', 'marital', 'children', 'N.F.A.' (no further action) and so on. As Raffel (1979: pp. 48–9), in line with Macintyre, notes, again in a study of medical records,

> It is not that records record things but that the very idea of recording determines in advance how things will have to appear.

On the other hand, records also stylise clients and events through the stereotypes which are a major resource in the decoding process.

In short, the authority of various documents is made accountable in terms of the routine, organised ways in which the unremarkable projects are geared to one another under the auspices of typified, generally known interests and motives, and with adumbrated reference to the more or less standardised procedures that presumably control the gearing.

(Zimmerman 1969b: p. 345)

Zimmerman concludes (p. 354) by describing how the ability to proceed along these routine paths in decision-making is a part of the welfare worker's stock-in-trade.

The taken-for-granted use of documents is dependent on an ordered world – the ordered world of organisations, and the ordered world of the society at large. When simply taken for granted, the features of these ordered domains are matters of mere recognition for which no accounts are called for or given. Indeed, such routine recognition, and the action and inference proceeding from it, is the mark of the competent worker.

A further reason for anticipating the routine character of professionals' decisions lies in the problem which social workers refer to as 'bombardment'. It is a crucial feature of welfare agencies that, like many other service organisations, there must be a regular and continuous flow of the 'referral', through to 'client', through to effective 'discharge' (even if this does not take the form of a clearly 'closed' case). Most social workers certainly report that the demands placed upon themselves and their agencies are excessive and leave them little time to engage in what they regard as the most important aspects of their professional practice. For they, like all other staff of an organisation, must, as Zimmerman (1971: p. 237) points out, 'bring off the day's work with respect to the constraints of timing, pacing and scheduling represented by the described "actual task structure"'. But professional discretion is, by its very nature, a time consuming, irregular and generally troublesome activity. Bureaucratically speaking (without perjorative connotation), routine rules, standard categories and automatic procedures are simpler, smoother and generally much more efficient at ensuring the continuous flow of clients through the several stages of an agency which require co-ordinated and sometimes quite tightly synchronised activity on the part of several groups of staff. The problems are akin to those of continuous production in an industrial setting. There is a tendency for professionals to categorise and routinise their work in situations that entail similar constraints.

These grounds for believing that professional decisions are more highly routinised than they purport to be are supported by a certain amount of material in the research literature that reports this to be the case. Of course, as the ethnomethodologists have pointed out, it is one of the more absurd features of the study of occupations in general that, although we may be told a great deal about recruitment to a profession, the social class correlates of a profession, its pay structure and much else besides, we often remain ignorant about what the professionals actually do. The main weakness of the argument of those who claim that social work cannot be justified because it has not been precisely described is that that is true of most professions. It is particularly noticeable that so many of the accounts of professionalism, in social work and elsewhere, as entailing autonomy and discretionary powers are quite lacking in empirical evidence. But, as Chapman (1978) has shown in the context of the civil service, simply to enter the branch of an organisation and find out just exactly what each person is doing at that particular point in time, can be extraordinarily revealing. He concludes (p. 109), on the basis of his working experience in the Property Services Agency, that 'there are many of them [staff] in the higher reaches of the Civil Service, who have made a very pleasant career for themselves without taking a single decision'. Certainly, when we turn to the comparatively limited body of work which offers some data-based (especially ethnographic) statement about the nature of decision-making by professionals in social work and medicine we see a picture which contrasts in important ways with the public image.

Rees (1978: p. 60) comments on the basis of his research in Scotland, where legislation lays upon the social work departments of local authorities a general duty to 'promote social welfare':

> The wide terms of reference of the Social Work (Scotland) Act have been regarded as giving social workers the chance to use discretionary powers in some novel ways (Carmichael 1969, 1977). But staff from both agencies [studied] were concerned to parcel their responsibilities in ways which conformed to familiar routines.

Blaxter (1967: p. 9) makes a related observation on the basis of her study of the operation of services for the disabled:

> Ideally, in the medical model, as in the social work model, there is no categorisation of the patient or his needs; each is individual. Yet in so

complex a structure and with much of the work so specialised and differentiated, labels are necessary, and the organisation is likely to categorize in the ways which best suit the task in hand.

In noting the following points she also refers (p. 5) directly to one aspect of the paradox that I have been discussing:

> At one and the same time there are pressures towards integration, and towards specialisation and differentiation. Thus, while a movement towards loosening of categorisation is taking place, paradoxically, administrative definitions become more and more important.

The structural roots of this paradox have been more fully discussed in the context of medical practice than in relation to social work. Clinical autonomy for both consultants and general practitioners has long been a hallowed principle but with the rising costs of medical care and the increasing political significance of these costs, the principle is no longer immune from criticism (if it ever was).

> The whole rationale of clinical freedom may be increasingly questioned. The clinical freedom to differ widely as to their [doctors'] conception of need has led to inconsistencies of treatment between patients and to the allocation, without challenge, of scarce resources to medical practices of no proven value. The doctor stands in the rather unique position of being both a supplier and an arbitrator. This gives him enormous discretion. Certainly such heroic individualism is inconsistent with modern management.
>
> (Cooper 1975: p. 59)

Certainly rationing takes place and certainly the doctor–patient relationship, as McGlew and Robertson point out (Chapter 10 below), is embedded in the social and economic environment of the health service. But there is some evidence to suggest that rationing practices are by no means the monopoly of professional staff. In a discussion of 'The informal rationing of primary medical care', Foster (1979) points, for example, to the way in which GPs use appointment and other systems staffed by clerical workers and receptionists to limit 'excess demand' on their services. Decisions within these systems are based more upon the common-sense judgements of untrained staff than upon the clinical discretion of professional practitioners.

Thus the observation with which I am suggesting we may usefully begin to plan research on discretionary decision-making in social work (and it may be useful to approach the study of comparable professions in similar terms) is this. There is an apparent paradox that those who are thought to occupy discretionary positions (and they do court that image) may well not, whereas those who are thought to occupy more mundane positions (and generally they abnegate a discretionary label) may in practice effect a discretionary service. The particular irony is that a number of those factors that seem to promote the routinisation of supposedly discretionary decisions are those that also promote the exercise of discretion within the apparently routine clerical and administrative aspects of the social work services. I have mentioned some of those factors in passing. The continuous flow of clients and the paperwork of bureaucratised practice limit social workers' freedom to perceive and categorise their clients in some ways rather than others. Yet as Zimmerman (1969b), Hall (1974) and Macintyre (1978) (in the context of medicine) have shown, it is precisely in generating the records on which subsequent service may be based, and in controlling the flow of work through an organisation (especially by defending or overloading professionals) that clerical and administrative discretion is so important. I shall be suggesting that further research designed to identify crucial features of decision-making situations would be fruitful. This, then, is the observation, and I have spent some time making it for what ensues seems to be important for a programme of research in the following ways.

(1)   The complex relationship between policy objectives and organisational dynamics may mean that mandatory rules become effectively discretionary or may mean that discretionary judgements become routinised. Although the first half of this equation has provided a focus for some research in social policy and the sociology of welfare, the second half has been studied less frequently. The whole enterprise will require a combination of 'macro' and 'micro' techniques (in both theory and method) which is not typical of this field of research.

(2)   It is clear that the meaning of 'discretion' varies between groups. Sometimes 'discretion' is courted and sometimes it is repudiated. Discretion is displayed by some groups in some situations but is disguised by other groups on other occasions. We need to understand more fully how the idea of discretion is employed

instrumentally for varying purposes. In any expansion of this point it will also be important to consider the ways in which clients as well as staff can be seen to exercise discretion in their decision-making. Blaxter (1976: p. 11) makes this point:

> It must not be supposed that the individual, the patient is passive. In one sense the clinical labels and the administrative categories are facts: the medical records, the pieces of paper giving assessment of money entitlement are true and real. But the reality of the individual's situation is a different sort of truth – an amalgam of official facts and private realities, of emotions and intentions, impressions and opinions. To him, the only reality is his own definition of the situation.

(3)   The automatic prescription that discretion is a 'bad thing' is to be avoided as the basis of research. The research task is at least initially, to study this debate rather than to enter it. This is not, of course, to argue against the policy and practical relevance of research. But prejudice is no basis for this relevance. It may be quite as important to promote as to control discretion. That is something to be investigated when we understand the phenomenon.

(4)   It is clear that the definition of discretionary decision-making for research purposes is far from precise. In the study of social work, at least, it seems most helpful to regard this as an empirical task rather than as an *a priori* definitional question.

Some Outstanding Issues

In the light of these comments it may now be useful to return to some of the main issues which feature in discussions of discretionary decision-making, asking ourselves how helpful the debate is for clarifying research designs and proposals in the field of social work. Several questions have featured particularly prominently;

(1)   How is discretion to be defined?
(2)   How is discretion to be controlled?
(3)   What are the consequences of widespread discretionary decision-making?
(4)   What models of service agencies provide a basis for studying discretion?
(5)   What factors influence discretionary decision-making?

A great deal of discussion tends to be devoted to the issue of how 'discretion' should be defined and in general I have found the apparent supposition that we can settle upon a definition, before research begins in social work, to be unhelpful. There are several reasons for this. As I have mentioned, the notion of discretion (and associated concepts) in social work seems to be used by different personnel, on different occasions, under different situational constraints, in different ways, for different purposes and to different effects. (There may be other differences as well.) Any attempt to provide a firm *a priori* definition rides roughshod over these differences. Adler and Asquith (Chapter 1 in this volume) are right in referring to a difference between 'professional' and 'administrative' discretion in social work if what they mean is that these notions are used by different groups in as yet unexplicated ways. But that is an empirical question. The clearest strategy is to retain discretion in social work as a topic rather than as a resource and that means that we must treat the *language* of discretion in relation to the *action* of discretion. It is the interaction between the two which is so important. As Bittner (in Salaman and Thompson 1973: p. 270) explains:

> The meaning of the concept, and of all the terms and determinations that are subsumed under it, must be discovered by studying their use in real scenes of action by persons whose competence to use them is socially sanctioned.

The alternatives are either that the researcher, 'must use that which he proposes to study as a resource for studying it' or that he 'attach to the terms a more or less arbitrary meaning by defining them operationally', in which case, 'interest in the actor's perspective is either deliberately abandoned, or some fictitious version of it is adopted'.

But even if we take the definitional debate to be aimed only at some rough working definition, there are problems. It is very hard in social work to see what a non-discretionary decision might look like, operationally. It would presumably be totally programmable. But that is quite uncharacteristic of the field of social work as a whole and in practice there would be minimal if any difference between the study of discretionary decision-making and simply that of decision-making.

Perhaps this confusion is inevitable if we try to consider definitional questions without reference to a problem for research. Overall I imagine that a programme of research on decision-making in social work would centre on a question of the general form: 'What are those factors which explain why and how particular decisions are taken about clients and potential clients, and what are the consequences of these decisions for the services which ensue?' The merits of any typology of different kinds of discretion must rest upon its utility in categorising the data in revealing ways. But in terms of this general question there is a danger that 'discretion' simply becomes a residual category for unexplained variance or else a statement of the view that we can never explain all the variance anyway because human beings exercise volition (depending upon one's philosophical position).

There is one further point about the definitional issue. Just as it is not readily apparent what 'discretion' looks like in social work as opposed to 'non-discretion', so neither is it clear that we can readily distinguish a 'decision' from other kinds of activity. Certainly the legal notion of being able to pinpoint precisely where and when a decision was made, what exactly it was, who made it, under what authority and so on, is quite uncharacteristic of social work. There is evidence in Rees (1978) and Mayer and Timms (1970), for example, of client frustration at the initial interview when clients feel that the social worker should be 'doing something', while the social worker feels that he should be 'assessing the problem'. Browne (1978) shows that the formalities of 'contract theory' in social work bear scant relationship to empirical practice. Impressions from the field of social work suggest that both the terms 'discretion' and 'decision' may be equally problematic.

On the problem of controlling discretion in social work I have already indicated that I can see no particular justification for posing the problem thus rather than as one of promoting discretion. So far as policy debate and public interest is concerned there may well be equal anxiety at the 'bureaucratisation' of decisions, the 'rubber stamping' and standard procedures and the general absence of professional judgement and individualised treatment. The terms of debate seem to have been heavily influenced by issues within the field of supplementary benefits in particular and these do not necessarily characterise social work. The more general point is that policy related research must contribute to the empirical accuracy and conceptual rigor of public debate. It will not help to build partisan precepts into the research design.

Any answer to the question of the consequences of widespread (discretionary) decision-making must remain, as I have suggested, an empirical one. The only point I would wish to make at this stage is to question Adler and Asquith's claim that the exercise of discretionary powers in social welfare takes place on a face-to-face level between individuals. In fact it is very noticeable in social work that many decisions are apparently made when the client is *not* with the social worker. The importance of the point is that any programme of research on decision-making in social welfare may need to range rather widely across contexts, situations and levels of the organisational hierarchy.

The issue of what models of service agencies provide a basis for studying discretion is one on which it is possible to comment more fully in advance of data collection, and a review of the literature in preparation for a programme of research in social work would encounter three issues which frequently arise in discussions about discretion. The notion of rule guided behaviour has, for the most part, been used with the implication that behaviour is a function of the rule. But research in the fields of health, welfare and juvenile justice, has given rise to the view that the meaning of the rule is equally determined by the situated actions which are deemed to constitute that rule. Certainly few studies now place any variable such as 'formal rules' as a significant determinant of decision-making activity. Indeed the whole trend of research on the organisations of social welfare has been to display the impotence of that view, and thus to suggest alternatives, in which the welfare worker's role in constructing his task under situational constraints, features prominently.

The so-called 'black box' model of bureaucracy (see Jowell 1975) which concentrates on 'objectives' and 'outputs' and implies that it is relatively unimportant to understand what goes on in between, has also proved deficient as the basis for research in welfare agencies. The idea that objectives go in and outcomes come out, however eminently reasonable that may seem, is in fact too rational to be true. Albrow (1970) sired the debate in sociology and the journals of public administration have featured a more or less parallel discussion

(Castles, Murray and Potter 1971). The particularly relevant point here is that the empirical difficulties that researchers have encountered in their attempts to define precisely the 'objectives of social welfare' have been most especially significant in displaying the conceptual limitations of any model that rests at all heavily on 'rational' notions of the goals or objectives of social work services.

In spite of denying the sociological nature of his contribution, Watson (chapter 11 in this volume) offers a framework which is essentially functionalist in character and a criticism of his chapter could well follow the lines of that debate. For example, the analysis borders on the kind of argument which insists that parties in battle integrate society because they reinforce the principles which dictate when one of them has won, a kind of argument that closely parallels the classic discussion in Coser's (1956) *The Functions of Social Conflict*. Certainly the specific illustration of the Children's Hearings as 'a policy which aims to sustain and promote forms of social integration' has been strongly criticised both in analyses of the policy basis of the system and in studies of the system in operation (Brown and Bloomfield 1979). But the more general point is that a view of social policy as 'aim[ing] to create moral relationships between individuals, relating them as members of a moral community' is now rather hard to defend. The potential of pluralist (Hall et al. 1975) and 'radical conflict' (George and Wilding 1976) models have recently been quite fully explored in the field of welfare policy and, although these debates in their present form may be far from satisfactory, the major weaknesses of the functionalist framework, especially as a guide to empirical research, have been well rehearsed. Specifically in relation to the concerns of this chapter, in so far as a functionalist model rests upon notions of an ideational consensus it does not begin to cope with the research problems that we will encounter in studying discretionary decision-making within social work. Rather, we require a framework which allows for dissensus, confusion and ambiguity in ideas about discretion, and which structures the empirical study of variation in actors' ideas under specific situational constraints and the relationship between these ideas and discretionary activity.

Finally there is the question of which factors influence discretionary decision-making. Suggestions have been made about the importance of bureaucratic factors, the political environment, power relationships, situational factors, organisational variables, professional reference groups, client influence, the economic climate, lay and professional ideologies and other matters. No doubt these topics would feature in the research designs for studies of discretion in social work as in other fields. But it is by no means clear that, when we come to this level of debate, the idea of 'discretion' has any particular merits for guiding research over and above the idea of 'decision-making' in general.

This later topic (simply 'decision-making') has long been a focus within research on social work. A recent example is a study by Lawson (1979) on 'Taking the decision to remove the child from the family' in which she concludes: 'it was clear that these social workers were not merely acting as tools of the law, but positively contributing to its interpretation'. She refers to the studies summarized in Packman (1975) which have examined how the notion of 'the welfare of the child' is in practice worked out. Lawson discusses the 'child's needs', 'parental history', 'general environment' and 'social workers' beliefs' and suggests that 'these particular groups of factors take on the weight they do because the judicial process, the rules of evidence and the statutes themselves demand certain kinds of proof' (mimeo). The point here is that one has no operational need of the idea of a specifically *discretionary* decision to undertake factorial research of this kind.

Research on Social Work Practice

Although there is not a *very* strong body of research reporting in detail what the practice of social work entails I have already mentioned a number of relevant studies (Hall 1974; Blaxter 1976; Mayer and Timms 1970; Stevenson and Parsloe 1978; Rees 1978; Zimmerman 1969a, 1969b, 1971) and there are further examples (e.g. Sainsbury 1975; Vosey 1975; Scott 1968; Jackson and Valencia 1979). These studies do not take decision-making as a central topic but they are relevant. Indeed there is a sense in which almost any empirical research report in the field of social welfare will contain material relevant to the topic of discretionary decision-making. For this reason it is likely that a literature review with the tasks of research design in mind will be more useful if it takes a small number of major studies and re-examines the data in some detail. It is clear that 'discretionary decision-making' is a rather slippery concept and a very wide-ranging, and thus necessarily superficial, review might not pin down the problems which are apparent when the detailed links between theory and method, data and policy implications are critically reviewed. In the last section of this chapter I wish, therefore, to offer a preliminary illustration of the kind of discussion that a literature review, along the lines that I have suggested, would entail.

Jackson and Valencia (1979) is one example of a study that considers decision-making explicitly. Chapter seven of their book is based on research into the way in which financial aid is offered through social work. They begin by referring to the model suggested by Donnison et al. (1975) to explain why 'effective policy frequently was made not by the controllers of resources but by the providers of service'. There are four reasons for this. First, social policy is rarely precisely defined. (The meaning assigned to social work objectives is crucial.) Second, controllers recognise providers as professionals with skills and knowledge on which to base decisions. ('Discretion' is perceived as an attribute of 'profession'.) Third, administrative structures militate against day-to-day control. (What it takes to constitute conformity to the rule is constantly negotiable.) And fourth, service providers claim close contact with those who demand a service. (Professionals perceive themselves as discretionary.) Within this framework Jackson and Valencia identify four groups whose attitudes towards discretion and whose decision-making activities must be explored separately: local councillors, social workers, clients and other relevant agencies (primarily the Supplementary Benefits Commission and the fuel and housing authorities).

In spite of the fact that 'Responsibility for formal policy-making on financial aid has been devolved from the national to the local government', Jackson and Valencia conclude that councillors do not have 'policy objectives'; 'At this level there appears to be what might be termed a "policy vacuum"', for a majority of councillors doubted their own ability to make judgements on social work matters. They felt that these decisions were best left to professionals and the professional social workers encouraged that view. Yet it was not quite that simple, for councillors of all political persuasions, although reluctant to decide 'broad policy', felt happier about making decisions about individual clients on whose behalf they had intervened.

Within the community of social workers, Jackson and Valencia point out (p. 95) how important it is to distinguish between different levels in the professional hierarchy. Senior staff may lay down 'policy' (one professional is conceived of as being capable of limiting the discretion of another) but in practice team leaders, area officers and the like are crucially important.

> In certain circumstances they may be able to reinterpret official policy; at the very least they can put their own gloss on it or adapt it to meet their own particular needs.

Much depends upon the way in which perceptions of the various rules interact within the administrative structure of the agency.

So far as the public in general and clients in particular are concerned Jackson and Valencia note (p. 101) that they have a very sketchy conception of social work.

> The absence of a firm body of rules or guidelines governing financial aid in many social work departments means that the way a claim or approach is proceeded with will depend, to a large extent, on the relationship between the social worker and the client.

Two factors which I mentioned earlier in this paper are noted in particular. The way in which a social worker categorises a client's 'problem' is crucial. Frequently a request for financial aid is seen as a cover for a more deep-seated personal problem. Alternatively a client's problem is not redefined but simply extended. Jackson and Valencia refer to the argument that social workers may in effect coerce clients into accepting additional guidance. The impact of bombardment is also discussed (p. 103):

> The sheer number of clients approaching a social worker for aid of any kind may have an effect on the decisions he makes; if he feels under pressure, then a social worker might well be persuaded to give financial aid to clients to 'get them off his books' or as an alternative to other aid.

Finally, Jackson and Valencia consider the influence of other agencies upon the way decisions are made within social work. Other agencies may refer clients to social work, they may cause or precipitate the 'problems' that clients present at social work agencies and they may influence social work by providing (or not) alternative sources of assistance.

In conclusion the authors set out the following broad hypothesis (p. 107):

> The more extensive the influence of senior personnel the more likely it is that the issues considered will involve broad matters of principle, whereas the more extensive the influence of junior personnel the more likely it is that decisions will be based on immediate pressure considerations, pressure exerted by determiners of demand or agencies in contact. The belief underlying this hypothesis is simply that it is easier for senior personnel to ignore day-to-day pressures because they are not closely subject to them.

Obviously a study of financial aid in social work is particularly relevant to related issues within the income maintenance services. But many other social work decisions could be and have been taken as subjects for similar research; decisions about children in care, about allocating home helps, about assigning places in homes for the elderly, and about fostering and adoption are examples. The research discussed in more detail in this section is just one example of a study which indicates how important it is to grasp the notions about discretion which are held by different parties to the situation, and understand the way in which these meanings interact, influencing and being influenced by the administrative and broader social environment.

Conclusion: Future Research

In essence, I have been trying to make two points in this chapter designed to suggest how we may best approach research on discretionary decisions in social work, drawing some comparisons also with medicine and other related services. First, the merits of specifically 'discretionary' decisions as a weapon in the research worker's conceptual armoury are dubious. It seems likely to backfire and give rise to a great deal of definitional debate which confuses as much as it clarifies. The *a priori* definitions of discretion tend to be either arbitrary or prejudiced.

Second, however, in social work at least, it is apparent that 'discretion' as a participant's concept constitutes a potentially most fruitful topic of enquiry. I have suggested that 'discretion' and a number of associated ideas are used by politicians, secretaries, administrators, clerical and professional staff and clients in different ways, on different occasions, in different situations, for different purposes and with different effects. Moreover these differences are displayed and disguised in different ways. It is these differences which should initially be the prime focus for research. The central research question then becomes 'What is the meaning of discretion for politicians, professionals, clients and other groups whose inter-action constitutes the provision of the personal social services?' And two further questions immediately ensue: 'What do these differences reveal about the social structure in which they arise?' and 'What effect do these differences have upon the way in which decisions are made and the consequent provision of social work services?' The fact that I have not dwelt upon these later questions should not be taken to imply that I consider them unimportant. The significance of the meaning of discretion lies in the part it plays in answering them. But I consider the issue of the meaning of discretion to be the prior issue.

Of course, much remains to be done by way of research design. It will be necessary to traverse the artificial barrier that divides 'macro' and 'micro' research. It will be necessary to supplement the official statistics and interviews with social workers with substantially more ethnographic material than is currently available in social work research. The methodology of triangulating data (Denzin 1978) is at a rudimentary stage. However, the great merit of the approach I am suggesting is that it does encourage us to move rather quickly to the stage of collecting some empirical material, while offering a way around some of the conceptual difficulties which otherwise seem likely to bedevil research in this field.

4 'What Type of Case is This?' Social Workers' Decisions about Children Who Offend

Henri Giller and Allison Morris

In this chapter, we report on a preliminary investigation into social workers' decisions concerning delinquent children in the care of the local authority.[1] It is based on a series of interviews with seventy social workers who were responsible for eighty children made the subjects of care orders over a three-month period in one large city. Each social worker was interviewed at least three times over the six months following the order. The interviews were unstructured, tape recorded and lasted, on average, one hour on each occasion. In addition to these interviews, we sat in on case conferences, assessment meetings and reviews of the cases.[2]

In the research we avoided traditional organisational analysis in favour of interpretative techniques which seek to 'assign a significant role to the organisational members' own subjective ideas about the phenomena in question' (Smith and Harris 1972: p. 28). By studying social workers' 'professional ideologies' (Strauss et al. 1964), we have sought to elucidate what decision-making means to social workers within the legal rubric of the care order. This, in turn, led us to look at social workers' 'operational philosophies' for this was the means by which their professional ideologies were mediated by the exigencies of practice. As Smith (Chapter 2 in this volume) has noted, this approach has gained increasing favour among those studying decision-making in organisations of social control (Bittner 1967, 1973) and has been developed in the area of social workers' decision-making most notably by Smith and Harris (1972) and Rees (1978).

The introduction of a care order for criminal offences was one of a number of measures introduced by the Children and Young Persons Act 1969 which was intended to de-criminalise the English juvenile court (see Bottoms 1974; Clarke 1980). Delinquent children were assumed to share the same pathology as other troublesome children; the offence *per se* was to be an insufficient ground for intervention. Only where the child was in need of care, protection or control were compulsory measures of intervention to be used. There was also said to be a need for variety and flexibility in the measures of 'treatment' to be applied and so traditional methods of disposal available to the juvenile court – approved schools, attendance centres, detention centres and recommendations for borstal training – which were primarily responses to the child's conduct were considered to be inappropriate. Responsibility for meeting the 'needs' of delinquent children, as with other children in 'need of care', was to be with the local authority. Its legal responsibility for the child was to last until his 18th birthday, although it could terminate the order at any time within that period. The exact nature of the particular measures of treatment to be applied was, however, to be totally within the discretion of the local authority. How this is put into practice is the focus of our research.

Care Order as Remedy?

The dominant assumption in debates about care orders is that they should provide a remedy for juvenile delinquency. But this view of the care order as a remedy for a defined agenda of problems did not seem to be shared by those who made decisions within the framework of the order. For the local authority social worker responsible for a particular case, the granting of a care order frequently marked the stage at which his own abilities in dealing with the child were exhausted. Requests for care orders (a care order had been recommended for over 70 per cent of the children in the sample[3]) were not, therefore, part of a planned programme of intervention. Indeed, many of the social workers talked of a 'treatment plan' emerging only *after* the order had been made. The following responses to the question 'When the care order was made did you have a firm plan in your mind?' illustrate this:

> *S.W.* No, and I still don't have a firm plan. I mean the only clear thing I
> have is that it was right for him to come into care and that a proper
> assessment needed to be done in terms of, well, educationally, what

was right for him and just generally what the right kind of place-ment was.

S.W. A care order is necessary to get access to things, to put things in focus, you have to have a starting point.

What seemed more important in the request for a care order was the power it gave social workers – a coercive power which could be used against the wishes of the parties:

S.W. I think that if things had been left, we would have not been able to persuade (the mother) to either get him to school regularly, or to keep him off the streets and keep him out of trouble. Neither would we have been able to persuade him to go away voluntarily somewhere.

S.W. Well the only reason I took a care order over John was it was the only way I could get him to a community school [sic]. For a start, it is very difficult to get him in under section 1 (of the Children Act 1948), I think, partly because they can't keep the boys.

Although the majority of children went through some sort of residential assessment after the order was made, it was clear that the social workers themselves had already made a preliminary assess-ment. This initial assessment was vital both to immediate and subsequent decision-making. In essence, social workers first evaluated the moral character of the child and the family, in social work terms, 'the case', and then constructed a 'logical' plan for intervention.

The Search for Moral Character – What Type of Case is This?
The concept of moral character and its use as a guide for action by social welfare decision-makers is not new. Stuart Rees (1978), for example, in his study of social work practice found that social workers regularly used the concept to justify different levels of intervention in seemingly similar work. He writes (p. 112) that social workers

made sense of these job issues through the development of practice-oriented ideologies, those sets of ideas about categories of cases and means of dealing with them. These incorporated work routines, typified people's problems and staff's roles. They enabled the staff to manage what most regarded as an occupational hazard of having large caseloads and too little time and other resources to deal with them.

It was not surprising, therefore, to find that the social workers interviewed by us had developed notions of 'typicality' and 'atypicality' in care order cases. For example, over half the children in our sample were made the subject of care orders at their first appearance in court. In each of these cases, the social workers said that the use of the care order in this way was atypical.

> *H.G.*   How typical, in your experience, is Steven's case of a child who has a care order for offences?
>
> *S.W.*   I think its untypical [*sic*] really. I don't see him basically as being a delinquent kid. I don't know what the proportions are but certainly over 50 per cent of the kids who come into care for that sort of reason are probably delinquent. With Steven, I feel that his delinquency is very much related to his relationship problem and it's not always as clear as that with the other kids.
>
> *H.G.*   How typical is Veronica's case of a child who comes into care after committing offences?
>
> *S.W.*   I don't think that Veronica is typical in terms of offences and the care order in that this was her first time in court although she had been cautioned before and I feel that it's only because there were very very different reasons within the family set-up that made me feel we should go for a care order.

As to the typical case:

> *S.W.*   Normally there are three or so offences, or seven or eight. I would see a normal pattern of a care order for a kid who is committing criminal offences is that it starts off as fairly minor when the kid is twelve or so. It's much more normal to look at the situation and say this is the kid's first offence and that hopefully he is not going to re-offend. There's conditional discharge and then there's fines and then there's deferred sentences and then you're going to have attendance centre orders and then eventually, if the kid's still offending and not responding to anything then you might start thinking well we're going to have to try removing the kid from the family situation and, therefore, recommend a care order or the Bench taking it upon themselves and saying we really think there has been quite enough of this and want this person on a care order.

Despite the widely different backgrounds of the children in our sample the social workers concerned talked in a very similar way about how the moral character of the case was established: by reference to the nature of the child's offence and the nature of the child's parental relationships. Unlike the juvenile court judges described by Emerson (1969) social workers did not seem to be solely concerned with 'what kind of youth are we dealing with here?'. Neither did social workers seem to adopt the techniques which Matza (1964) suggests of elevating the offence *sub rosa* when deciding on the nature of their intervention. By talking in terms of 'the case' rather than 'the child', social workers broadened their ambit of moral enquiry so that matters outside the child's behaviour were assessed in their own right.

The Offence as Symptom

As many sociologists of deviance have pointed out, not all delinquency needs the attention of social welfare professionals; were it otherwise, the machinery of criminal justice would quickly come to a grinding halt (see Cicourel 1977). Social workers, therefore, are sensitised to look for 'real trouble'. How is this assessed?

Our interviews suggest that, where the offence can be explained by notions of 'family trouble', then it will pale into insignificance. One social worker, for example, when asked about the reason for the care order, catalogued in great detail the breakdown of the mother's marriage, consequential housing problems and the child's school refusal. After ten minutes on these issues, the social worker was asked:

H.G.   How does the offence fit into this?
S.W.   The offence took place when all this was going on. It seemed to me
        to be all part of the same thing, of being an especially confusing
        situation for Paul (the child). He isn't able to explain anything. At
        the same time as he couldn't explain why he isn't going to school or
        didn't want to think about it, he also didn't want to think or
        explain about the offence. But, in fact, when you look at the offence
        it is a very minor thing. It involved a garage attendant. He was
        kind of helping out there on Saturday morning or something like
        that and there was £10 lying around in a pay packet, lying around
        on the table, and he took the £10. Well he actually gave £8 of that
        back, so the offence is actually only stealing £2. But the thinking
        there was tied in with the fact, with the idea of taking the care
        proceedings anyway because – well to back track – I was liaising
        quite closely with education welfare about it and our joint thinking
        on it was that it seemed quite clear that the situation at home for
        Paul was too much for him, it just wasn't right and he was just

getting worse. The school attendance and the offences were all tied up with it. What was obvious was that he did need to be removed from the home and at the same time that is what he had asked for all along.

The offence became subsumed into the 'family troubles'. The social worker minimised the significance of the offence and allowed alternative explanations to be used. Paul was not seen as a 'real delinquent'.

A similar picture emerged in Steven's case. Steven was a 14-year-old boy who was charged on his first appearance in the juvenile court with six counts of burglary and had seven other offences taken into consideration. The social worker thought that this level of delinquency was 'unusual in a lad of his age' and recommended that a care order be made in order to see what the problem was. Soon after the care order was made, however, the social worker began to ignore the offences and concentrated on what was seen to be the 'real trouble' – Steven's parents.

> *S.W.*   Well, I suppose I don't feel myself that kids behave in that way without there being some problems for them, either within the family, within the school or in other places and there didn't seem to be that much problem with the school for him and I felt having met his mother and father there was a problem.

The influence of this assumption that 'something was wrong in the home' is well documented (see Cicourel 1977; Emerson 1969) and was frequently referred to by the social workers interviewed by us. Implicit in this approach is the belief that early intervention provides the social worker with increased scope for preventing matters from becoming 'worse'. Thus a first offence justified a care order as it was seen as symptomatic of wider 'problems'. This meant that the moral character of the parents became a major issue in determining whether or not 'problems' existed.

Matters such as a recent death or divorce, homelessness, poverty and the like provided ready indicators of moral character. Barry's case provides an example of this:

> *H.G.*   Can you tell me how you reached the conclusion that Barry was acting out these conflicts about his father by committing offences?

S.W.   Well it's circumstantial in a sense, you know, there's a lot of supposition really. You listen to what was said: the mother presented a whole picture of a marriage which was a total disaster, alcoholism, aggression, violence, the whole thing. She's had two other fairly stable relationships and these had ended similarly, they had been disasters. I don't know, it's a question of gut feeling I suppose, it's not terribly professional but you get a feeling and also there was the woman's manner. When she was with me there was a sort of edginess, a restlessness and it just occurred to me that if this is her normal manner or at least when she's unable or feeling herself to be unable to cope, to manage, I would think she probably doesn't contribute much to the stability of a relationship, that there would be a lot of unease and my guess is that Barry might well have been responding in a way that her husband had.

In other cases, less tangible indicators were relied upon. In Brian's case, for example, the social worker could find no explanation of why the boy, who came from 'a very united sort of family', would not attend school. By chance, the social worker discovered that Brian's parents could not read or write and that they had rejected school. For the social worker this proved sufficient explanation:

S.W.   When we had discussed that his parents had both had bad school experiences it then emerged that his mother when telling him to go to school was really identifying with his fear of school and wasn't making him go at all. If she could say to him without ambivalence that he must go to school then he would have gone. In fact, she shares his worry about his failure. She is very ambitious for him and fears that he is going to fail and, therefore, he doesn't go and I think that is the crux of the problem.

The focus upon the family as the basic unit of 'need' has been documented by others who have examined social work practice (see Smith and Harris 1972). The outcome of the use of this ideology in practice was that the family rather than the individual child became the object of intervention.

An ideology of individual need emerged, on the other hand, where the social worker's assessment of the moral character of the parents made it difficult for the social worker to co-opt them as clients. Martin's social worker, for example, concentrated her attention on the child because of her difficulty in making a relationship with the mother:

> H.G. Do you see the main thrust of your work with the child, the mother, or whom?
>
> S.W. Well, with Martin I suppose. I suppose partly because of my experience of the mother I don't think really we will get far with her; not unless you have got a lot more time than I've got. It would take so long to build up any kind of relationship with her in which she would be actually able to talk. I think she is so untrusting of anybody in authority it makes working with her very difficult.

But despite the social worker's inability to work with the family, the case remained a 'care' rather than a 'delinquency' matter.

The Real Delinquent

There remained a minority of children in which an individual need ideology arose in a different form: intervention was directed towards the child because of his delinquency. This ascription of the child as a 'real delinquent' seemed to occur in three instances. First, the child was seen as the product of a family whose moral character was so totally damning that it was beyond remedy. An example of such a child is Gary. The social worker summarised the position in the following manner:

> S.W. [The family] are just a bunch of crooks really. They're all into stealing and fencing and Gary's been brought up in that way. He's just a socially conditioned, amoral delinquent and there's precious little I can do about it.

Alternatively, the child's delinquency could be seen as a product of environmental pressures, which were beyond remedy by the social worker. In Bruce's case, for example, the mother, despite initially being seen as unable to provide the boy with consistent standards, had co-operated with the social worker to a degree which was thought to be sufficient for all practical purposes. The boy's continued offending, therefore, required alternative explanations:

> H.G. If it wasn't his immediate family background which was causing his offending what was?
>
> S.W. The peer group. Bruce obviously was a very established member of a fairly healthy delinquent sub-culture in the part of [the town] that he lived. It became increasingly clear that Bruce was taking much more of a leadership role than his tender years implied. The

mothers of the sixteen-year-olds with whom he associated would complain to me about how awful this little tearaway was, leading their charges into a life of crime. It became increasingly clear that there was an element of truth in that. But quite clearly the peer group being there and being in this sort of delinquent culture didn't help.

The final category of 'real delinquents' were those children whose acts defied explanation or gave rise to speculative interpretations:

H.G.   What lies behind Simon's offending?
S.W.   That's a very difficult question because it came on so suddenly. We never heard anything of him until he was twelve. He seems to have had quite a normal childhood within the confines that he was fostered. But we never heard anything at all and then all of a sudden last summer he started to get into trouble and started acting up at school and things like this, and then the child guidance thing started which was a normal sort of progression and then suddenly he was in care and then suddenly he was offending the whole time and to try and work out why has just been very difficult. I really don't know.

H.G.   What would you say are the reasons for his recent offences?
S.W.   No idea. No idea honestly. It's quite a nice school. I mean there is no regimentation, he comes home officially every three weeks. I think he needs to be contained. I think that he may be asking us to contain him.

By interpreting the reasons for the child's behaviour as beyond his remedy, the social worker began to see the child as a 'real delinquent'.

In assessing moral character, social workers located the 'case' on what we shall call a 'care-delinquency continuum'. Two examples illustrate the polar extremes of this construct. Care cases were those in which the imposition of a care order after the commission of an offence was merely ancillary to personal or family problems which would have been sufficient for all practical purposes for the care order to have been made on other (non-criminal) grounds. The care order on the offence condition was, as it were, merely a legal convenience.

Lee, for example, was in care under S1 of the 1948 Children Act after his parents had died. The boy was to be made the subject of a S2 resolution (which vests parental rights in the local authority) when he committed an offence of taking and driving away a car which led to the making of a care order under the 1969 Act. When the social worker was asked about the boy's offences she replied in the following way:

> *S.W.* Lee's care order is not because of the offences. Lee came into care because of his family circumstances, because he was an orphan and because he needed someone to look after him.

At the other end of the spectrum are the delinquency cases. Here, the offence is the sole ground for the care order and the social worker's intervention is concentrated on that 'fact'. Kelvin, for example, had been found guilty of indecent assault and incest in the Crown Court. A probation officer had recommended the care order without prior consultation with the social services department. Because the social worker assigned to the case did not see the offence as abnormal, he justified his action on the basis of the offence alone.

Social workers initially located the child between these two extremes by ascertaining the moral character of the parties involved. By typifying persons and problems in this way, categories of cases emerged and, also, categories of practical solutions.

Routine Remedies – What Do I Usually Do?

Broadly speaking, the closer the case was to the care end of the continuum, the more likely the child was to remain in his home and the more likely the whole family was seen as the client. Conversely, the more the case was seen as 'really delinquent', the greater the likelihood was of the child being removed from home, placed in a residential facility and seen as the client. Intervention became ordered; the application of certain resources became routinised and was made manageable.

In care cases, for example, intervention commonly took the form of returning the child home on trial and attempting family casework or therapy. Where an immediate return home was not thought practicable, a children's home or reception centre placement tended to be used. Also, in some cases, where the child could not be found a day school place because of previous truancy, alternative forms of education – such as intermediate treatment units or free schools – were arranged. Where this could not be arranged, a boarding school placement (organised by the local education authority or a private body) would usually be applied for.

In delinquency cases, on the other hand, the most commonly sought placement was a Community Home with Education on the premises (CHE). Social workers' taken-for-granted assumptions about these placements were that they were schools for young offenders which would provide structure, discipline, education and job opportunities. While those social workers who had prior knowledge of the CHE system added some refinements to their categorisation (for example, CHEs which were described as therapeutic communities were seen to be suitable for the child who, while delinquent, had some overt care problems, whereas CHEs which were described as schools were seen as suitable for 'real delinquents'), there were quite clear differences in the way different forms of provision were viewed. As one social worker put it:

> I wouldn't think of sending Chris to a community home because I suppose I see CHEs for the delinquent, that's why I wouldn't think of that for him.

Another social worker elaborated on the distinction between boarding schools and community homes:

> S.W. What I would prefer for Paul is a boarding school, whereby he can come home regularly for holidays and he wouldn't feel that he is actually in a place as punishment, he's not being deprived of his home full stop. A community home is much more like the old approved schools; I think that the community home is seen to have a kind of atmosphere of a thieves' den. Basically children go to community homes because they committed offences. Boarding school is very different. Kids are not all there because they have committed offences. A lot of kids are there because they have family problems and the parents have asked for the children to have an education away from home. They can only cope with them at home during holidays, for instance, where they are a one-parent family, where the mother may be very disabled. I prefer that [Paul] should have that kind of experience than one where it is lots of other kids who have committed offences.

Having located the moral character of the case, the social workers were able to respond with a repertoire of provisions which routinely met the case as portrayed. In this way, social work with offenders became ordered and rational and a work priority was established.

Decisions were not 'made'; they emerged as natural, logical, even inevitable, responses to the social worker's interpretation of the case. But these interpretations were part of a dialectic. What 'explained' the moral character of the case also provided evidence of its nature (see Emerson 1969).

Decisions and Ideologies

In examining decision-making in this way, we have tried to set out what social work with delinquent children means. We have treated such concepts as 'rules', 'decision-making' and 'the organisation of social work' as problematic in order to make them empirical issues (Zimmerman 1971). In developing the notion of moral character, we have attempted to show how social workers' ideologies are put into practice in determining such questions as 'what type of case this is?' and 'what actions are necessary?'[4] These processes cannot be ascertained merely by analysing the intended policy of the 1969 Act, the formal organizational arrangements of social services agencies or the letter of the law (see Smith, Chapter 3 of this volume). As Grace and Wilkinson (1978) have previously illustrated, social workers (and, we would argue, similar decision-makers) use the law as a resource to negotiate desired practices and outcomes. In the present context, the ascertainment of the moral character of the case and the application of the appropriate routine remedy typically accomplished competent social work for all practical purposes. It provided social workers with a set of practice-oriented ideologies which guided the competent exercise of discretionary power and enabled social workers to produce a 'normal state of affairs' (Zimmerman 1971).

The 1969 Act in particular and social welfare legislation generally are examples of what Tay and Kamenka (1975) describe as 'bureaucratic–administrative' law. This, they argue (p. 139), in contrast with other legal modalities (*gemeinschaft* and *gesellschaft* law), seeks

> to regulate activity and not to adjudicate in collisions between individuals; its fundamental concern is with consequences rather than with fault or *mens rea*, with public need or public interest, rather than private rights and individual duties.

It is clear from our interviews that these dictates influence social workers' 'operational philosophies'. But, at the same time, it is evident that social workers retain and use concepts of responsibility and non-responsibility, or individual rights and duties: *gesellschaft* concepts. Identifying dominant legal ideologies, therefore, is insufficient to inform us of the nature of discretionary decision-making. What is necessary is an examination of 'professional ideologies' and 'operational philosophies' including their internal contradictions and inconsistencies and the rhetoric which conceals them. These must be treated as research issues in their own right. An analysis of social workers' decision-making in relation to children in care provides an example of this.

5   The Political Economy of Administrative Discretion
J. T. Winkler

The issue of administrative discretion must be set in context. Why has it become a matter of public concern in Britain now? It is not as if the discretionary exercise of power is something new in human affairs. The capacity to give or withhold rewards, to apply or abrogate penalties is intrinsic to the exercise of social control, by the state or anyone else. Those who have no options are impotent. In Crozier's pithy definition, 'Power *is* the control of discretion'. (Crozier 1964). What then has turned an enduring human universal into a contemporary social problem?

The current concern with the administrative discretion of state officials is one manifestation of long-term structural changes in British society which are now reaching a cardinal point. The first part of this paper seeks to spell out two of these trends that have served to make the exercise of discretion both more frequent and more contentious: first, the expanding and changing role of the state, which involves officials not only in increasing intervention in society, but also in more selective intervention; and second, the retreat from the concept of a comprehensive welfare state, which involves officials increasingly in the denial of citizens' claims on the state.

Neither of these trends is as yet more than partially developed, neither publicly acknowledged, much less affirmed. They may or may not continue further, although there are good grounds (which will be elaborated below) for believing that they will persist. If so, the changing role of the state will bring with it changes in the methods of public administration. The second part of this paper seeks to document two of the most important of these changes, now inchoately emerging, controls over the primary distribution of real income and the off-loading of welfare provision onto the community. Taken together they may alter the form, the scope and the locus of administrative discretion.

It has frequently been observed that much of the current concern about administrative discretion was initially stimulated by the operation of the supplementary benefits scheme. The papers in this book demonstrate the significance of discretionary decision-making in many other fields of social policy. But if the macro-trends in political economy described here continue much further, then the issue of administrative discretion may soon appear in a very different form than that which motivated the compilation of this volume. Those concerned about its consequences must be alert to the changing ways in which they may manifest themselves.

Emergent Trends in Political Economy
The changing role of the state

The most conspicuous development in British political economy over the past two decades has been the expansion in the role of the state. This recent growth is, of course, only the latest phase in a long-term process of increasing activity by governmental and related agencies. From the very beginning of the capitalist era in Britain, the state has played an active role. *'Laissez-faire'* is a relative concept. But for over a century now there has been an obvious and well-documented trend, albeit with many vicissitudes, of increasing state intervention in economic and social affairs. Even in this historical perspective, however, the past twenty years have been a particularly expansive period.

That there is a connection between the growth of the state and the issue of administrative discretion and legalism has long been clear, both in the grand theoretical and the immediately practical senses. The predominant interpretation in Britain for many years was that one of the defining characteristics of the liberal state was the rule of law, not of men. The application of this idea to social policy is best known in Marshall's theory of the growth of citizenship rights, first civil, then political, and most recently social (Marshall 1963). This development has been extrapolated into the future in Macpherson's analysis of the reassertion of communal property rights, effectively a right to full participation in a culturally legitimated life style (Macpherson 1975). Similarly the rule of law has been seen, by sympathisers and opponents alike, as a prerequisite for a market economy, at the bare minimum to protect the rights of private property and to provide certainty about the enforceability of contracts. At the mundane level, private industry persistently complains about the increasing volume of government regulation and compulsory requirements for information disclosure. This businessman's grumble finds reflection in the concept of economic law propounded in the 1960s by Schmitthoff (1966), who may claim to have founded the academic study of the subject in Britain; 'economic law comprises the regulation of state interference with the affairs of commerce, industry and finance' (p. 315) and is 'of mandatory rather than permissive character' (p. 319). In the social field, Jones, Brown and Bradshaw (1978) have concisely summarised the prevailing interpretation, 'The development of social policy can be characterised by a movement from discretion to legalism', (p. 140), and later, '[This movement] has been associated with the increasing intervention of the state in human affairs.' (p. 141). In sum, there is a substantial tradition, preponderant if not hegemonic, which sees a strong association between the growth of the state and the growth of legalism.

In discussions of state economic activity, academic as much as popular, it is commonplace to focus on the extent of intervention, to treat it implicitly at least as a quantity, something of which there is simply more or less, something which only advances or recedes. But the important point about the recent expansion of the state in Britain is that it has involved not just an increase in its activity, but also a qualitative change in its role. The change that is taking place, under both Labour and Conservative governments, is from a supportive to a directive role for the state. The relevance for the issue of administrative discretion is that when the state attempts to give positive direction to private economic activity, more discretionary forms of intervention are necessary.

In *the supportive role* the state attempts to sustain and improve the functioning of a market economy. It does this by trying to smooth out the cyclical fluctuations to which markets have historically been prone. The means to this stabilisation is the manipulation of national aggregate economic variables. Since the Second World War, there have been two versions of the supportive approach, Keynesianism and monetarism. Keynesians make countercyclical adjustments to aggregate demand; monetarists try to steady the growth of money supply. Despite all the self-aggrandising acrimony between the two camps, they are but variants of the same strategy; they just choose to regulate different national aggregates. The logic by which both are supposed to be effective is that if the state manages to stabilise the macroeconomic environment, then individuals, responding with only normal cupidity, will ensure that market processes operate as theory prescribes they should − for better or worse according to one's preferences in these matters. This stabilisation is supplemented by various aids and incentives, general subsidies designed to stimulate investments, exporting, research and development, productivity, industrial relocation and other shifting national priorities. But private economic actors (entrepreneurs and workers, corporations and trade unions) remain free to act independently, pursuing their own interests as they see them. The state attempts to support them, influence them perhaps, but does not tell them what to do.

In *the directive role*, the state attempts positively to guide and control the economy in the name of improving national performance. Business remains predominantly in private ownership and interest associations (trade unions, professional societies, employers federations) remain independent, but the state attempts to direct their behaviour. It does so not by regulating the economic environment but by trying to specify, or at least set limits around, the internal decision-making of these formally autonomous private organisations.

The most conspicuous means to this end recently have been controls over prices and incomes, but the range and mechanisms of direction extend well beyond these. The clearest and most effective example of the directive state intervention in British experience is the role played by the government during the Second World War. It then assumed responsibility for the four principal functions of any economic system: the establishment of national goals, the allocation of resources, the coordination of production and consumption for important goods and services, and the distribution of rewards. This was an extreme case. How much private economic activity is controlled and to what degree will vary. In practice, the apparently state-imposed constraints are, even in wartime, the outcome of continuous formal and informal bargaining among multiple state agencies and the principal economic interests, notably capital and labour (hence 'tripartism'). But in these negotiations, the state attempts to take the initiative in directing national effort or, with the more modest aspirations of the late 1970s, stopping the collective rot.

For the purpose of conceptual clarification, we may contrast the supportive and directive roles of the state in pure form. It is the difference between a pattern of state intervention that operates at the macro level and one that works at the micro level, one that manipulates national aggregates versus one that changes specific institutional decisions, that seeks stabilisation or aspires to direction, that works only on the demand side or includes supply as well, that tries only to influence private economic activity or attempts to control it. Ultimately the contrast is between a strategy that would sustain a market economy and one that would supplant it. A directive role for the state leads on to one version of a planned economic system, a particularly interesting and administratively difficult one, because private ownership and private economic association remain the norm.

The supportive and directive roles of the state are thus logically incompatible. However convincing that conclusion may appear to an outside analyst, in practice British governments of both parties for the past twenty years have been attempting to pursue both simultaneously. A contradictory mixture of intervention devices has evolved because the old supportive instruments were not sufficiently effective, and governments gradually added directive elements to their policies as *ad hoc*, coping responses to immediate, pressing problems (balance-of-payments deficits, inflation, Celtic nationalism, unemployment, etc.). The assumption of a directive role by the British state has not come about through the conscious implementation of any economic theory or ideology, but as the result of pragmatic, incremental adaptions to the obduracy and intensification of the country's difficulties, introduced with reluctance and recurrent promises that 'free enterprise' and/or 'free collective bargaining' would be restored as soon as economic conditions allowed.

The latest phase in the growth of the state began not with a burst of socialist appropriation, but with the frustration of the Federation of British Industry and the Conservative government at the consequences of 'stop–go' policies in the late 1950s and their acceptance of the need for some type of economic planning. This led to the establishment in 1962 of the National Economic Development Council (Organisation), its four exercises in 'consensus planning' (of which the best known was the National Plan 1964/65), followed by more rigorous attempts in 'planning agreements' and 'sectoral planning' during the 1970s. Chronologically, the most visible events in the development of the directive role were, under the Labour government 1964–70, the imposition of price and wage controls, the requirement of advance deposits as a form of import control, the establishment of the Industrial Reorganisation Corporation to create large internationally competitive British companies through organising mergers, and an unsuccessful attempt at the legal regulation of industrial relations.

The Conservative government that followed succeeded in passing an Industrial Relations Act. It initially suspended the other controls on private economic activity (the 'Selsdon phase' 1970–2), but felt compelled to reintroduce them and several more by 1972, establishing controls over prices, profit margins, dividends, incomes, capital movements and office rents. It also created several other, less celebrated interventionist instruments concerning investment, insurance and housing. Overall, Anthony Wedgwood Benn ungrudgingly observed, the Heath government created 'the most comprehensive armoury of Government control that has ever been assembled for use over private industry, far exceeding all the powers thought to be necessary by the last Labour government' (Benn 1973). The succeeding Labour government retained most of these instruments for most of its tenure, either in statutory or 'voluntary' form, substituting housing rent controls for those on offices. Thus, over the decade and a half up to 1980, in what purports to be a market economy, some kind of price and income controls have been in force for over 70 per cent of the time.

Less conspicuously, throughout the 1970s both governments proliferated neo-mercantilist devices for export stimulation and import substitution and control (the so-called 'invisible barriers to trade'), continued state management of industrial reorganisation and location, heavily subsidised selected advanced technological developments, both on the grand scale (e.g. nuclear reactors) and the miniature (e.g. electronic watches), directed government purchasing to develop British industries (most successfully in computers and oil-related equipment), and increased state provision of industrial capital through various forms of public expenditure and the less visible but more important 'tax expenditures'.

Throughout all this period British governments have also been pursuing a supportive strategy, recently changing from the Keynesian to the monetarist variant. But one can see, even in this very condensed summary, the development of a substantial directive role for the state. However, three characteristics of this trend need immediately to be noted. First, the directive strategy has not been noticeably successful. While in certain areas (like the control of North Sea oil development) state control has achieved much of what it set out to do, and while governments have gradually become more sophisticated in the use of directive instruments (particularly incomes policies, of which more shortly), overall the substantial growth of state intervention has not improved national economic performance. Britain is a slightly richer country than she was twenty years ago, but her situation relative to other advanced industrial nations has, if anything, worsened.

Second, the directive strategy is still very incompletely developed. Compared with the role of the British state during the Second World War, the scope of recent directive intervention is very restricted, its instruments of control very much weaker. On the other hand, compared with the activities of previous governments in peacetime, there has been a substantial increase in both the scale and potency of intervention. We are concerned here with a trend, not a finished process. It has developed considerable momentum. Whether it will continue leads to the third point.

In the process of development described here, there have been two obvious interruptions, two attempts to reverse the expansion of the state. The first occurred in the early 1970s during the Selsdon phase of the Heath government. It did not last long. This 'failure' may be interpreted in several ways: as a mere interregnum in the recent trend, as incompetence or a failure of the will in carrying through a difficult and prolonged change of policy, or as evidence that the expansion of the state is a response to long-term structural changes in the nature of a capitalist economy and cannot be reversed at the whim of governments.

The present government will provide further evidence on these questions, for it too is attempting to reduce the size and change the role of the state, and in a much more truculent manner. The first draft of this chapter was written during the closing phase of the Callaghan government, which was certainly, if not consciously, furthering the directive role of the state. The final draft was written under the Thatcher government, which most certainly and consciously is not. Will it make its monetarist–supportive approach work, or will it too be forced by mounting problems to return to the more directive approach that has characterised its predecessors? Will Margaret Thatcher prove the Edward Heath of the 1980s? Or is this paper proclaiming a trend at just that moment when the regress has begun? The only honest answer to those questions is that one cannot answer them yet.

However, the resolute determination with which the government is pursuing its policies is providing a fair, rigorous test of the directive hypothesis. If it succeeds for a substantial period, then the analysis presented here would be falsified. But such a formidable change of direction takes time; and so the test takes time. For those who like their political economy presented with certitude, now is a most unsatisfying moment to be publishing on the subject. Better two years hence . . . or two years ago.

But because the future of administrative discretion/legalism is clearly linked to the future size and role of the state, it is incumbent to specify, however briefly (Winkler 1976), why it is probable that the directive trend will continue, despite this second attempt to reverse it. The issue turns on two questions. Why has the role of the state been expanding and assuming a directive character? How adequate is the present government's strategy to deal with these causes of the state's growth? State intervention in society has fluctuated with wars, and the booms and slumps of the trade cycle, but the long, slow, generally upward trend throughout the capitalist era indicates that the causes are structural, not conjunctural. For over a century, the economic structure of Britain has been undergoing a number of changes, each of which, for a different reason, has been evoking state intervention. All of these long-term changes have accelerated markedly in the past twenty years.

First, the increasing concentration of industry has now made Britain one of the most oligopolistic economies in the world, seriously weakening the effectiveness of the market as an allocative, coordinative and distributive mechanism in most manufacturing sectors, and provoking state intervention as a partial corrective

Second, the profitability of private manufacturing industry has been falling, pre- and post-tax, at least since 1950 and probably, except for the war period, since the 1930s. In Britain (as in the United States, but unlike the Federal Republic of Germany and Japan), most capital investment has traditionally been funded by retained earnings. The private sector has thus become increasingly dependent on the state both as a direct provider of investment capital and, more importantly, as a guarantor of profits through numerous and varied mechanisms.

Third, the balance of power between capital and labour has shifted. The present combination of high unemployment and high wage settlements is merely the most visible of many indicators that employers can no longer rely on the labour market and traditional notions of authority to control their workforce to the same extent as in the past. The state is being called in to mediate a new relationship between capital and labour, if not to restore the old one.

Fourth, the cost and risk of much advanced technological development has escalated to the point where the private venture capital market is no longer able or willing to provide finance. The state is having both to provide research and development capital and to guarantee a profitable market for the resulting products.

Fifth, the competitiveness of British industry in world markets has been deteriorating for a long time, whether measured by the balance of payments, the share of the world exports, control of the domestic market, flows of direct investment or many other indicators. The state is increasingly having to protect and sustain British companies against international rivals, by every possible means bar the raising of tariffs.

These are five of the principal causes of the growth of the state in Britain. All are long-term structural processes; none are likely to reverse themselves spontaneously in the foreseeable future. The present government is attempting to reduce the size of the state by cutting public expenditure and the public sector borrowing requirement, by decreasing the numbers of civil servants and quasi-governmental agencies, by hiving off portions of the nationalised industries and by eliminating or restricting some regulatory activities. None of its principal policies touch on any of the structural causes that have evoked state intervention in the first place. It is attempting a symptomatic rather than a causal cure to what it perceives to be a problem. The strategy is not logically adequate to solve that problem. It will fail, sooner or later. The subsequent change of policy may not be called a U-turn; there may be a new metaphor for the 1980s. But the most likely result is a reversion to the directive pattern of intervention.

It is no purpose of this paper to argue that a directive role for the state is better than a supportive one, by any standard of value, nor that it will prove more effective in the long run in solving Britain's problems. The aim is merely to demonstrate that there has been a substantial trend toward direction, and for structural reasons this seems likely to continue. It is one consequence of this trend that is relevant here: direction leads to discretion. Once one recognises that there has been a qualitative change in the role the state is attempting to play, then one may appreciate that there will be a qualitative change in administration as well.

The straightforward association of the growth of the state with the growth of legalism can no longer be sustained. Strategies to regulate or stabilise a market are insufficient because, in all the areas just described above, the market mechanism has been significantly debilitated by structural changes in the economy. When the state has to provide a partial substitute for the allocative, coordinative and distributive mechanism and also to give positive direction to an economy in difficulty, then selective, discretionary intervention is necessary. This change may be described in two ways, theoretically and empirically.

Legalism in administration, mandatory rules which prescribe the state's behaviour towards the private sector, weakens its capacity to direct the economy. For the state to guide the economy effectively, it must be able to make prompt and flexible responses to changing circumstances and problems, towards achieving the prevailing national priorities, which themselves must change with time and conditions. Rules encumber this adaptive process in several ways, introducing both delay and rigidity. The elaborate formal procedures of legal enactment, promulgation, amendment and repeal, intentionally designed to be lengthy and arduous as a control on the rash use of power, are one source of delay, retarding response. Another lies in the technicalities of 'due process' which may hinder the restoration of activity in the event of disputes. Rights of appeal or redress for aggrieved parties are a particular obstacle, as the clarification of what the state may or may not do often waits upon a precedent-setting judicial interpretation, as the outcome of a lengthy process of trial and retrial.

More importantly, all rules are constraints. They fetter the state as well as the subject, restricting the range of permissible responses to economic problems. This is obvious with prohibitions, but prescriptive rules are also constraining because they enjoin some alternative actions rather than others. One cannot direct an economy that remains predominantly in private ownership if a substantial realm of citizens' economic activity is protected against state intervention by formal rules that are difficult to amend. A directive state will seek discretionary powers.

The general principle has been hammered home again and again in microcosm by organisation theorists, most memorably by Burns and Stalker (1966). Those who seek positive action (direction) in a changing or 'turbulent' environment will incline to 'organic' (flexible, discretionary) rather than 'mechanistic' (rule-bound) forms of organisation and administration. The point applies at the level of the state as well as the corporation.

One counter strategy of those subject to discretionary power is equally clear: to bind up the ruler in rules, be they called laws, rights, precedents, universal regulations, natural justice or whatever, whether in the field of social security, the economy, or any other. Rules provide a defence for subordinates who conform to them. They also legitimate claims. They thus obviate both arbitrary punishment and arbitrary reward, which is to say they constrain superior authorities' discretion. As Crozier (1964) vividly illustrated, if this counter strategy is successful, the outcome is, for long periods, stasis, with all change from either side blocked by rules. For the citizen, this provides at least elementary protection or equity. For a directive state, it means the inability to give direction.

The same theoretical point can be made in more conventional political economic terms. If, as so many ideological enemies have agreed, 'the rule of law is a pre-condition of capitalist competition', then we also may recognise, with Neumann, the obverse:

> The theory that the state may rule only through general laws applies to a specific economic system, namely, one of free competition . . . the conclusion is obvious that with the termination of free competition and its replacement by organised state capitalism, the general law, the independence of judges, and the separation of powers will also disappear.
>
> (Neumann 1957, pp. 7–13)

What will take their place is, in language appropriate to the present context, discretionary power disguised and legitimated in many ways.

Viewed from the perspective of a jurisprudent, Unger, increasing state intervention in both welfare and economic affairs, and the consequent erosion of the liberal separation between state and civil society, gradually 'undermine the relative generality and the autonomy that distinguish the legal order', 'break down the traditional distinction between public and private law . . . (and) . . . the very distinction between the law of the state and the spontaneously produced normative order of nonstate institutions', and 'encourage the dissolution of the rule of law'. Again, what will follow this destruction of positive law in practice is clear: 'As government assumes managerial responsibilities, it must work in areas in which the complexity and variability of the relevant factors of decision seem too great to allow for general rules, whence the recourse to vague standards. These standards need to be made concrete and individualised by persons charged with their administrative or judicial execution'. (Unger 1976: pp. 196–201). In a word, discretion.

The economic basis for the growth of administrative discretion should by now be at least theoretically apparent. All planned economic systems, even privately-owned ones half-wittingly planned by a directive state, build mechanisms of flexibility into their planning. The most absurd thing any economic planner, corporate as well as governmental, can do is to make a plan and then follow it, that is, without regard to the changed conditions and problems that arise during its implementation.

These mechanisms of flexibility may take various forms. In the case of French indicative planning, they involved the use of vague targets and unformalised 'quasi-contracts' with producers (Shonfield 1965). Much more interesting, administratively, is the device employed in the apparently highly bureaucratic Soviet system of planning. Flexibility is created by the selective, but systematic non-enforcement of many of the rules by which the system is supposed to work, the normal, persistent toleration of economic practices that are formally illicit, indeed criminal, some to the degree of being punishable by death. Planners and implementers are, in effect, continuously bargaining over which bits of the plan, which targets, which rules will be enforced with how much priority at the moment. Very bureaucratic, very flexible, very discretionary (Nove 1969).

Britain is developing rather different mechanisms of flexibility. The movement toward discretionary forms of administration which theory predicts is empirically well advanced. Very early on in the development of the directive state described here, Ganz (1967) noted a 'retreat from law' in the government's relations with industry. 'We are moving even further away from law to an "administration of things". This is the inevitable outcome of increasing governmental control over industry which must be flexible and selective to achieve the desired results' (p. 106).

The subsequent growth of discretion has assumed three principal forms. First, greater use of the traditional mechanism, building discretion into legislation. Second, the use of the state's general financial instruments for purposes with which they are neither legally nor logically connected. Third, delegating the enforcement of public policy onto private organisations. Full documentation of each of these mechanisms would require a full book in itself. The most that can be attempted here is to state the general principle of what is happening and illustrate it with a few examples, as seen from a political economist's perspective; then describe the consequences for discretion, as summarised by the small body of economic lawyers working on the subject, with further references.

The most conventional device for expanding discretion is simply the inclusion of *discretionary formulae* in the statutes and regulations that empower state action. Intervention is made optional. Rather grander is the adoption of an *enabling act* model of the law. The essence of the enabling act is that it describes its aims so abstractly as to be uncontentious, its applicability so broadly as to be unrestricted, and leaves the content and powers to be filled in later. Enabling acts appear under many names: in France they are known as 'outline laws' (Rendel 1970); Edward Short, defending their increasing use in a rare Parliamentary debate on the subject, called them 'framework legislation' (Hansard 1975: col 967), the Renton Committee in advocating them still further referred to 'general statements of principle' (Report of the Committee on the Preparation of Legislation 1975). Whatever they are called, their effect formally is to legitimate unrestricted state intervention in a new field. In practice, they establish a permanent new arena for bargaining between the state and private interests.

Many of the instruments of directive state control created in recent

years have been exercisable at the discretion of ministers or their
agents: price controls, merger control, grants and loans, industrial
location permits, oil development licences, credit control, research
and development support, import controls and export subsidies.
The principal instrument of economic policy under the last Labour
government, wage control, was not even circumscribed by so much
as an enabling act. It was a 'voluntary agreement' negotiated
between the state and the trade unions, not expressed in formalised
rules of any kind.

What is evident here is 'the substitution of discretionary powers
for mandatory duties', with the rules made purely by administrative
action and implemented through informal procedures (Ganz 1967).
Surveying interventionist schemes of the 1970s, Sharpe proposes a
'declension' of instruments, ranging from specific statutory authority
through statutory instruments, guidelines, published schemes, down
to 'the secret rules which govern the award of many discretionary
benefits' (Sharpe 1978: p. 4). The movement down this declension
has meant that 'The significance of recent British experience lies not
in the steady growth of public expenditure on subventions to industry,
but in the selective character of that expenditure.' (Sharpe 1978:
p. 1).

The cumulative effect of this trend in Britain is pungently
summarised by Daintith: 'the golden metewand of the law (is)
reduced to an economist's bludgeon . . . the public law framework
for economic policy is so loose and flexible as to be hardly worthy of
being called a framework at all . . . public law seems called upon to
play an exclusively instrumental role in relation to economic policy.
This imbalance may threaten values inherent in the legal system
itself . . . generality, publicity, predictability, freedom from
arbitrariness' (Daintith 1974, pp. 21, 16–7). The erosion of the rule
of law by state intervention, anticipated above in theory, is being
realised in practice.

But changes in public law are only the beginning. The most
significant change under a directive state is that the preferred means
of control shifts from legal regulation to financial manipulation. The
logic is as follows. Any modern state possesses many general
financial powers – to tax, spend, lend, grant, subsidise, borrow, levy,
license, insure, purchase, raise tariffs and charge for state-provided
services. To these, the fully directive state may add numerous other

financial controls – over prices, incomes, dividends, rents, credit, interest rates, investment, capital movements, exports and imports.

It is theoretically obvious and practically inescapable that all these financial powers and controls have differential effects on the income of constituent groups in society. Changes in any of them raise the income of some groups and lower that of others. The 'groups' involved here are not just capital and labour (that is, we are concerned not only with the shifting division of the national income between profits and wages, but also with the more mundane, if more celebrated 'pound-in-your-pocket'). Some types of company, in certain industries or regions gain, while others elsewhere lose. Some occupational groups, their trade unions and their members benefit, others suffer.

Within these financial powers and controls, there is an important distinction to be made. Some financial instruments, such as interest rates, rent controls and many taxes, have a broad effect through much of society, at least as they have been recently used in Britain. Others, such as tariffs, employment subsidies, or levies, affect whole industries, regions or occupational groups. Still others, such as price controls, investment grants, industrial development certificates, loans, export credits, exchange controls, government contracts and licences, can be brought to bear on a single company and its employees. These are crucial, because they make possible selective control of the internal decision-making of private organisations.

Thus, the state already possesses considerable capacity to manipulate people's incomes up or down, and to focus this control on specific targets. This is, potentially, a potent bargaining lever for the state in dealings with groups it is trying to bring into harmony, or at least acquiescence, with its wishes. Since the war and its aftermath, this potential has never been developed to anything like the full; the financial powers and controls of the state have never been used in a coherent and comprehensive manner. There has been a vague, intermittent commitment to redistribution and equity, but the individual financial instruments have always worked at cross purposes and were seldom coordinated in a broader economic policy.

Nonetheless, we may appreciate the general principle here. The financial strategy of a directive state involves the systematic exploitation of this capacity to manipulate corporate and personal income. In plain English, the state trades income for compliance. In political–economic English, the financial strategy consists in the state employing its financial powers and controls to modulate the net real income of private businesses and occupational groups, thereby applying positive and/or negative sanctions, which are bartered for conformity to public policy.

The financial powers and controls that existed in Britain for most of the 1970s were crude and incomplete. But in a strictly technical sense, they were more than adequate. The liquidity crisis of 1974/75 proved that. Without being aware of what it was creating, the then Labour government was applying moderately strict price controls in a time of high inflation, and taxing paper profits through the existing treatment of stock appreciation. The result was a historically unique cash flow crisis, forcing heavy corporate borrowing and threatening large sections of British industry with bankruptcy. The Government had neither a plan nor the political will to make use of the financial pressure it had unintentionally applied; it simply relaxed price controls and tax regulations. But there can no longer be any question that the financial strategy of a directive state is technically feasible. The real questions are political; who determines how the financial instruments are used and the capacity of those who suffer to resist.

The point of all this for the issue of administrative discretion is that the financial gains and losses that the state can create for private economic groups can be used in support of almost any policy it wishes to enforce at the moment. Because the financial instruments bear on that most important and negotiable of commodities, money income, they can be exchanged for conformity to policies with which they have no apparent relationship, either in logic or in law. The resulting arrangement need not even take the form of a contract; it can be presented as another 'voluntary agreement'. This financial strategy massively expands the realm of discretion for a directive state.

To be sure, financial powers and controls may be used for their nominal purpose; wage controls were certainly used to control wages. But the administratively interesting applications are the ones for unstated purposes. To choose just a few of the more extreme, and therefore illustrative, examples from the 1970s: dividend control was used to stimulate industrial reorganisation, export credit guarantees to bolster incomes policy, employment subsidies to induce companies into negotiating planning agreements, and state purchasing contracts to encourage racial equality in employments and workers' participation. Because it bears so directly on corporate income, price control has been a particularly popular instrument. The nominal purpose of price control legislation was the containment of inflation, but from the way the changing regulations were formulated during the course of the decade, it became clear that price control (and exemption therefrom) was also intended to stimulate exports, management efficiency, and industrial investment, especially employment-creating investment. So much became more or less explicit over time. But it was nowhere made clear that price control would also be used, as it was, to enforce import control or wage control or consumer protection or economic planning.

These extended applications of financial instruments were often *ad hoc*, weak and ineffective. Sometimes slightly more coordinated sets of financial pressures were put together. The most conspicuous was the 'blacklist' under which the government attempted to deny state contracts, industrial grants and loans, export credits and employment subsidies to companies in breach of its 'voluntary' income policy, which was never backed by statute. The ploy failed. Less obvious but more effective was the way the government combined its powers to award North Sea exploration and production licences and seaworthiness certificates for oil rigs, to induce applicant companies to buy British capital equipment, hire British labour, recognise British trade unions, establish industrial training facilities, control the landed price of oil, and much else besides.

All these examples are meagre relative to the theoretical potential of the financial strategy, and even compared with the control actually exercised by the government during the Second World War. But they do serve to illustrate empirically the development of financial controls by a directive state in Britain and their extremely discretionary character.

The same phenomenon may be described from the perspective of a lawyer. After a survey of interventionist legislation in the 1970s, Daintith (1979) summarises the emerging pattern:

> Two major trends can be distinguished . . . in the implementation of economic policy . . . [First] Government is placing ever-increasing emphasis, in its policy-making and policy implementation in the economic sphere, on its power to dispose of wealth and property . . . its economic

power, if you like . . . and less emphasis on its power to rule (p. 15) . . .
[Second] a steady shift from generalised to particularised interventions . . .
an individual relationship is developed between government and assisted
enterprise (p. 19).

In terms of discretion, there are two great advantages to an interventionist state of using economic power rather than law as its
control mechanism: first, the state is thereby

> able to introduce these regulatory measures without either the discipline
> of the intensive and detailed debate associated with legislative procedure,
> or the restraining framework of a set of formal rules laid down by Parlia-
> ment for the purpose of facilitating its own political control [and second, it
> may] displace legal coercion and with it the protection for the subject
> which stems from the precise legislative delimitation of the powers of
> coercion, and his consequent ability to appeal to the independent arbitra-
> ment of the courts to secure respects for the terms of the legislation.
>
> (Daintith 1976b, p. 77)

This second advantage has certainly been realised in full. In a
detailed examination of the protections available to the citizen who
suffers through discretionary economic intervention, Sharpe finds
them ineffective, where not actually non-existent. And not only is
protection absent from the courts; it is also absent from the
administrative process, Parliament and the European Community.
He concludes: 'Recent history has seen a steady accretion of the
power of the state as benefactor, without any corresponding
strengthening of the means of securing redress in the event of any
abuse of that power.' (Sharpe 1978, p. 41).

He also hints at something even grander.

> The older stereotype of state intervention through ownership or more
> general assistance to an industry is giving way to more recent develop-
> ments where the state's influence is brought to bear on the level of the
> enterprise and where the enterprise, whatever its juridical form, acts as an
> instrument of government economic policy.
>
> (Sharpe 1978, p. 8)

This provides a link to the third mechanism of flexibility for a directive state, the delegation of enforcement.

The general principle here is that when the state does reach agreement with private organisations, by financial pressure or any other
means, it may then oblige them to implement the bargains them-

selves. It is effectively delegating the enforcement of public policy, and the state may ensure that this delegation is efficiently carried through by the prompt and flexible manipulation of its company-specific financial controls should the private partner stray from its agreed obligations. The relevance for administrative discretion is that the state may, if it chooses, thereby avoid the procedural requirements, minimum standards and public law remedies that would apply if the same policy were implemented by government agencies.

The most contentious example of this recently has been in the field of wage control As, over time, Britain moved from statutory freezes to voluntary incomes policies, governments attempted to make both unions and employers implement its policy. Most recently, under the 'social contract' the unions did, more or less, keep their side of the bargain. The 'blacklist' described above was an attempt to double bank the enforcement of incomes policy by getting companies in receipt of government contracts to enforce it, not only on their own employees and unions, but on those of their sub-contractors as well. Administratively, this was a chain of delegation.

This was a singularly dramatic example, but the principle also applies in a literally everyday sense. When the state is pursuing a directive strategy, it is in continuous negotiation with the major oligopolies over numerous aspects of economic policy simultaneously. Agreements between state agencies and the few, large dominant companies become critical both to the welfare of the companies and the effectiveness of public policy. The distinction between the public and the private sector blurs and the company may indeed become the instrument of the government. Or the other way around.

Often the state creates new, formally autonomous bodies precisely in order to delegate the enforcement of a contentious public policy to them; these are the quasi-governmental organisations. These have been so much the subject of public controversy recently that they need be no more than noted here. What is relevant in the present context is that the debate has concentrated on their 'accountability', rather than their effectiveness, which is to say, it has been concerned with their discretionary power. There has been no corresponding interest in the results or value-for-money achieved through its use.

None of this delegated enforcement is new. British governments have long used 'chosen instruments'. As the debate on quangos made clear, they are an administrative device with an extensive pedigree. The most important of them, the Bank of England, has been functioning as the instrument for monetary policy for a long while, and delegating some of its enforcement to private banks by very discretionary means (see Daintith 1976b). While measurement of historical trends in the use of quangos is difficult, even apart from the idiosyncrasies of competing definitions, their number appears to have increased significantly in recent years, while the directive role of the state has been developing (Hague, Mackenzie and Barker 1975). This is only to be expected; they are one mechanism among several for avoiding the constraints of law and putting flexibility into the direction of the economy.

The delegated enforcement of policy is commonplace in the social field as well. But it is administratively more interesting there, because more substantial and expanding rapidly: the state is off-loading the actual provision of services. This issue is therefore better developed more fully below (pp. 123–31).

The purpose of this section has been to demonstrate the expansion of administrative discretion in economic policy caused by the changing role of the state. That effect has been emphatically summarised by Ganz.

> The greatest challenge which has been presented to administrative law in recent times is the development towards selectivity and discrimination. This is nothing but the old problem of discretionary power in a new guise and it, therefore, raises the fundamental distinction between discretion and arbitrariness.
>
> (Ganz 1972, p. 307)

This is true, but it also looks at the problem from a certain perspective, a concern for the citizen subjected to the discretionary exercise of power.

This is the same concern which has dominated the field of social administration generally. In recent years, many commentators on social policy have pointed to the advantages of rules over discretion, 'universal' as opposed to 'selective' benefits and the need to strengthen the rights of recipients of the welfare services.

This is a compassionate concern for the well-being of ordinary and relatively disadvantaged citizens. It makes still more credible those analyses of the growth of discretion by economic lawyers, who are objectively recording the destruction of values they cherish. But it is possible to look at the same phenomenon from another, not unsympathetic, perspective. In this view the real problem lies not with administrative law, but with the faltering performance of the British economy. In coping with that problem the old, unselective, non-discretionary interventions of the supportive strategy have been a conspicuous failure. The consequences of that failure for social policy are the subject of the next section.

The retreat from the welfare state

For the last thirty-odd years, Britain has been working towards a certain conception of how social welfare ought to be organised, i.e. the welfare state. The idea never accurately represented the complexity of actual welfare provision in this country; Titmuss (1958) noted three systems of welfare, Wolfenden (1978) yet three more. But the phrase flooded into the political rhetoric of opponents as much as advocates, despite Beveridge's preference for a different label. The expectation of statutory services and benefits became integrated into the majority of people's lives. As Marshall (1963) has observed, the concept of the welfare state, emerging in Britain out of a unique collective experience of the war, achieved a popularity here which it never attained in other countries. Through all the dreariness of the initial postwar years, and despite the imperfections of the real welfare state on the ground, the ideal long retained its appeal.

Sometime during the 1970s that goal of a comprehensive welfare state was abandoned, even as a long-term aspiration. There were, of course, many who never believed that a full system of universalistic social provision by the state was either feasible or desirable. But for those who did, the decade brought to fruition four types of pressure which, taken together, logically meant that their ideal would never be attained, no matter how vaguely one defined 'welfare state'.

First, there was the continuing accretion of evidence from social researchers about the quantitative and qualitative inadequacies of existing services, about territorial injustices in provision, and about the endurance of multiple deprivation among substantial sections of the population. This created an articulate awareness of how much of the grand design had yet to be built.

Second, public resistance to taxation strengthened and broadened. It was no longer just the rich and the propertied who protested, but also the comparatively poor, those who passed over the unindexed lower thresholds of the income tax system during a decade of high inflation in which wages spiralled up with prices. The tax-cutting campaigns in Britain were mild and ineffective compared with those in Denmark and the United States; and tax evasion here through 'the informal economy' grew to only 5–7 per cent of gross domestic product, compared with an estimated 20 per cent in Italy (O'Higgins 1980). Still, the 1970s made certain that no substantial expansion of the welfare state would be funded through increased taxation. The 1960s had already made it clear that it would not be funded through economic growth.

Third, toward the end of the decade cuts began to be made to the budgets of social programmes under the Labour government and these were increased under the Conservatives. Even the inadequate, existing level of provision was to be reduced.

Fourth, and most importantly, the social definition of 'need' expanded greatly. This owed less to the earnest researches of social scientists, than to the activities of what Seebohm called the 'new style' voluntary organisations, the campaigning social pressure groups. They drew attention to new types of client groups and to larger numbers of the old types, they defined higher standards of adequacy in provision, and brought existing shortcomings to the attention of a broader public. They also mobilised claimants of many sorts, turning 'need' into demand.

At the start of the welfare state in Britain there existed an idea, which with the dispirited hindsight of the 1980s seems naïve, that the guarantee of a reasonable basic standard of living for all through the welfare system would gradually lead to a reduction in the requirement for state services. This expectation of social prevention has proved demonstrably false; all social programmes grew rapidly throughout the postwar period. In the last decade the social perception of 'need', far from disappearing, has grown dramatically. It gradually became clear that the 'need' for social provision was potentially infinite and the satisfying of it through a statutory welfare service therefore impossible.

There was no single moment when hope expired. And, of course, no official renunciation of the goal by the political figures responsible for the system. The slogans continue, but during the 1970s the financial problem of the welfare state, the disparity between the funds available and the calls upon them, became insurmountable. As with a man sprinting after a departing bus, as the gap between the effort one can muster and that which is required acceleratingly widens, the determined quest decomposes into the realisation that one is not going to make it. Britain has missed that particular, public service bus.

The ineluctable financial problems of the statutory welfare system have consequences for administrative discretion – short-term consequences which will exacerbate the problems of discretion as presently conceived and long-term consequences which may transform the issue utterly. For the state is responding to the financial problem in two very different ways. To clarify the distinction, it is necessary to analyse the main factors in the problem in a little more detail.

Public expenditure rose more or less continuously from 1950 to 1975, in money terms, in real terms and as a proportion of the gross domestic product. There are many ways of measuring this, but the most recent and most conservative estimate (using market prices and excluding nationalised industries) shows that public expenditure increased from 34 per cent of GDP in 1950 to a peak of 50 per cent in 1975 (Gould and Roweth 1980). The government itself, using a different measure, once estimated that it was spending 60 per cent of GDP (Public Expenditure to 1979/80: p. 1).

Within this, the percentage devoted to social programmes has also increased. Considering only the five principal areas of social security, personal social services, housing, health and education, social expenditure rose from 48 per cent of total public expenditure in 1950 to 63 per cent of a much larger budget in 1977. If, under the rubric of 'social programmes', one is willing to include portions of the spending on transport, environmental services, and law and order, then the proportion rises to around 70 per cent, give or take a large bit. There was surprisingly (to those who take their ideologies seriously) little difference in the spending patterns of Conservative and Labour governments (Gould and Roweth 1978): both were trying to buy a welfare state.

However, in doing so, the government was getting deeper and deeper in debt. Faced with a relatively slowly growing economy and hence with relatively slowly growing tax revenues, government income fell persistently short of expenditure and public sector borrowing increased to fill the gap, exacerbated by a *de facto* bias toward spending in Keynesian economic management. By the mid-1970s, government indebtedness had become a major economic issue, forcing resort to rescue loans through the International Monetary Fund and cuts in public expenditure. Under the present government, the reduction of the public sector borrowing requirement, the containment of public spending and the control of the money supply have become the principal instruments of economic policy. This is having a noticeable effect. Public expenditure in Britain (in 1979/80) has been reduced to 42 per cent of GDP, the lowest of any country in Europe (Labour Research 1980), and the government hopes to get it down to 40 per cent by the mid-1980s.

There was a brief attempt to insulate welfare provision from these cuts, but with so much of public expenditure absorbed in social programmes, they had to become the principal area for economies, whatever the preferences of the government in power. In the event, the programmes in housing, personal social services and education have been reduced the most. The practical outcome is that the statutory services can no longer plan or hope to meet even present demand for them.

At the same time, the changing social definitions of 'need' were beginning to find their place in government planning. In 1977, the Central Policy Review Staff concluded, with a concision appropriate to the bluntness of the point, '"Needs" in the social services are virtually insatiable and resources cannot possibly match them.' (Central Policy Review Staff 1977). More recently and just considering health alone, the Royal Commission on the NHS noted 'the almost unlimited capacity of the health services to absorb resources. We had no difficulty in believing the proposition put to us by a medical witness that "we can easily spend the whole of the gross national product". To believe that one can satisfy the demand for health care is illusory.' (Report of the Royal Commission on the National Health Service, 1979).

Not unnaturally, the political figures most acutely aware of the implications that expanding 'need' has for the future of the statutory welfare services are those ministers in charge of social programmes. Their public acknowledgement that the state will never be able to meet people's expectations has, however, taken a disguised, but significant form: eulogies for the voluntary organisations whose activities they describe as supplementing statutory services. To illustrate with just one citation selected from a very large number: 'Whatever the scale of statutory provision, we cannot do without the extra contribution from the voluntary sector.' (Merlyn Rees, Home Secretary, The Government and the Voluntary Sector, 1978).

The point has got through to some that even if Britain were an extremely successful economy and the financial constraints greatly relaxed, the statutory services still could not meet all plausible 'need' for welfare provision.

In this brief outline of the present financial problem, four quantities are tidily arranged in ascending order of magnitude: resources, supply, demand and 'need'. Resources available to pay for statutory services (basically from taxes and charges) are less than the current cost of supply – hence the financial problem of debt. The supply of statutory service is less than the existing demand for them, hence a political problem of competing and dissatisfied clients. Finally, the current level of demand is less than the socially perceived level of 'need' which is growing rapidly and is theoretically infinite, indicating the logical impossibility of ever solving the problem – at least as currently conceived. It is against the reality of these quantities that the idea of a comprehensive welfare state has foundered. Quite simply, the supply of state services is not meeting and never will be able to meet the demand for them. The current situation may be represented graphically:

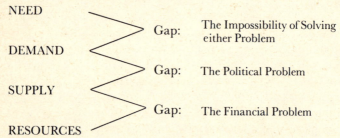

NEED

Gap: The Impossibility of Solving either Problem

DEMAND

Gap: The Political Problem

SUPPLY

Gap: The Financial Problem

RESOURCES

The situation analysed here, of declining resources in a time of expanding need, should be seen not as a sudden crisis, but as the acute state of Britain's chronic problem with her welfare state; scant means to realise great aspirations. The building of the welfare state began in a time of great deprivation. High expectations of social services were created while basic commodities were still on ration. Ever since, Britain has had an economy which grew slowly, relative to those other nations with whom she compared herself and her standard of living. Thus, despite the significant changes in public expenditure described above, the funds available for the statutory services have always seemed sparse when set in the context of so grand and so popular an ideal as a welfare state. There has always been a financial, as well as an ideological, base to the running confrontation over selectivity, 'concentrating scarce resources on those most in need'. Britain has always had to spend her welfare monies with discretion, in both senses of the phrase.

That puts the point in the decorous language of the present debate. Wilensky (1976) makes it more robustly when, after an international comparative study of welfare systems, he summed up Britain's welfare state as 'a welfare mess characterized by inadequacy, inequity, punitiveness, and inefficiency'. The social rights of citizenship have never been fully established. There has always been a strong discretionary element in Britain's welfare system. The sharpening throughout the 1970s of the abiding financial problem has served to expand and strengthen it, creating pettiness in the name of frugality.

The most visible response of both the last two governments has been to cut social expenditure. Effectively, what they have been trying to do is bring the level of supply down to the level of available resources. This is clearly a short-term response to the immediate financial pressure. It does not attempt to deal with the demand side of the problem at all. Indeed, economic ministers in both governments have explicitly avoided this, on the logic that cuts now will lead to more economic growth which will make possible better state services later. Hence the deprivation will only be temporary and there is no need for a permanent lowering of demand. The contrasting presentations of the problem by economic and social ministers is perhaps an indicator of the still incomplete understanding about the future of the welfare state. Or perhaps just an indicator of hypocrisy.

One immediate consequence of this cost-cutting response has been a vast increase in the exercise of administrative discretion, and in precisely that form which has been the focus of most recent controversy: the denial of citizens' claims against the state. For much of the debate on discretion has not really been about discretion *per se*, but about denial, the negative exercise of discretion. Few in Britain recently have complained when state officials said 'yes', when they exercised their discretion positively. At other times and in other places, it is the abuse of positive discretion, in the forms of nepotism, favouritism or corruption, that has been the issue. But the form that recent reductions in public expenditure has taken has compelled the negative exercise of discretion at all levels of the administrative hierarchy. The Cabinet and the Treasury have set gross targets for savings, leaving the choice of where specific cuts should fall (or which charges should be increased) to be made at subordinate levels. Officials in national and local government and front-line workers in direct contact with clients have all thus come under heavy pressure to exercise discretion in the direction of economy, that is, to restrict welfare provision to citizens.

The three most common choices they have made, not filling posts that become vacant, closing residential institutions, and delaying the opening of new facilities of all kinds (Weir and Simpson 1980; NCSS 1980a) all lead quickly to more negative discretion in face-to-face interaction between fieldwork staff and the public. A recently leaked DHSS internal report traced the chain of staff shortages leading to increased workload pressure, yielding 'short cuts', 'defensive procedures' and 'forms of rationing' which are 'deliberate departures' from Department rules, instituted by local officers but 'less visible to management or to regional office or headquarters' (Moore 1980, pp. 68/69).

Fewer places available in residential units and other facilities, be they old people's homes, pre-school nurseries, day care centres, special education units or whatever, lead to more selective entry criteria operated by local caseworkers.

The 970 new fraud investigators of various sorts hired to make savings in social security budget are pressured into negative discretion in a more explicit way, as another leaked DHSS document made clear (*Observer* 1980). They were not just told to be more vigilant and literal in the enforcement of existing rules, but were set monthly targets for savings. This not only led some officials to 'falsely inflate the figures on which the financial effectiveness of the operation is judged', but as an official of the Society of Civil and Public Servants suggested, 'The whole emphasis of social security work has changed. People are involved in policing the system and producing statistics instead of helping claimants.'

Fraud investigations have always been contentious, financial pressure only makes them more so. Other forms of increased negative discretion are more covert and respectable: more rapid discharges from hospital to increase patient turnover in a shrinking number of beds is done at a doctor's discretion and legitimated in the name of 'clinical freedom'.

These are all examples from the front-line. Negative discretion of broader impact is exercised at higher levels of administration: the decisions about which budgets will be cut how much (for example, that state health provision will be relatively protected but state housing provision reduced by half), decisions to preserve staff employment and cut services to clients, decisions about how much to increase the charges for which services (prescriptions, public transport, school buses, etc.). All these choices, made at the discretion of administrators and elected officials at various levels, effectively deny citizens' claims against the state.

The examples are myriad; they could go on and on. The cost-cutting response to the financial problem of the welfare state has led to a vast increase in negative administrative discretion. It has proliferated niggardliness. But there has been a second response to the problem, less obvious but likely to have an even greater effect on the issue of administrative discretion: the off-loading of welfare provision back onto the community. If ever fully developed, this would amount to a fundamental revision in our organisation of welfare. It thus leads into the second part of the paper, concerned with emergent trends in social administration.

Before moving to the future, let us summarise briefly where we have got to so far. This essay began by asking why, when discretion is so abundantly and constantly with us, has it become a social issue now. Two answers have been advanced to that question, drawn from the political economic context in which Britain finds herself at present: the changing role of the state leads to more discretionary intervention and the financial problem of the state means that discretion is increasingly exercised negatively. In plain English, people are more concerned over discretion now because there is more of it about, and it is being used to deny them what they want.

Many readers, and not just the perspicacious ones, may by now have sensed a conflict between these two answers. One refers to an expanding state, the other to a contracting state. Is this perhaps a contradiction? An oversight? A paradox? Only if one cleaves to a traditional notion of how the state works, in which state control implies state administration, and state administration implies bureaucracy. But if one can imagine a society which combines state control with private administration, through the delegation of implementation, and in which that delegation is made effective not by an army of civil servants enforcing laws, but by the manipulation of financial pressure through continuous bargaining between the state and the principal economic interest groups, then the apparent conflict resolves itself, at least at the level of theory. The next part describes two of the most important mechanisms by which such a society is now being created in Britain, the resolution in practice.

Emerging Trends in Public Administration

From a secondary to a primary distribution policy
In Britain, attempts at the redistribution of income (or more broadly welfare) have taken two principal forms: the application of progressive tax structures and the establishment of social programmes to make transfer payments or provide services. They have not been successful, certainly not relative to the hopes held for them by their advocates.

The two mechanisms are complementary parts of a particular approach to the task of redistribution. Both are secondary or *post hoc* corrections to a primary distribution of income and life chances already determined by competition in a very imperfect labour market. Taxation takes back from those who did relatively well in the initial distribution; welfare provision in general, and social security in particular, eke out the first receipts of those who did poorly.

Taken together they involve a double transfer of resources; first from the citizen to the state and then back again. This means that private welfare becomes highly dependent upon public spending, and therefore subject to all the caprice and parsimony described above. But there are other unintended consequences. Both mechanisms involve enormous administrative costs. Both have proliferated elaborate and arcane bodies of rules defining obligations and entitlements, which are too complex to be used or even understood by many who are subject to them, necessitating a supplementary system of information and advice services (NCSS 1980b). Both stimulate fraud, necessitating a substantial investigatory and surveillance apparatus, which nonetheless fails grossly to enforce the regulations. Both evoke in their participants venality, corruption, suspicion, cynicism and meanness – all in the name of social justice.

Britain's welfare system has become a spaghetti bowl of entangled strands of universal rights, means-tested entitlements, discretionary benefits, partial subsidies, retrospective rebates, fiscal allowances, earnings-related supplements and specialist services administered by multiple, multi-tiered state agencies, employers, voluntary organisations, commercial services, neighbourhood associations and self-help groups. This dish is then covered in a thick sauce of incomprehensible bureaucratese (Dalglish 1979) which makes the system opaque as well as labyrinthine. Like the 'spaghetti bol' served up in many a shadowy restaurant, you don't know what you're getting, even if you have enough stomach to try it.

And still the system does not work. The social history of Britain and other advanced capitalist societies in the twentieth century indicates that neither of these secondary correction mechanisms for redistribution is effective. Neither is able to make a sufficient alteration to the primary distribution of income to bring about even an approximation to the conceptions of equity held by their advocates. Yet worse, they trap people in poverty rather than liberating them from it.

Of course, there is no incontestable reason why Britain or any society should be concerned with redistribution. Indeed, at present, restoring differentials and exposing scroungers rank higher on the political agenda here than improving the lot of the lowly paid. But those who are concerned about guaranteeing citizens' welfare claims against the state are committed to redistribution, unawares if not knowingly.

For them, the first point is that secondary correction does not work. The second point is that the issue of discretion, as presently conceived, is focused on the administration of one of the secondary correction mechanisms, the social programmes. Thus, as a reform strategy, improvements to the delivery systems of the social services will not suffice to deal with the original and real problem, the poverty and consequent hardships caused by the inequitable initial distribution of income. Campaigning against the stingy exercise of discretion by front line officials may ameliorate a portion of the problem for some, but will not solve it. This is to misapply one's passion. Redistribution will be achieved by altering the primary distribution of income or not at all.

The emergence of a directive state creates an opportunity to do this. Any government which is exercising some measure of control over prices, incomes, rents, dividends and employment is, willy-nilly, whether it knows it or not, in corresponding measure operating a primary distribution policy. For these are the principal variables that determine the initial allocation of real income, for both those who live by labour and those who live off capital. Directive state controls make possible a radically different approach to the social organisation of welfare.

The two great moments of state intervention in the provision of welfare in Britain both incorporated such controls in their design, only to see them abolished in practice. Hennock notes:

> the [Elizabethan] Poor Law was therefore part of a bigger and more ambitious policy, which included the fixing of maximum wages, the price of bread and the quality of products . . . and . . . the universal obligation of apprenticeship. . . . Originally, the Poor Law had formed part of a society in which production was regulated. It survived into a different world.
>
> (Hennock 1968, pp. 301–2)

The same might be said of the welfare state. Harris (1979) has said it (p. 190):

> The legislation of 1945–48 was in many respects a reflection of the highly regulated and mercantilist nature of the British war economy. Wartime discussion of social security need had been based on the assumption that postwar price levels would be strictly stabilised.

Harris traces this assumption back to the Beveridge Report:

> In addition to his substantive proposals, Beveridge obliquely referred to a range of additional policies that would be necessary. . . . Quite what these further policies were to be was never made clear in the report; but Beveridge's private papers suggest that he had in mind a quite astonishing degree of economic collectivism [including] permanent peacetime control over prices and wages.

The report itself was explicit, of course, on the necessity of a state policy for full employment.

In this original conception then, 'the welfare state' was not just a secondary correction system, but part of a more comprehensive scheme grounded on the principal controls over the primary distribution of income. Seen in that context, it was not naïve, but reasonable to anticipate that the income-maintenance duties of the National Assistance Board toward the destitute would be 'residual and likely to wither away into an occasional crisis service' (Harris 1979, p. 190). If one can guarantee fixed prices, fixed incomes, and full employment, and all employed persons and their families are covered by National Insurance, then this becomes a logical deduction. Such a system attempts to prevent destitution from arising in the first place, so the state does not have to relieve it afterwards.

The economic foundations for this approach to welfare were destroyed in the 'bonfire of controls' in the 1950s. In the ensuing years, one of the most persistent criticisms of the welfare state has been that it has overwhelmingly concentrated on the *post hoc* relief or treatment of social problems, rather than on their prevention. A directive state, in theory, has at its disposal the instruments for a preventive approach in its purest form: the control of poverty through control of the primary distribution of income. The slow, pragmatic, timorous, incomplete re-establishment in recent years of a directive state on the wartime model is simultaneously recreating the possibility of that preventive approach to welfare.

One of the consequences of developing control over primary distribution is that some of the secondary corrections would no longer be necessary. Parts of the state's social security, housing and transport programmes would be affected directly. The effects of a more equitable initial distribution would work through indirectly, over a longer period to the health and personal social services. One part of the welfare state that would become largely redundant is, as its wartime designers anticipated, the income-maintenance programme for the poor, known in the latest euphemism as supplementary benefits. This is the programme which has precipitated much of the concern about administrative discretion.

Indeed, the most relevant consequence of the directive approach to welfare in the present context is that if the secondary correction social programmes are gradually eliminated, so too is the discretion of front line officials – and without proliferating administrative rules and regulations. For the antidote to discretion here is not 'legalism', but the financial controls of a directive state – themselves discretionary, but exercised at a different level altogether.

Control over primary distribution also affects the other secondary correction mechanism, taxation. The administratively complex redistributive elements in the tax system, particularly in personal income taxes, would no longer be necessary, leaving the system to work principally as a revenue-raising device. But here too the directive approach changes things dramatically.

It is a hyperbole of commitment when Wolfe (1978) writes, 'In the final analysis, only one thing causes welfare spending: the existence of poor people.' (p. 299). There are, of course, the 'natural dependencies' of age and handicap as well as the 'man-made dependencies' of the political economic system (Titmuss 1958). But one can allow the dramatist a bit of sociological licence (at least, I can), because the policy conclusion he draws from it pragmatically expresses another consequence of the directive approach. 'A strategy of economic development that would have sharply reduced the number of poor people would also have reduced the welfare burden.' (Wolfe 1978, p. 299).

By controlling the initial distribution of income, one reduces the need for the double transfer of resources that is such an administratively catastrophic part of our present approach to welfare. If the state reduces the amount of money it puts into society through the secondary, corrective social programmes which absorb such a large portion of the national budget at present, then it could also reduce the amount of money it takes out of society through taxation. A fully directive state would not have to spend 50 per cent of the gross domestic product to make its control effective. By determining the behaviour of the privately-owned economy at source, it creates a situation which, in the prevailing conventions of British politics, is thought to be impossible: more state control with less state expenditure – perhaps even more welfare for less expenditure.

What happens under the directive strategy is that many of the problems which we have customarily coped with through social policy can be dealt with through economic policy. One of the traditional liberal interpretations of the welfare state is that it is a means of dealing with the social problems created by a market economy. A directive state could use its economic control to try to prevent some of these problems from arising, and in so doing also pre-empt some of the consequent difficulties created by the bureaucratic messiness of our welfare state, including among others, administrative discretion.

Such a strategic reversal is immediately relevant to the current debate on the future of social policy. As Britain's economic problems mounted throughout the 1970s and government thinking became dominated by economic policy concerns, supporters of the welfare state have tried to protect social programmes from being decimated by budget cuts made in the name of improving national economic performance. The first line of defence was to resist all cuts: it did not work. Next, many tried to jettison 'fringe' activities and thereby preserve the core programmes; but the cuts proved too large for that. Another defence has emerged: to recast social programmes so that they deliver direct economic benefits. Social programmes might survive if they could be shown to be economically useful.

Thus, David Donnison, then Chairman of the then Supplementary Benefits Commission predicted:

> Funds for services operating only on the demand side . . . redistributing resources without claiming to generate any . . . will be harder to get. . . . Public services which have hitherto been confined to the demand side of the economy will in future have to play a larger part on the supply side. What we produce, where we produce it, how to keep people working, what to retrain them for . . . these questions can no longer be left to the economic motor to resolve.
>
> (Donnison 1978b, p. 70)

Similarly, Schreiner (1978, pp. 2–11) in an overview of social policies in all OECD countries starts from the recognition that in the 1980s

> the expansion of the welfare programmes can be expected to be constrained [and hence] there is little room for the creation of new programmes.

From this he goes on to recommend that

> To a much larger extent than today social policies ought to focus upon the general efficiency and functioning of the economy . . . social policy evaluation should be made in a wider context than has so far been done (e.g. by taking into account, for instance, its effects on the labour market).

By such means social policies 'will move from debit to credit'.

In both cases the impulse was humane, but in practice such instrumentalism will only serve to confirm that other interpretation of the welfare state, namely that it is a subsidised means of reproducing labour power for a capitalist economy. A directive strategy for welfare, in contrast, does not try to save social programmes, it strives to eliminate most of them. It seeks to substitute ineffective secondary correction mechanisms with direct control of the primary distribution of income. Social policy is absorbed into economic policy.

Everything in this section up to here has been an attempt to demonstrate the potential that the directive strategy creates for achieving the original goals of the welfare by other means. Having done that, it must immediately be repeated that there is no insuperable reason that guarantees that the real directive state that is emerging in Britain will actually use its powers to these ends. Directive financial controls are instruments merely; they can be employed for many purposes. Any fully directive state inevitably acquires control over the primary distribution of income, but there is no need for that control to be exercised for redistribution. Directive controls could be used to pre-empt poverty, but they could also be used to keep the poor more firmly in their place. And there is no reason why they must do anything about the issue of administrative discretion. The eternal human battle over who gets what does not disappear under a directive state; it is merely fought with different weapons.

For most of the 1970s, British governments had in operation, in dilute forms, many of the financial controls necessary to control the primary distribution of income. They were nominally being used for another purpose – to control inflation – but they nonetheless had the effect of producing some historically unusual short-term fluctuations in differentials, first compression (Brown and Sissons 1976), then expansion. By the end of the decade, however, the broad pattern of income distribution had not changed significantly. This is hardly unusual. As Routh (1980: p. 55) concludes in his study of twentieth century income patterns in Britain, 'the outstanding characteristic of the national pay structure is the rigidity of its relationships'. But why, precisely, did directive controls over income not make some difference?

Analytically, one must separate the two types of reasons for this outcome, the technical and the political. On the technical side, the controls themselves were weak, intermittent and incomplete. This was manifested in the sharp vicissitudes of income movements within the decade and, particularly, in the growth of fringe benefits, or 'occupational welfare'. Even more importantly, there was no institution to plan and co-ordinate the application of the financial instruments. As mentioned earlier, the directive role of the state was far from fully developed. Even if it were, the real world technical task of restructuring the primary distribution of income in the society as large as Britain would be a difficult and complex one. But it would be less difficult and complex, vastly less so, than administering the kind of welfare system we have at the moment. As an elementary test of that unqualified assertion, imagine trying to establish in similar circumstances, that is from scratch in the 1980s, the administrative structure for our existing welfare leviathan. The real issue, in welfare as in the economy, is not technical, but political.

The history of British incomes policy is filled with appeals for 'being treated as a special case', 'catching up', 'establishing comparability', 'maintaining relativities' and 'correcting anomalies' (i.e. restoring differentials). This was only to be expected. People who have been socialised in a market economy understandably do not like having a ceiling put on their earnings, most especially in a time of high inflation. They become even more resentful when the controls, however unintentionally, widen the distance between them and their economic reference groups. Those overtly objecting to the unintended redistributive consequences of incomes policies included not just the rich and the affluent middle class, but also the skilled working class, since traditional craft differentials were narrowed. It seems patently obvious that most people in Britain do not like incomes policies and they have had the power to break them.

To be fair, no one every tried to make the people like income policies. The political leaders who imposed them and most of the trade union and employers' leaders who acquiesced to them, have always publicly presented incomes policies as a temporary unpleasant necessity in the struggle against inflation, never as a means to a more equitable society. And few of the believers in redistribution contested that interpretation. In sum, there is an overwhelming political and ideological resistance to any attempt at controlling, much less restructuring the primary distribution of income. The incomes policies and other directive controls of the 1970s did not result in any redistribution because no one tried to use them for that purpose, in turn because very few wanted them to be used for that purpose and because very few appreciated that they could be used for that purpose.

In the face of such opposition and incomprehension, what is the likelihood that a directive approach to welfare, approximating to that theoretically outlined above, might actually develop in Britain? Is one to conclude, as Routh (1980, p. 220) did, 'that justice, equality and order will remain beyond the reach of policy as long as present ideas and institutions persist'? More concretely, is there any reason to believe that, as a practical matter, there will be established, in the foreseeable future, a new institutional structure that exercises conscious and positive control over the distribution of real income? There is. Indeed, there are two such reasons, the two best possible reasons: in the medium term ahead, those who presently oppose such control have no other choice, and, it is in their interests to participate in such an institution. In fact, for much of the 1970s their representatives have been participating in rudimentary, transitional versions of such an institution. These are so rudimentary that they compare to the theoretical potential much like an ovum to an elephant – quite different but nonetheless identifiable as the same species.

As noted very briefly above the balance of power between capital and labour has been shifting, and quite rapidly since the depression of the 1930s. Employers are no longer able to contol their workers to the same extent as before, and they have been asking the state to do the job for them. The problems, from an employer's perspective, have appeared in several forms.

First, strikes. Even though by international standards Britain is not a particularly strike-prone country, both Labour and Conservative governments have attempted to control 'unofficial' strikes, make collective agreements enforceable with legal sanctions, control the shop stewards' movement and restrict picketing. To date it has not worked.

Second, low productivity. The long-standing priority given to job security in British trade unionism has resulted in the country having relatively low labour productivity in comparison with competitor nations. The state has intervened with redundancy payments and early retirement schemes to facilitate labour shedding, support for productivity bargaining in many forms and incentives for more productive capital investment.

Third, wage inflation. British trade unions have historically made very modest annual wage settlements and Britain is still today, compared with other advanced capitalist societies, a low wage economy. Nonetheless, the rate of increases during the uncontrolled phases of the 1970s has been much higher than employers were accustomed to, so most of them have been more than willing participants in state-imposed incomes policies, despite their public objections in principle. In all these key areas, and others, employers not only have a positive interest in state control, but are increasingly reliant upon it.

Parallel with this has come the growing dependence of trade unions on the state and their consequent interest in institutionalised access to state policy-making. Their concern is not for more 'legalism' in industrial relations, of course, but to protect their members' financial interests. As Turner and Wilkinson have demonstrated (1975), British governments of both parties have consistently pursued a clawback strategy toward traditional wage bargaining; that is, within the supportive side of their economic policy, governments regularly conceived an idea of the level of stimulation to aggregate demand or money supply that was tolerable through wage settlements. If the actual level of settlements exceeded that thought acceptable, the government then retrospectively attempted to reduce demand or money supply by clawing back some of the wage gains in either or both of two ways, by increasing various taxes and/or by reducing transfer payments. Further, other government economic policies which provoked or tolerated price increases could erode negotiated improvements through inflation. Thus, gains in money wages won in collective bargaining could be turned into losses in real income by subsequent government actions. Governments were playing an elementary version, using a limited number of instruments for a limited purpose, of the financial strategy described earlier, to manipulate the net real income of private economic groups.

Elementary, perhaps, but effective enough for unions to see the moral: collective bargaining is not enough. Like it or not, and despite all the ritual public testimonials to 'free collective bargaining', they have become aware that what a modern trade union movement is bargaining about is not wages, but net real income, and whom they are bargaining with is not just employers, but the state as well. This lesson is valid even when no incomes policy is in force. It only becomes more obvious when the state is trying to control wages directly. Corporate income can be manipulated similarly, of course.

Employers, unions and the state have thus come to see that it is in each of their interests to negotiate together. They all affect one another, whether they negotiate or not; better to do it systematically. Only they cannot yet admit that in public. So the negotiations throughout the 1970s have followed a fitful pattern: sometimes relatively formal, as under NEDC or 'tripartism', sometimes informal, sometimes at arm's length by circulating economic policy proposals, sometimes in pairs in sequence. The nominal subject under discussion was usually the control of inflation, but that led directly to general economic policy planning, including, among other topics, specific controls over prices, wages, dividends and rents, tax adjustments and employment creation or maintenance. All parties only wanted to protect their own interests, but they were quickly drawn into something much bigger. Under Labour it expanded further, to include social programmes explicitly.

The concept of the 'social wage' has existed for a long time. That is, trade unions have recognised that all the social programmes provided through the state were a source of real income which supplemented money wages earned through collective bargaining. While the trade union movement always had demands concerning social policy, these were pursued separately from normal wage bargaining. The government, however, linked the two, by means of its clawback financial strategy. Initially this linkage was a two-stage or retrospective one; first money wages were negotiated, then the government adjusted the social wage.

In 1976 the financial strategy evolved into a more advanced phase; it became anticipatory. In advance of the coming pay round, the government offered to negotiate a comprehensive settlement with the unions in which it would agree to reduce taxes and expand social programmes if they would limit money wage claims. The government coordinated its financial instruments into a single, pre-emptive stage. Originally, the social side of the proposed package included increased subsidies on council housing, public transport, basic foods and school meals, higher pensions, children's allowances and unemployment benefits, plus more spending on the health services and facilities for the elderly. The promise was that union members would be better off on balance, even though they settled for less in wages. The consequence was that the unions were led to integrate their social bargaining with the state and their economic bargaining with employers. It was the first round of comprehensive national net real income bargaining.

In the event, the government reneged on most of the social spending promises. Nonetheless, an agreement was reached. In theoretical terms, it was clearly a hybrid; it included not only direct controls over the primary distribution of income, but also adjustments to both the secondary correction mechanisms, taxation and the social programmes. In practical terms, it was a transitional arrangement, a combination of the old approach to welfare with the new, appropriate to that phase when the directive state is still only being formed. Appropriate also to that ideological condition when incomes policies are interpreted only as a limit on earnings, never as a means to redistribution; hence their enforcement has to be lubricated with a bribe in the form of the social wage. Here was an example of the state, consciously and successfully manipulating the net real income of a major private economic interest group to bring it into line with the public policy of the moment. It was, in embryonic form, that new institution which could exercise positive control over the primary distribution of income and establish a directive approach to welfare.

Some saw the potential. Proposals flourished for annual, tripartite negotiations to determine 'what the nation could afford' in terms of wages, taxes and social expenditure. They were never institutionalised, and this approach to bargaining has now lapsed. But it will reappear in some form. Employers, unions and the state are interdependent, and they need some mechanism for organising their relationships. When it does re-emerge, it will probably still be a hybrid institution, but gradually the emphasis will shift toward primary controls rather than secondary corrections. It is economically cheaper, politically emollient and administratively simpler to arrange welfare that way – even if one does not wish to redistribute towards an egalitarian society. In the long term, some kind of directive approach to welfare is practically likely as well as theoretically feasible.

This chapter began with a description of macro trends in political economy, the changing role of the state, and by this point has deduced from them the prediction that Britain will sometime soon develop a comprehensive social and economic planning institution. Some students of social administration may find this route to their concerns unfamiliar and/or uncongenial. It is therefore perhaps worth taking a moment to indicate that Townsend (1979) starting from a more usual social policy perspective, has arrived at an almost identical prediction.

After surveying the present chaotic arrangements for determining Britain's social policies, he concludes that (pp. 320–323), 'More integrated social planning is the chief priority for government in the 1980s.' He proposes a new institution to do this ('a social development council'), combining specialists, consumers and providers, backed by a staff, and linked directly to the key political actors, the Prime Minister and the Cabinet. The task of this body would be 'to define the relationship between employment and dependency', because he recognises that 'more than a quarter of the population are at any one time principally dependent on national insurance and other benefits'. That is, they are living in 'ill-financed dependency on the state'. However, it is also clear that, 'Through its policies, any modern government sanctions the net disposable incomes of different groups of the population.' Thus, he concludes that,

> The 1974 problem of attempting to define a 'social contract' is bound to recur. Sooner or later, Britain will have to accommodate itself to a more comprehensive incomes policy than any tried in the 1960s and 1970s. [This would include] 'Policies on taxes, prices, subsidies, employment, incomes and social benefits [which] all interact to determine living standards.

In short, he is advocating/predicting an institution that will develop a directive approach to welfare.

The implications of the directive approach for administrative discretion are enormous. Reducing the use of secondary correction mechanisms will reduce much of the discretion exercised by front-line administrators. It will however create much more, and more potent, discretion over many more variables that affect people's lives at the level of the peak national bargaining institution. The phrase 'administrative discretion' will no longer be an accurate description of the main issue; something more like political discretion. Private parties, particularly employers and trade unionists, but perhaps representatives of other economic interest groups as well, will have a share of this discretion along with state officials and politicians. There will be real bargaining over the distribution of national income. Hence the concern over discretion will no longer be with negative discretion – the denial of citizens' claims against the state – but with positive discretion – which group's net real income is going up most this year? And why?

Off-loading welfare provision

Across the whole range of social policy, recent British governments, both Labour and Conservative, have been developing institutions for involving 'the community' in the provision of welfare services. These developments are commonly presented as being better for the recipient, more cost-effective and, more grandly, a superior form of social organisation as well.

Stripped of these rationales, however, in straightforward descriptive terms what the state has been doing is off-loading some of its heretofore accepted welfare obligations back onto its citizens. At the minimum, this off-loading process means simply that the provision of certain services is being transferred from statutory agencies to the populace, in various guises – voluntary organisations, community groups, user cooperatives, non-profit corporations, mutual aid societies, therapeutic communities, 'natural helping networks', spinster daughters, or even the clients-in-need themselves.

Complementary to this is the refusal to accept new welfare obligations – to provide new forms of service or to take on new types of client. Examples include single-parent families, thalidomide babies, the single homeless, cystitis sufferers, or the regulation of hostels. The state is attempting to pre-empt increased demand for statutory services. The consequence is that the community must continue to deal with the problem, which is now much more explicitly recognised than before.

Further, there are often also attempts to mobilise, stimulate or exhort the development of extra capacity within the community to meet the new obligations off-loaded onto it. These new forms of community self-provision appear under various names perfumed with the ambiance of the *gemeinschaft* – voluntary action, neighbour-hood development, self-help, community service, primary preven-tion, informal care, reciprocal giving, intermediate treatment, good neighbouring, or most commonly, in what seems to be gaining precedence as the generic term, community care. 'The community' in this context takes two forms: the voluntary sector and the 'informal sector' (networks of kin, neighbours and friends).

Cutting through the euphemisms, the off-loading process thus consists of three linked operations, the *transfer* of existing services to the community, the *pre-emption* of new demand, and the *mobilisation* of new community provision. It is important to recognise that what is being off-loaded is not just statutory services, but obligations to deal with social problems. The process signifies the renunciation of the attempt by statutory agencies to provide a comprehensive welfare service. This is the principal form of the retreat from the ideal of the welfare state.

The mere fact of community provision is not in itself new or unusual. Historically, and even throughout the growth of twentieth century statutory welfare systems, the bulk of service has always been provided by kin, neighbours and friends. Charitable organisa-tions and self-help groups were the two great Victorian responses to the problems of urban industrialism, and even since the establish-ment of the welfare state, voluntary organisations have continued to play a significant role. What is notable is that during the last decade and a half in Britain, the state has been actively promoting or passively facilitating the expansion of this community provision.

The most one can do in the present space is to provide a few illustrations of the off-loading process in the principal social policy areas, selected from a long list of examples gathered over the past few years. In the *housing* field, there has been the stimulus through grants and advice to housing associations; the organisation of tenants on council estates to involve people in maintenance, rent collection, tenant selection and sometimes general management; pump-priming grants for rehabilitation by owner-occupiers; mounting support for the voluntary hostel movement.

In *education*, economising on nursery places has been made possible by inexpensive encouragement to the pre-school playgroups; the adult literacy campaign was based on extensive use of volunteers;

disruptive pupils are increasingly sent to voluntary 'alternative' education units.

In the *penal* field, there has been a policy to try to deal with as many non-professional criminals as possible in the community through 'diversion' schemes of many sorts: community service orders, intermediate treatment, cautioning, day training centres, more generous bail, greater use of probation, supervision orders and conditional discharge.

The *health* services have been a particularly active field for off-loading: community care is now the officially preferred form of provision for all the priority groups (elderly, mentally ill, mentally and physically handicapped, and children); stimulation of self-help groups for a large number of patient categories; extensive use of volunteers in general and mental hospitals; voluntary family planning services for difficult subjects (infertility clinics, young people, sexual counselling); right down to the supply of breast milk for premature baby units through collection by a voluntary agency.

In *personal social services*, there has been an intensive effort to recruit and organise volunteers, by establishing the Volunteer Centre, the Voluntary Services Unit, and volunteer bureaux; sub-contracting service provision to voluntary agencies on an increasing scale; development of 'fostering' as a generic concept, not just for children but also for the elderly and handicapped; peripatetic services to help keep the dependent in their own homes; organising 'good neighbour' and 'paid volunteer' schemes to assist them while they stay there.

From these few examples and others, one can discern a pattern to what is being off-loaded. First and foremost are the inmates of expensive custodial institutions; then come services where the voluntary sector is already well developed, labour-intensive services, low skill tasks, services for new types of clients, politically or socially controversial services, the 'difficult' cases, and experimental projects.

Off-loading is a response to the financial problem of the welfare state. The state reduces the services it provides by shifting some of them to the community and thereby reduces its expenditure as well. In this sense, off-loading is similar to the other response to the financial problem described above, straightforward budget cutting for the social services. Both are means of bringing the cost of supplying services down to the level of resources available. If that was all that off-loading managed to achieve, it would be no more adequate a response to the problem than the other. Cutting back the supply of state services actually widens the gap between supply and demand/ 'need' which was part of the original problem. It is a very limited response which exacerbates people's sense of deprivation.

A more logical response is to try to narrow the gap between supply and demand. This may be achieved by raising supply or lowering demand or both. Off-loading manages both. That is its attraction for an economising state. The gain on the supply side is the more obvious of the two. Mobilising the community generates additional resources in two ways, not just extra funds, but extra labour.

By off-loading provision onto the voluntary sector, the state usually thereby mobilises the unpaid labour of volunteers. The Wolfenden Committee estimated that at present only 15 per cent of adults over 16 take part in voluntary activity at all, some of them only for very brief periods (Wolfenden 1978). There is enormous potential for extra labour resources here. In off-loading onto the informal sector, the state could mobilise an even larger pool of labour, toward the goal which it once candidly expressed in the title of a DHSS publication, *50 Million Volunteers*.

Off-loading can also generate extra money. Most of the voluntary agencies onto whom the state shifts services are also charities, and therefore raise additional funds through donations. A voluntary agency such as Dr Barnardo's, for example, now receives 100 per cent of its children in care through local authority placements, for which it is paid standard fees, and then is a major charitable fund-raiser besides. The present government is trying to stimulate the fund-raising activities of voluntary organisations. It has suggested putting a limit on the proportion of any voluntary organisation's budget which can be funded by grant-aid from the state, as an incentive for them to find additional money from other sources. David Ennals, Secretary of State for Health and Social Services in the previous government, concisely summarised the supply advantages of off-loading: 'Pound for pound, we can buy more services through the voluntary channel than through the statutory. I am ready to prove it if there are some who doubt it.' (1976).

Actually, that isn't the half of it. The potentially most important benefit of off-loading comes through its effects in lowering the demand for statutory services. The mechanism here is much more complex. The approach to 'community care' presented here so far has been very strictly from the perspective of the state, and the stress has been on the instrumental advantages it may gain through off-loading. In fact, behind every form of community care project there always lies a treble rationale, therapeutic and ideological as well as economic. This enormously widens the appeal of community welfare provision, generating popular support for what, in the eyes of a state under financial pressure, is basically an economising device.

The *therapeutic* rationale is that service provision in and by the community is thought to be better for the recipient: children develop more fully in the care of natural or substitute mothers; the slide into senility by the elderly is forestalled if they continue normal lives in their own neighbourhood, rather than in old people's homes; psychiatric patients behave more normally if we treat them as normal in normal communities than if we treat them as sick in special institutions; etc. etc. There are two strands to the therapeutic case. On the one hand, there is the negative reaction against the dehumanising and iatrogenic effects of institutional provision. On the other, there is the positive belief in the theory of 'normalisation', that care by 'natural' helpers in 'normal' settings is the most effective form of therapy. The evidence for this claim varies greatly from field to field, but in each area of social policy there is genuine belief in and enthusiasm for community provision among substantial numbers of specialist experts as well as the general public.

The *ideological* rationale is that community self-provision is claimed to be the institutional manifestation of certain moral or political values. What is practically significant is that some form of justification for community care can be found in the political philosophies of the contemporary Left, Right and Centre in Britain. For the Right, community provision is a means of reversing the growth of the state, encouraging self-reliance, and facilitating choice among consumers. For the Left, it offers an institution under popular control and a hope of correcting the quantitative and qualitative inadequacies of statutory provision for the working class. For liberals, voluntary and community groups are a form of secondary or intermediate associations, providing a bulwark between the citizen and the state, preserving individual liberty. Their proliferation facilitates pluralism. Community care is provided through smaller-scale units and so seem to be more comprehensible, accessible and humane.

Therefore, the community approach to welfare provision has a very wide appeal across the political spectrum. The most conspicuous characteristic of current public discussion of community care is its one-sidedness: almost everyone approves of it.

The *economic* rationale is that community provision is thought to be cheaper than statutory, in part because of the use of unpaid voluntary labour mentioned above. The appeal of this argument extends well beyond the economising state. It is attractive to those who believe the state bureaucracy is wasteful and to those who hope that efficient use of resources in one area will make possible extra provision in some other field that they favour. The evidence on the economic point is scant and ambiguous. For good reason; the cost of community care is highly dependent on the level of support for the community carers provided by the state (in the form of peripatetic specialist services, respite facilities, finance for those who must stay at home to provide the care, aids and adaptations, day centres, meals on wheels, home helps, etc.). If support services are generous, then community care is dear; if they are mean, it is cheap. What the economic argument really means is that if the state scrimps on support, then low quality community provision costs the state less than doing the job well itself. Nonetheless, at present community care is believed to be an economical form of provision and this further widens its appeal.

The combined effect of all these arguments is that a substantial number of people believe, for a mixture of reasons, that welfare is better provided through the community than by the state. They may be right. However, the immediate concern here is the potential such a developing belief holds for the state and administrative discretion.

To the extent that clients come to accept that community provision is therapeutically more effective and morally preferable, they will actually choose non-statutory forms of welfare and demand less from the state. For centuries, the basic technique of niggardly governments for containing the demand for welfare has been to stigmatise the recipients of public benefits – drive them into the workhouse, put them through inquisitorial means-tests, call them scroungers. Community care offers the potential for a positive resocialisation; people may genuinely come to want less service from the state. What is more, to the extent that state policy-makers also believe the therapeutic and ideological rationales, they can off-load statutory services in good conscience, and cut public expenditure in the bargain.

Off-loading welfare provision in the name of community care thus offers the state a much more comprehensive, positive and logical response to its financial problem. Simultaneously, it lowers demand for state services, cuts the cost of their supply, and mobilises extra resources within the community. As Britain retreats from the concept of a comprehensive welfare state, it appears to be moving positively toward a community-based welfare system. That is still a long way off, but it is clearly feasible to organise a modern welfare system in such a way. The Netherlands has one already. There are many implications for the issue of administrative discretion.

First there will be less administrative discretion of the sort that has traditionally raised concern, the negative discretion of state officials. As people make fewer claims on the state, fewer of them will be denied. There will still be plenty of administrative discretion to be exercised, only now it will come from the members of community organisations. It is no longer a state officer who exercises the mean spirited discretion which deprives the citizen of what he needs.

It will still be the discretion at the front line, just different officials. It may be no less negative or painful. Indeed, it may be much worse. Henry's critique of self-help groups is applicable to many communal organisations. 'Because groups are informal, they are free to exercise their own controls arbitrarily. They are insulated from the contraints of moral justice demanded of formal organisations and are under no pressure to respect the individual rights that are offered by the wider society'. (Henry 1978: p. 656).

There is another transfer of discretion away from state official, however. It falls onto potential claimants themselves. If people actually come to believe that community care, including informal care, is the superior form, then when they are faced with some problem and feel the need for assistance, they are confronted with a question: To whom do we turn for help? To the community? To ourselves? To the state? If the statutory option is rejected because it is seen as inferior, then it is citizens who deny their own claims against the state.

Some may reconcile themselves to these costs of community-based welfare systems, because at least they eliminate the discretionary power of the state. Perhaps somewhere, but not in Britain. The government's future relationship with the voluntary sector was spelled out with remarkable candour in its submission to the Wolfenden Committee and in its subsequent consultative document. The voluntary sector is seen straightforwardly as an extension of the state: 'essential partners in the provision of services'. The aim is 'greater harmonisation' and a 'joint approach'; that is, a common policy for the two sectors. Any off-loaded services are expected to be provided in a manner consistent with government policy. The mechanism by which national policy decisions will be transmitted to the local level for implementation is clearly spelled out.

> If more formal links were established between central government and national intermediary bodies some machinery would be needed to enable the national intermediary bodies to consult with local voluntary organisations. This might suggest some form of hierarchy of intermediary bodies to which other organisations were affiliated.
>
> (The Government and the Voluntary Sector 1978, p. 14).

The government envisages more monitoring of the quality of voluntary organisations' performance and more 'oversight'; that is,

> procedures which enable a funding agency [i.e. some branch of the state] to play some part in the policy planning or management of an organisation . . . the greater the support from public funds for the voluntary sector, the greater the need to ensure that public money is used to best advantage. The Government believes that responsible voluntary organisations will recognise this truth and cooperate in devising and implementing such procedures as seem appropriate in the circumstances.
>
> (op. cit., p. 27).

That belief is well placed. There is no need to posit coercion or state repression of the voluntary movement. The Wolfenden Report was one long appeal from voluntary organisations to be co-opted by the government. It concluded:

> We address an appeal to the government, as the central strategic makers of social policy. It is for them to take, urgently, the initiative in working out, with the variety of agencies which are now operating in this field, a collaborative social plan which will make the optimum and maximum use of resources.
>
> (The Wolfenden Committee 1978, p. 193).

Cousins' researches at the local level confirm the same point (Cousins 1976). Service-providing voluntary organisations keep within limits set by the local authority and never criticise those limits in public. They willingly accept control over their internal decision-making and become agents of a directive state.

The off-loading of welfare is not the social analog to 'hiving off' in the economic world. The essence of 'hiving off' is that the state cuts asunder some nationalised body and forswears responsibility for what happens thereafter.

The key to the welfare off-loading process, in contrast, is that the state attempts to keep control of the service it has transposed to the community – what is provided and who receives it. It is simply delegating the provision of welfare. The state does not off-load control. What it off-loads are the services, the obligations and the exercise of negative discretion.

Two Conclusions: the Immediate and the Transcendent

This has been an essay in applied political economy. Its brief was to draw the implications of certain emergent trends in economy and society for the issue of administrative discretion. This final section will summarise those implications and then, very briefly, indicate the longer-term significance of the political economic trends that lie behind them.

For those who see administrative discretion as a source of problems for the citizen rather than as a means by which the state can realise citizens' collective goals, then those problems are likely to become larger and more acute in the medium term ahead. Structural trends are leading the state to develop new discretionary instruments and to use the existing ones in new ways. This exacerbates the issue that has been the principal focus of the debate over administrative discretion so far, the denial of people's claims for welfare provision at that point where the citizen directly confronts the state, through contact with front line officials. This is, however, but part of a more general trend for the state increasingly to direct and control the activities of private individuals and groups.

The main thrust of the analysis here is that the form in which administrative discretion manifests itself is being transformed in several ways simultaneously. The locus of discretion that really matters to the individual citizen is not at the front line, but in the decision-making institutions of a directive state. Of course, the higher reaches of the state hierarchy have always had more power and discretion than the lower levels, even if it has been less visible to welfare claimants. But as the state gradually assumes a more directive role, so the scope and potency of economic decision-making expands and comes to bear on the individual more forcibly, most obviously in the determination of his/her net real income, the cash that gets into one's pocket from all sources, not just social security benefits. As the directive approach to welfare develops, so the area of discretionary decision-making that affects the individual most shifts from social policy, as traditionally conceived, to economic policy. And here it is the winning of positive discrimination for interest groups which counts, not the negative discretion that is exercised in denying a citizen's claim on the state.

Because directive state control of the economy is exercised by determining the internal-decision making of private organisations rather than by regulating national aggregate economic variables, the immediacy of the constraints that the state puts on the individual is increased. But because the policies of a directive state are worked out through continuous bargaining between the state and the powerful economic interest groups, the important discretion is exercised not only by state officials, whatever their level, but by private individuals as well. At the macro economic level, this means only a few key representatives. But private citizens are involved more broadly through the off-loading of welfare provision. Here again the locus of discretionary shifts away from the front line state official toward the community. Ultimately that involves, in a practical and not just a theoretical sense, the vast majority of adult citizens.

These then are some of the changing forms in which discretionary decision-making may present itself in future. But the issue of administrative discretion may be viewed in a wider context of social change. The concern about the niggardly discretion of state officials embodies and makes specific several other, broader concerns about trends in British society: about a movement from openness to secrecy, about a loss of individual freedom, or most grandly, about a reversal of the long development in modern society towards universalism, back towards particularism.

It would be surprising if such abstract issues as these did not show themselves in other forms besides a debate about administrative discretion. And, of course, they do. They are manifested in campaigns for a Freedom of Information Act or for 'open government' generally, and for 'participation' in a great variety of forms. They show in the double-barrelled proposals, from liberals and conservatives alike, for a Bill of Rights that would guarantee civil liberties, restrict the activities of the state, and restore Parliamentary control over the government. They show in almost daily demands for increased 'accountability' of state agencies, most contentiously in the worries about the spread of 'quangos'. A large number of people, in a large number of different ways, are concerned about the growing size, power, secrecy and discretion of the state.

They have good reason to be. The first part of this essay, translated into other words, presented evidence that the state is indeed growing larger and stronger, operating in more covert and selective ways. To acknowledge this is not to condemn it. It is not to slip into unquestioning agreement with that strong anti-statist strand in Anglo-Saxon political culture, which shows itself equally strongly on the individualist Right, in the libertarian Centre, and on the syndicalist Left. In Britain, of all places, the growth of the state has been pragmatic, a coping response to problems that sufficiently large numbers of people no longer found tolerable. The state grew, in part, because people wanted it to. Whether they want it to continue growing and whether they want a further development of its directive role are quite different questions.

For a fully developed directive state implies a very different type of society. Not, in simple black and white terms, a clearly better or worse one, but certainly a different one. It would involve a more planned economy and a more organised society, in which the state controlled and directed, even if it did not administer or provide, more emphasis on the collective national good and less on individual freedom or prosperity and a greater stress on civil duties than civil rights. It would again be surprising if many people, and not only those who do well out of the current system, were not concerned about what such a society would mean for them. The debate over administrative discretion is just one manifestation of that concern, one of many arenas in which the decision about how British society develops will gradually be formed.

In political economic terms, Britain is now in a transitional phase, *en route* towards a fundamentally different society, impelled by structural changes in the economic system on which it has been based for the last two centuries. If the British people do not like the prospect, they will have to do something more substantial about it than cutting public expenditure or establishing firmer rights to welfare benefits. They will have to do something about the structural causes that are creating the directive state. To return whence this essay began, that is the context in which the issue of administrative discretion must be set.

6 From Discretion to Rules: the Experience of the Family Fund
Jonathan Bradshaw

On 29 November 1972 Sir Keith Joseph, the Secretary of State for Social Services, announced in Parliament that he would establish a fund of £3m, 'to ease the burdens of living for those households containing very severely congenitally handicapped children' (Hansard 1972: col. 498).

This unexpected announcement was one result of the public campaign on behalf of children damaged by the thalidomide drug. To administer the fund, the Government by-passed all existing statutory agencies and sought the help of an independent charitable trust – The Joseph Rowntree Memorial Trust, based at York. The fund was named the Family Fund and began operations in March 1973. Its terms of reference were extended to include the non-congenitally disabled in December 1974 and by December 1978 the fund had received applications from 48,000 families and distributed grants in cash or kind worth £13m. The Fund was established for three years in the first instance and is now operating on an open ended contract.

The Family Fund is a small policy innovation in terms of resources; nonetheless it is a particularly interesting subject for research. The manner in which it developed is unusual; it was announced suddenly in response to a crisis; it was devised and established with great rapidity; and the administrative form it took was and is unprecedented in British social policy. Never before have such large amounts of public money been given to an independent body to distribute directly to the public. Because of the research opportunities presented by the Fund a research project was mounted to monitor and evaluate its work. Research workers were given the most unusual opportunity of observing and evaluating an agency developing from its inception.

The Origins of the Family Fund

The Family Fund has been described as a 'classic example' of one of Winkler's propositions about state behaviour towards the social services (see Winkler, Chapter 5 in this volume). It might be helpful to give a thumbnail sketch of Winkler's ideas. The role of the state is expanding. In the economy this has been accompanied by a movement from supportive state intervention to directive state intervention. The implications of this trend for the social services are profound. First, attempts to redistribute income by means of taxation and the social services having failed, the state may acquire enough power through control on prices, incomes and employment to exercise control over the primary distribution of real incomes. Second, because of the state's control over real incomes through taxation and welfare policy, the trade unions are forced to negotiate with the state as well as employers over their real income. Third, as a result of these negotiations, the state gets more in debt. The main way in which the state copes with this is then to involve the community in the provision of welfare services by 'off-loading' responsibility from statutory agencies to various non-statutory bodies, by getting people to help themselves, and by refusing to accept new welfare obligations. However, although the state delegates service provision, it maintains control through co-optation.

There is little doubt that 'a retreat from the welfare state' is taking place. However the reasons for these developments are not always those put forward by Winkler. According to Winkler, 'off-loading' is a mechanism for narrowing the gap between supply and demand for welfare services. This has economic and political advantages. Government is able to cut back on public expenditure and can deflect antagonism about the under-supply of services to other organisations. Thus 'it is no longer a state officer who exercises the mean-spirited discretion which deprives the citizen of what he needs'. Although the Family Fund may well have had these functions, they do not provide an explanation of why it was initially established.

Hood (1974) has written elegantly about the possible motivations of the state for operating through 'quangos', and Hood and

Bradshaw (1977) after analysing the origins of the Family Fund have considered which of these motivations operated in that case. It is worth briefly rehearsing the findings because they do not lend support to Winkler's thesis. It was concluded that the decision to establish the Family Fund was taken only the day before the debate in parliament in which it was announced. It is likely that Sir Keith Joseph, the Secretary of State for Social Services, having decided that it was necessary to provide some sort of assistance to thalidomide damaged children turned to his officials to work out speedily, without prejudicing the private litigation and without discriminating against other families with equally handicapped children the form such help should take. He may himself have thought up the idea of using an independent trust. Such an idea would have fitted into Conservative philosophy which favours voluntary action over government action. The Conservative government was also interested in controlling the growth of the civil service. There was also a fashion in British public policy to hive off purely executive operations from Ministerial departments. However, although a Labour minister might not have instinctively turned to an independent trust for assistance, given the requirements for speed and flexibility, it is unlikely that it was the hiving off mood in public administration or the niceties of Conservative philosophy which influenced the decisions made at such short notice.

There were in fact few other options. Among the candidates from central government, the Supplementary Benefits Commission was already hard-pressed and anyway had limited legal powers to help families where the head of the household was in full-time work. Although the Commission's staff had experience in making discretionary payments to families, their traditions and procedures were wedded to providing for the essential needs of poor people rather than the generous and imaginative support encouraged by the Fund. The Attendance Allowance Board was similarly pressed because of having to cope with the applications both for the higher and for the newly introduced lower rate allowance and their staff had no experience of distributing *ad hoc* payments. Officials knew from experience with supplementary benefits and the attendance allowance how difficult it was for government agencies to administer discretion flexibly and justify decisions in marginal cases. The DHSS had had recent experience in the Jimmy Martin case[1] of the public outcry which can result from being forced to make invidious distinctions between different categories of severely handicapped children.

The civil servants may also have considered distributing the money through the local authorities. In one sense the necessity for a fund at all was because of the inadequacy of existing services. But experience in implementing the Chronically Sick and Disabled Persons Act 1970 had shown how difficult it was to get local authorities to maintain equivalent standards and it would have been impossible to ensure through the rate support grant that the money would reach families with handicapped children. To use local authorities to disburse the money would anyway have required special legislation and even then the project would have foundered on the rock of the rate support grant and the administrative divisions between health, housing and social services. The Fund clearly had to be a complement to existing services but the decision to establish an independent fund was probably made because speed was imperative rather than for the purpose of out-flanking existing agencies already operating in the field.

The officials might have considered establishing a new trust with its own trustees and organisation, but it would have taken time to establish. The principal political consideration facing the Department was to provide help for the thalidomide children quickly. The demands in press and parliament were for immediate help. A solution requiring legislation would have taken too long and provoked long and bitter arguments and the civil servants must presumably have reasoned that it would have taken too long to establish an organisation of their own.

One reason why government may choose to operate through an unorthodox agency is that the policy area is experimental. In these circumstances, a voluntary organisation may be used as a trailblazer. The DHSS was certainly operating in the dark when it established the Family Fund. There was no planning or thinking about this type of operation prior to the thalidomide affair, and there was little information available to officials at short notice about either the numbers or the needs of handicapped children. The experimental notion of the Fund was taken up by the press after the announcement and was perhaps the most important factor influencing the Rowntree Trust to assume responsibility for the administration of the Family Fund. However, it is not likely to have been the reason for turning to the Trust for help in the first place. The view in the Department at the time of the announcement was that the government was making an *ad hoc* response to political circumstances and it was only after the announcement that ministers and officials became aware that the Family Fund had potential as an experiment in the administration of social services.

This account of the origins of the Family Fund suggests that it can be dangerous to attribute motives to those who established the Fund from the form it took. The establishment of a fund to help families with handicapped children was an unpremeditated response by government to external demands. It was announced without clarity of purpose, with uncertainty about its clientèle and with little or no consideration of how it would operate or what would be its long-term implications. Although it was subsequently hailed as a new experiment in social policy, this was a *post hoc* rationalisation designed to raise the status of something that had a more expedient purpose.

Thus, the form which the Family Fund took was not determined by a strategic preference for 'off-loading' – it was simply the best device available to the government for dealing with a political crisis. Once established, it may well have facilitated cut-backs in public expenditure and functioned to take the heat out of additional demands on government. Demands for help for vaccine damaged children, for compensation for children damaged *in utero,* for the attendance allowance to be paid to foster children and for general demands for improvements in policies for the handicapped have all been met with the assurance that, *inter alia,* the Family Fund exists to provide help for such families. However, that in itself does not (in this instance) explain why this particular social policy initiative originated or took the form it did.

Discretion and the Family Fund

An earlier paper on this subject (Bradshaw 1975) depicted discretion as a matter of degree. Most agencies making decisions do so in a manner which can be located on a continuum somewhere between discretion at one end and rules at the other. Competing values push the character of the decision between these two ends of the continuum. Thus accountability, efficiency, rationality and entitlement push the agency towards rules, and generosity, relevance, individuality, sensitivity and choice push it towards discretion.

As Adler and Asquith have pointed out (in Chapter 1 of this volume) it is usual for agencies such as the Family Fund that give things to people rather than to do things to them to operate on the basis of a body of rules. One of the most interesting aspects of the Family Fund was that it set out to place itself at the discretion end of the spectrum − to operate not by rules but by the individual discretionary decisions of professionally trained social workers. The rest of this chapter describes how the Family Fund developed: how external pressures and internal bureaucratic constraints conspired to turn what began as a flexible operation staffed by professionals into one that was much less flexible and staffed by clerical or administrative personnel.

In establishing the Family Fund the Joseph Rowntree Memorial Trust had little to go on. Little was known about the numbers of families that might ask for help or about the nature of their needs. The Trust had very limited office accommodation and no staff available to run the Family Fund and they only had three months between the end of December 1972 when they agreed to take on the Fund to the beginning of April 1973 when they began to deal with applications.

In seeking to allocate the money the organisation can be seen to have passed through three phases. The initial phase of exploratory development lasted from April 1973 to about April 1975. The second phase of retrenchment lasted from about March 1975 to about December 1975. The third phase from January 1976 has been a period of relative stability.

The behaviour of the organisation and the timing of these phases was certainly the result of the evolution of thinking within the Fund but it was also determined to a considerable extent by three externally determined pressures: the number of applications received by the Fund, the number of cases processed by the Fund, and the rate of expenditure of the Fund. Broadly speaking the Fund developed in the first phase in response to the rate of applications and the need to increase the throughput of grants. As the throughput of grants increased so the rate of expenditure also increased and, with the rate of expenditure in danger of exhausting the resources available to it, the Fund entered the phase of retrenchment. Having found a level of expenditure which fell within the limits of the resources available to it and established an organisation which would cope with the steadied rate of applications the Fund settled into the third phase of stability.

The Family Fund aimed to respond flexibly to the individual needs of each family without recourse to a body of detailed rules. They therefore employed social workers who were felt to have the training and expertise to make decisions using their own professional judgement. However, the Management Committee of the Family Fund also decided to appoint a panel to provide the social workers with an interpretation of the guidelines set by the Department of Health and Social Security.

The decision to employ social work staff to exercise their discretion in dealing with individual applicants was crucial in the development of the Fund. A social work ethos dominated the approach to applicants and the Fund's managers found it difficult to direct them as a professional group. The Trust's Director later regretted the decision to employ social workers to process applications at York. While he valued the caring approach which they brought to the work he felt that the pressures on the Fund were too great for it to operate on social work precepts: case work could not be done at a distance. He felt that administrative skills were all that were really necessary to make decisions. Later, the Fund reduced the proportion of social work staff at York. The decision to employ social work staff in the first place was the result of the influence of the DHSS Social Work Service in the establishment of the Fund. They believed that professionally qualified social workers would be needed to seek beyond the initial item requested for unmet needs, to negotiate with social work and other agencies in the field and to appreciate the nature of the problems of families with disabled children. The social work staff who were recruited to the Fund were attracted because they were expected to be able to use their professional judgement flexibly to the benefit of families with handicapped children. In the early days of the Fund, before the number of applications to be dealt with built up, the social work staff were encouraged to urge families and visiting social workers to think of new and interesting ways of relieving stress, they were encouraged to enquire into needs beyond those covered by the initial request, to advise families of other benefits and services that they might be entitled to, to advocate on

behalf of families and, in borderline cases, to give the families the
benefit of the doubt. This degree of discretion was soon limited by
three developments:

(1) *Pressure of work.*   The growth in the rate of applications and the
backlog of cases to be assessed soon made it very difficult for social
workers to spend the time on each case to carry out the detailed
enquiries necessary for them to use their discretion. The Fund's
managers, alarmed by the backlog, began to introduce measures to
routinise procedures and urged social workers to reduce the time
spent on each case. Cases that could be routinely processed were
taken out of the hands of the social workers and given to staff without
social work qualifications; the staff were urged to respond only to the
item requested and not to try to do case work at a distance. The
social work staff were not happy with these developments: they felt
that the problem had arisen as a result of delays in recruiting staff,
they were unwilling to accept limits imposed on their professional
judgement, and they were not happy in seeing needs that they had
recognised in others go unmet because they did not have the time to
make a full assessment. The conflict between the social workers'
unwillingness to have their discretion restrained and the Fund's
managers' wish to increase the output of grants continued throughout the phase of exploratory development.

(2) *Panel decisions.*   The social workers' discretion was not only constrained by the pressure of work but also increasingly inhibited by
the body of rules that began to emerge from the Panel about what
could be given and which children were eligible. Decisions of the
Panel became another source of conflict within the organisation.
The conflict arose when the social workers disagreed with the
Panel's decisions in individual cases or the guide lines that emanated
from the Fund. The Panel's judgement on individual cases had the
effect of undermining the social workers' confidence in their own
discretionary decisions. This confidence was further undermined
when social workers' decisions were altered without consultation.

(3) *Equity.*   It was not that some clear guidance from the Panel was
not generally welcomed by the social work staff. Guidance was
welcomed because it gave staff confidence that their judgements
would not be challenged, that they would be upheld in case of a

dispute and most important of all that the Fund was operating with some consistency. One of the lessons that was learned by the social workers in the Fund was how difficult it was to operate individual discretion without some limit and without some guidelines. The Fund managers took the view that

> there is no entitlement and because we are using discretion flexibly we cannot be called upon to show that our grants are equitable. (Notes of Guidance to Social Workers, undated).

However, evidence began to be produced that the amounts that families got from the Fund varied considerably and that the better off and more articulate families were getting larger grants than poorer families with lower aspirations. It became difficult to justify these inequities in terms of flexibility, speed, ease of administration and general responsiveness of the system.

In the absence of guidelines from the Panel social workers developed their own unwritten principles and, despite the resistance of the staff to many of the constraints put on their discretion by the Panel's guidelines, they did become able to operate their discretion with more speed and confidence as the body of internal guidelines built up.

For the time being the organisation remained staffed predominantly by social workers exercising a considerable degree of individual discretion within these guidelines. However, in the period of retrenchment this discretion was further constrained by budgetary pressures, until the social work staff found themselves left with little freedom to operate discretion.

It was inevitable that budgetary pressures should begin to affect the work of the Family Fund. The Fund developed its procedures without the discipline of a budget. Apart from the costs of administration, the only financial consideration that had any real effect on the early policy making of the Fund was the need to increase expenditure. Until the end of 1973 the Fund had still not succeeded in spending the interest that had accrued on the first £3m it had received from the government. By mid 1974 the Fund's managers began to consider their rate of expenditure. The management committee were told in June 1974 that

> The Trust's finance officer had calculated that at the present rate of expenditure the Family Fund will be reduced by the end of 1974 to

approximately £900,000 bearing in mind the number of applications in the pipe line. The Trust would be unwise to invite further applications after the end of 1974. (Family Fund Note to the Management Committee, June 1974).

In October 1974 this situation was relieved by the announcement that a second £3m would be made available and, replete with these extra resources, the criteria of eligibility were extended by DHSS to include the non-congenitally very severely disabled.

The first form of retrenchment, the decision to withdraw from the giving of aids and adaptations which could be given by social services departments, came as a result of the belief that local authorities with pressure on their own resources were transferring their responsibilities to the Fund and that this might exhaust the Family Fund resources. The limited provision made by many local authorities, and the powerlessness of government to do anything about it, was one of the factors which had made it necessary to establish a Fund in the first place. The Fund was established both because there were gaps in provision and because of the inadequate level of existing provision. It was able to fill some of the gaps, but it found it could not take on full responsibility for the inadequacy of existing provisions. The position might have been different either if existing provision had been able to expand more rapidly or if the Family Fund had been financed to enable it to meet those needs which local authorities were unable (or unwilling) to meet. The dilemma of the Fund was that in abandoning the doctrine that it would provide for unmet needs, regardless of the responsibility of other agencies, the one feature which had made the Fund such an effective source of help for families was also abandoned. In attempting to avoid becoming the dustbin of other agencies' unwanted cases the Fund had either to refuse to help at all or only to agree to help as a last resort, and in withdrawing from this arena of provision the Fund further limited and constrained the discretion of its social work staff.

The second form of retrenchment came partly as a result of the increased awareness that the Fund might face a financial crisis and partly as a result of the announcement that from July 1974 a mobility allowance was to be introduced. A decision was also made to replace grants for car purchase worth £750 with grants for car hire worth £200 per year.

The third form of retrenchment came soon after and was very explicitly the result of a need to work to a budgetary framework. In a letter to the trustees on 15 August the Director of the Trust wrote that the DHSS had agreed that the Fund should continue in operation until the end of 1978.

> It now follows that the administration of the Family Fund must be related to an annual budget and the Department's first anxiety was whether the Trust would accept such an arrangement as against the 'open ended' discretion and resulting demand on resources that has operated so far. The view that I expressed was that, whether or not there was a financial crisis, the time had come when some budgetary discipline ought to be introduced into the administration of the Fund and that this was not inconsistent with the discretionary aspect of the Trust's administration so far. I hoped that in discussions about this change the Department would not put the stress on the need for economy but on a desirable development following the period of two years' experiment.

In the event, grants covering a whole range of items and circumstances were limited or discontinued and these changes in policy were successful in reducing the rate of expenditure of the Fund. The range and level of help available from the Fund was greatly reduced and the discretion left to social workers was further constrained. The social work staff the Trust had recruited to exercise discretion began to leave and as they left they were replaced with administrative workers. They left for a variety of reasons but one important reason was that they no longer felt that they had sufficient freedom to exercise their own discretion. From early 1976 the Fund has been operating without significant changes, with mostly administrative staff, on the basis of criteria as revised during the period of retrenchment and to a budget of about £2m a year.

Discussion

Two conclusions, both of which will be familiar to students of organisations, can be drawn from this account. In the first place the bureaucratic machinery necessary to implement an innovation in social policy led to increasing rigidity. The characteristics of the task of the Family Fund (the distribution of money to large numbers of families) called for some of the qualities of a bureaucratic organisation (division of labour, hierarchy of offices, abstract rules and procedures) and the development of these inevitably led to increasing control over front line staff who exercised discretion. Secondly, these front line staff experienced many of the conflicts of professionals working in a bureaucratic setting. While social workers in the Family Fund eventually accepted that there had to be some limits on their discretion to enable cases to be dealt with more rapidly and to maintain equity, they were very reluctant to accept the procedures that were entailed. The managers of the Fund had to take decisions with administrative considerations in mind which often conflicted with the individual discretionary considerations of the social workers.

While these aspects of organisational behaviour are familiar, of more interest has been the experience of watching the administration of discretion developing within an organisation. The Family Fund was an example of an organisation operating with the very minimum of rules. At first, the social workers made decisions on cases constrained only by the guidelines agreed with the DHSS and their own self-imposed sense of what was fair and effective. The scope of their discretion became limited, first by the requirements of the administration, then by the developing body of internal guidelines and finally by budgetary constraints. Hill (1972: p. 62) has written:

> The exercise of discretion occurs when officials are required or permitted to make decisions without being given instructions which would in effect pre-determine those decisions.

As the Family Fund developed, more and more of the decisions that the staff could make have become pre-determined by instructions. Although the Fund never became rulebound, it was not able to maintain the flexibility which was hoped for at the start and it has become more and more 'rule guided'.

Much of the debate about discretion in the last decade has centred on the supplementary benefits scheme. Titmuss, when vice chairman of the Supplementary Benefits Commission mounted a biting attack on the 'pathology of legalism' (Titmuss 1971) and stoutly defended discretion as an area of flexible, individualised justice. But the administrative problems presented to the Commission in their efforts to administer their discretionary powers have become overwhelming: and Donnison (1977b) has intimated that the Commission should

Abandon the aspiration to match the benefits we pay to the infinite variety of human needs we encounter – the aspiration for creative justice.

In supplementary benefits, rules to control officer level discretion have been introduced for three main reasons (i) to ensure some degree of consistency or equity in the decisions made at officer level; (ii) because the kind of staff employed by the commission to make individual discretionary decisions are felt to lack the training and expertise to do so without considerable guidance, and (iii) because those who manage the scheme need to be assured that expenditure on discretionary grants is reasonable and can be predicted (for a fuller discussion, see Prosser, Chapter 7 in this volume).

The Family Fund sought to avoid detailed rules by the appointment of social workers. It was neither tribunals, courts, the press, the Public Accounts Committee, parliamentary questions nor any other judicial or quasi-judicial mechanism which constrained this discretion. Rather it was the need to process grants rapidly, to control expenditure and to maintain a degree of equity which eventually led to increasing rigidity in the administration.

The Family Fund is still largely a discretionary rather than a legalistic instrument. Social workers in the field and administrative staff in York make discretionary judgements but they (particularly the staff at York) are not practising 'individual private and personal discretion' (Donnison 1977b) but the type of administrative judgements inevitable in any organisation. The range and level of the help available from the Fund has been reduced. The Fund is no longer able to be as flexible and generous as it was, and through routinised administrative procedures the Fund may be operating with less individualised responsiveness than it did. However, there is now less variation in the help given to families, greater fairness and consistency, less delay and more clarity about what could be obtained on behalf of families. These may be the advantages of a less discretionary agency, but they also make the Fund a less exciting and creative instrument in social policy.

7 The Politics of Discretion: Aspects of Discretionary Power in the Supplementary Benefits Scheme*
Tony Prosser

There can be few areas of the welfare state in which discretion has performed a more controversial role than in that of Supplementary Benefits (SB). I believe it to be crucially important in advancing the debate to develop an understanding of how discretion fits into the broader political structure, of how its form and operation are determined by political, social and administrative constraints. Thus I will attempt to abstract certain key themes in the development of some forms of discretionary power in this field to illustrate some important political influences on discretion.

A crucial question prompted by the examination of the SB system and its predecessors is why they assumed a legal form which survived largely unchanged over forty years of hectic social development. This is particularly striking because at first sight the system seems highly inadequate, not only from the point of view of those dependent on it but also from that of bureaucratic administration and of the need to keep public expenditure within bounds. It is well known that the operation of the scheme may pose particularly difficult choices for relatively low-level staff (Hill 1972: Chapter 4) and that it is extremely expensive to administer: there are over 30,000 staff employed on SB work, more than half the total number

* I would like to thank all those who contributed to the discussion of an earlier version of this work at the SSRC Workshop on discretion in Cambridge on 11 July 1979, and in particular David Bull and Michael Hill. I am also grateful to Norman Lewis for valuable comments on the manuscript and to John Mesher for some useful source material and comments.

of staff in Department of Health and Social Security (DHSS) local offices, paying out in 1978 only 14.5 per cent of the total budget (DHSS 1978: para. 1.11). This applies especially to the well known discretionary powers to provide additions to benefit (or reduce or withhold it) in 'exceptional circumstances', and to make a lump sum payment to meet an 'exceptional need' (SB Act 1976, Sch. 1, para. 4(1), and section 3) which are used on an extremely large scale. Thus, in November 1978 1,666,000 claimants, representing about 57 per cent of all claimants, received 'exceptional circumstances additions' (ECAs) to weekly benefit. During 1978 1,119,000 'exceptional needs payments' (ENPs) were made (Report of the Supplementary Benefits Commission for 1978, 1979: 125).

What, then, have been the reasons for the continued existence of discretion in such a broad form? The reason commonly given has been that it enables the scheme to cater for individual needs not suitable for being met on the basis of general rules. There is some truth in this; however, anyone familiar with the administration of the scheme will know that individualised justice is not the dominant consideration in practice; it is subject to the often highly restrictive and complex body of rules made by the SB Commission and embodied partly in the now celebrated A-Code (see Hodge 1975). The existence of such powers can also be seen as a disguised form of rationing (Hill, 1972: Chapter 4), yet formal rules may be in many ways more effective in restraining expenditure (see Bradshaw, Chapter 6 in this volume). I will try to show that a central reason for the existence of apparently wide discretionary powers in this area is the conflict of political values in the development of a large-scale system for the relief of poverty.

This will involve examining the political functions of discretion rather than employing a 'legal' methodology in which exercise of discretion is compared with the norms of public law, or in which discretionary powers are seen as fields ripe for confining and structuring to achieve an agreed on purpose. In particular I feel unhappy with the 'black box' model of discretion often implicit in such accounts (Jowell 1975) in which the determined legislative purpose is 'shone into' an administrative agency, but then 'refracted' by the various influences affecting the exercise of discretion. Rather I will suggest that discretion may arise as an attempt to disguise conflicting purposes behind both legislation and administration; it may serve as a means by which the resolution of the value conflicts behind such purposes is deliberately fudged.

It should now be clear that, like Adler and Asquith (Chapter 1 in this volume), my central concern is the relationship between discretion and power. Of course this relationship has been the basis of much writing about discretion. Thus writings presenting traditional conceptions of the rule of law have arisen through disquiet at the power of the state to manipulate the affairs of private citizens. However, in the first part of this chapter I will see the relationship in a different way. I will not be concerned with the overt opportunities for manipulation opened up by the existence of discretion, nor with the content of particular discretionary decisions, but rather with the role of discretion in the presentation of policy, and in particular with its role in disguising contradictory pressures on government. In other words discretion can prevent the coalescing of open issues around which political struggle can take place. In this context the existence of discretion must be seen as part of the problem central to current debate about the administrative process, that of 'open government'.

This concern parallels recent developments in political and sociological theories of power; the now celebrated work of Bachrach and Baratz (1970) on 'nondecision-making' and the development of this by Steven Lukes (1974). Bachrach and Baratz begin from a critique of pluralist theories of decision-making which are concerned with the outcome of overt conflict in the making of decisions on what have emerged as key political decisions. This is criticised as being merely one face of the exercise of power; in addition power may be exercised by the confining of observable conflict to safe issues not posing a threat to the powerful. Thus the concern is with the visibility of decision-making as much as with its actual content. For the purpose of empirical study of this they develop the concept of 'nondecisions'. A 'nondecision' is a decision which results in the prevention of conflict. To quote Bachrach and Baratz (1970: p. 44),

> A non decision, as we define it, is a decision that results in suppression or thwarting of a latent or manifest challenge to the values or interests of the decision-maker. To be more nearly explicit, nondecision-making is a means by which demands for change in the existing allocation of benefits and privileges in the community can be suffocated before they are even voiced; or kept covert; or killed before they gain access to the relevant decison-making arena; or, failing all these things, maimed or destroyed in the decision-implementing stage of the policy process.

Bachrach and Baratz confine their discussion to decisions having the effect of excluding particular groups from participation in the political process. However, as Lukes has suggested, the potential of their work is wider than this. He stresses that 'nondecisions' need not be decisions consciously made to exclude challenge of those with power, for it is enough that they result in the suppression of latent or manifest challenge to dominant structures or values. He also stresses that there need not be observable conflict between the person or body exercising power and those who might have a grievance which is prevented from becoming an issue, and includes unconscious, accepted behaviour and the weight of institutions as exercises of power if they are in some way detrimental to the interests of those affected, even if these interests have not yet been articulated as a conscious grievance.

Despite the considerable methodological problems in applying these concepts, I have felt for some time that they can be useful in understanding some functions of discretion, and in particular the allocation of particular areas of decision-making to discretion or to published rule. If rules constraining administration are available it means that to a degree policy is made explicit and visible and so can be subject to political challenge. Moreover, the rule provides a resource for criticism of the decision eventually made. If no open rules are provided both these tasks are made more difficult, and pressure for change can be diverted through a lack of an object against which to direct it. In the first part of the chapter I will suggest that the emergence in the mid 1930s of the main discretionary powers in something resembling their present form was part of a process which was rather more than the political compromise inevitable in this area, and in particular that the emergence of these powers was part of a governmental attempt to disguise the issue of benefit reductions and to take the issue of the rate of benefit out of political debate.

The second part of this chapter will deal with the most important source of change in the legal structure of the SB system since the 1930s: the recent policy review carried out by a team of Department of Health and Social Security officials and published as *Social Assistance* (DHSS 1978). I will argue that from the mid 1960s various changes took place both in the numbers dependent on benefit and in the tactics adopted by groups working on their behalf which made the model based on the legislation of 1934–6 unworkable. These produced indications that the system might collapse by pressure of numbers and by the 'exploitation' (from the viewpoint of administration and government) of the discretionary powers and the powers of the appeal tribunals. Moreover, soon after the publication of the review a Conservative government determined to cut public expenditure was elected. These administrative and political pressures have had the effect of encouraging the development from discretion towards a rational system of rules.

Discretion and Unemployment Assistance

It was in 1934 that the discretionary powers under discussion first became incorporated in a national scheme for the relief of unemployment. The fundamental problem resulting in the establishment of this scheme was the inadequacy of the Unemployment Insurance Scheme of 1911 in conditions of major economic recession. In September 1931, after the report of the May Committee on National Expenditure (Report of the Committee on National Expenditure 1931), the Government limited the availability of unemployment benefit. Those not qualifying for this would receive means tested 'transitional payments'. These formed a new departure in unemployment relief for they were funded by the Exchequer but administered locally; the task of setting the scales of payment and of administering the means test to determine the amount payable in individual cases fell to the Public Assistance Committees of the local authorities.

Inevitably, the system gave rise to serious difficulties (Briggs and Deacon 1973). The main problems were inconsistency in scales from area to area and, more importantly from the government's point of view, 'lax' or generous use in some areas of the deeply unpopular household means test; for example, from February to September 1932, 98.7 per cent of applications were allowed at the maximum rate in Rotherham but only 11.8 per cent were in Oldham (Report of the Royal Commission on Unemployment Insurance 1932: para 106). Much of the inconsistency was a result of the deliberate refusal of some authorities to operate the test fully: sometimes this was inspired by political commitment, but it was also because of fear of disorder of the type illustrated by the widespread rioting in Birkenhead in September 1932 (*The Times* 19–20 September 1932) and fear of loss of votes in the local elections (Briggs and Deacon 1973: especially pp. 57–8). The Government's response was to issue warnings to many of the local authorities; where these warnings were ignored the Minister of Labour had power to supersede the Public Assistance Committees and to replace them with commissioners appointed by himself. This was done in Rotherham and County Durham in October and November 1932.

The Government was thus faced with a situation in which its determination to bring expenditure under firm control was threatened by strong political pressure for generous treatment. Moreover, the payment of relatively high sums by many local authorities had created expectations which would make the task of restraining expenditure peaceably much more difficult. How could the government implement its policy in such a way as to prevent benefit reductions becoming an explosive political issue? The strategy adopted was to take unemployment relief 'out of politics', or, as one recent writer has put it (Booth 1978: p. 140, emphasis in original):

> The coalition's main vulnerability lay in becoming involved in an auction at the polls over the level of unemployment relief. Thus [Chamberlain, the Chancellor] decided that the potential *political* weaknesses could be protected only if some *administrative* device could be found to take the whole topic of unemployment outside the scope of political argument.

There were to be two central elements in the structure of the new scheme: centralisation rather than local authority administration to enable more effective control of expenditure and administration not by a government department but by a formally independent commission to be called the Unemployment Assistance Board. It now seems clear that the independent status of the Board and the existence of its own appeal tribunals were designed to avoid pressure by MPs for more generous allowances (Millett 1940: especially p. 233 and Briggs and Deacon 1973: pp. 58–62). This Board was to be established by Part II of the Unemployment Bill which was introduced in November 1933 and received the Royal Assent in June 1934. However, the Act did not establish the rates of allowance to be paid, nor did it set out what discretionary powers were to be available to the Board: these were left for later regulations. Before the end of the year the regulations were introduced under the affirmative resolution procedure (for their framing see Lynes 1977).

In debate, the Minister of Labour (Mr Stanley) pointed to the importance of the discretionary powers provided in the regulations for meeting 'special circumstances' and 'exceptional needs' (Hansard 1935a: cols 841–2):

> The regulations . . . cannot lay down any arbitrary figures. All they can do is to lay down, first of all, a general standard of payment; second, to afford a minimum protection to certain resources; thirdly, to illustrate the various points at which discretion will be necessary; and fourthly, as far as possible, to place the exercise of that discretion within limits of which this House can be aware.

In dealing with the financial effects of the regulations he stated (Hansard 1935a: cols 855–7):

> You cannot expect, in attempting to get uniformity, that you will not get some decreases as well as increases. But the unemployed on transitional payments are going to get £3,000,000 a year more than they are getting this year.

Thus the impression given was that the discretion would be exercised widely and generously and that despite occasional decreases most of the unemployed would as a result be better off than they had been when receiving transitional payments (see Lynes 1977).

Speakers for the Opposition suggested that the discretionary powers would not in practice be widely used, and Aneurin Bevan accused the Government of using the discretion as an 'alibi' to disguise the fact that 'the Government are now engaged in carrying through the House regulations which will brutally impoverish the conditions of all the distressed areas' (Hansard 1935a: cols 884–6). On the resumption of debate the following day the Solicitor-General also stressed the discretion to increase payment; 'these figures are guides and only guides, and the overriding provision makes plain that the discretion remains to treat each particular case on its merits and consider all the special circumstances' (Hansard 1935a: col. 1015). The Government put the whips on to ensure passage of the motion of approval of the regulations, and they were approved in the Lords without a vote.

When one examines the regulations (*The Unemployment Assistance Regulations 1934*, 1934) the discretionary powers do indeed seem wide, and correspond closely to those in the 1976 legislation. Reg. IV provided that

(2) A final assessment may in any case where special circumstances exist, be adjusted by way of increase or reduction to meet such special circumstances.

(3) A final assessment may be increased to provide for needs of an exceptional character by such amount as is reasonable.

The explanatory memorandum on the regulations (*Memorandum on the draft Unemployment Assistance Regulations* 1934) gave special diets and high rents as examples of special circumstances warranting an addition and the deliberate resort to cheap lodgings to save more money for non-essentials as an example of an act to warrant reduction. It was envisaged that use of the power to make payments for exceptional needs would be rare, and it was stressed that all normal needs including clothing and household equipment were to be met from the normal allowance. Appeal against the exercise of these powers required leave of the tribunal chairman, and this could only be granted on limited grounds.

The Board were to take over their business on two 'appointed days', the first being 7 January 1935 when they took over those unemployed who had received transitional payment. There was an immediate outcry for it was found that the amount paid was reduced in a large proportion of cases. Members returning to Parliament were overwhelmed with deputations and public demonstrations took place almost daily, especially in South Wales and Yorkshire in what has been described as 'a political storm of the first magnitude' (Millett 1940: p. 52). When Parliament reassembled there was pending a supplementary estimate of approximately £5m for the Board's allowances for the remainder of the financial year. As this was proportionally far below the £44m annual cost estimated in the earlier White Paper, it produced a heated debate, as did the contrast between the actual reductions and the impression created earlier by the Minister that allowances in general would be more generous than transitional payments. Strong criticism came even from Government supporters; to give only one example Robert Boothby began by saying that 'when these Regulations were first announced I thought they were very good'. But on seeing their operation in practice he now thought 'the new administration is brutal. I can use

no other word. The cuts are brutal.' (Hansard 1935b: cols. 63, 66).
What were the reasons for so sudden a disillusionment? A National
Labour peer (Lord Elton) was later to tell the House of Lords that
he had based his

> very excessive optimism [concerning the regulations] upon the presence in
> the Bill of a discretionary power which I thought – wrongly as it proves –
> would be so important that I actually went as far as to say I understood it
> was an expert opinion that the number of families dealt with under the
> discretionary clause would come to be more numerous than those dealt
> with under the regulations. In that I was wrong. That forecast has been
> falsified.
>
> (Hansard 1935c: col. 955)

The initial government response was to claim that many decisions
would be revised upwards by the appeal tribunals. On the following
day, the Minister denied that the new scheme was an economy
measure and blamed the problems on the fact that there were new
men working the scheme so that their inevitable timidity resulted in
rigidity and a reluctance to exercise discretion properly (Hansard
1935b: col. 246). In fact it appears that most of the staff had been
taken over from those employed by the local authorities to administer
transitional payments, and the Minister's statement produced
protests from the Civil Service Clerical Association on the grounds
that the 'officers, who had day-to-day contact with the unemployed,
had been compelled to work very rigidly to specific regulations, and
that the margin of discretion allowed was almost non-existent' (*The
Times*, 17 February 1935).

The Government avoided the political problems by introducing
regulations, later embodied in the Unemployment Assistance
(Temporary Provisions) Act, establishing the 'standstill' during
which allowances were determined either by the Unemployment
Assistance Regulations or by transitional payment practices, which-
ever was the greater. This was effective retroactively and so restored
the money lost because of the cuts. It is interesting to note that it was
later admitted by the Government that expenditure in the first few
weeks fell far short of the level of the original claim that it would
exceed that on transitional payments by £3m (Hansard 1935c: col.
942; *Report of the Unemployment Assistance Board for 1935*, 1935/36:
p. 14).

Thus all this illustrates well how the apparent existence of discretion could be used by government as a means of avoiding conflict over unpopular change. If firm new benefit scales had been provided this would have made it plain that major cuts would have to take place; the ability to point to the discretionary powers provided a means for avoiding this, for preventing the possibility of large-scale cuts from becoming a clear issue of political debate. Yet it proved unsuccessful. One reason for this appears to be that the actual exercise of discretion was far more restrictive than government statements had suggested. At the time of the 'standstill' some MPs made strong claims to this effect. Dingle Foot stated that enormous reductions had been foreseen by the Opposition and were the inevitable result of the regulations. He pointed out that

> these scales do not constitute a sort of general guide or pointer to officers to give them an idea of the lines on which they are to proceed. They are, in the most important aspect, rather mandatory, and tell the officers exactly what is to be done. . . . You cannot expect local officers to invent special circumstances.
>
> (Hansard 1935b: cols. 1005–6)

These suggestions were echoed by later speakers, and the same thesis is presented forcefully in Millett's account of the establishment of the Board (Millett 1940: pp. 198–206). He states that 'it is preposterous to believe that the local officers of the Unemployment Assistance Board were expected to exercise discretion as they pleased in dealing with applicants' (p. 203). Reasons he gives for this are that too much authority would have been given to subordinate officials, inconsistency would have resulted and the sense of obligation to the Exchequer would have been lost. Moreover, psychological factors were also important, and the use of discretion was not effectively encouraged in the instructions from the centre;

> Is it any wonder the local officers decided to play safe and stick to the scale? The scale was objective. It could be calculated with mathematical precision. Discretion was subjective, and the officers were confused as to just what was its purpose or how they were expected to proceed. The local officials of the Unemployment Assistance Board can be entirely absolved from any responsibility for the situation which necessitated the standstill. They had no reason to believe that they were not expected to follow their instructions faithfully.
>
> (p. 206)

More recent work based on the Board's internal documents has confirmed this (*Report of the Supplementary Benefits Commission for 1976*, 1977: Appendix C based on research by Tony Lynes). The initial instructions issued to officers warned against administration becoming 'mechanical and routine'. (Para C7). However, there was little to assist officers in deciding what constituted 'special circumstances' and this must initially have led to caution. By the third week of the scheme discretionary additions were awarded in about 5 per cent of cases, and this was 'too few to have any real political impact'. (Para C17). Other instructions 'were more cautious in tone and hardly calculated to encourage generous use of the power to make single payments for exceptional needs' (*Report of the Supplementary Benefits Commission for 1976*, 1977: para C8), and stressed that 'weekly allowances are intended to cover all normal needs that can be foreseen, including those which arise only from time to time such as renewal of clothing and household equipment'. Most important of all, discretionary additions were not to be made on any large scale to mitigate the cuts as such. This had been suggested by the Cabinet as a possible means of making the cuts gradually rather than as a sudden reduction but was resisted by the Board as the reductions would result only from a 'progressive increase of illegal administration'. A second way in which restrictions on the exercise of discretion prevented a smooth transition to the new scheme related to the limited grounds on which appeals against the amount of allowances could be heard. Initially the chairmen were extremely reluctant to grant leave to appeal to the tribunals. This was remedied by memoranda sent to them and by a government amendment to the legislation creating the standstill which prevented them from refusing leave in appeals against allowances granted under its provisions (Lynes 1976).

In these events, then, the ability of the Government to point to the existence of discretionary powers was a central part of its attempt to justify unpopular change; yet this was unsuccessful partly because the reality did not match up to the claims. The role of discretion becomes more evident when one examines subsequent events. The 'standstill' was deeply unpopular with the Board and could clearly not last for ever. Yet ending it would mean cuts in allowances for it had enabled an increase over the rate set out in the regulations to apply in the majority of cases. Eventually regulations were presented to the House in July 1936, and after long and lively debate were approved (*The Unemployment Assistance Regulations 1936* 1936). 'This time no concerted protests greeted the execution of the assistance regulations. The Government and the Unemployment Assistance Board had learned some lessons.' (Millett 1940: p. 76).

There were several reasons for the lack of response to the new regulations. Firstly, unemployment was dropping and in June 1936 some 567,058 people were dependent on the means-tested benefit in contrast to 817,031 two years earlier. Secondly, reductions phased in over eighteen months and the use of local advisory committees enabled the process to be planned in such a way as to avoid cases of particular hardship. In addition two weeks' notice was given to enable an appeal to take place, and as the Board itself stated, this together with the fact that reductions were recommended by local people 'undoubtedly helped to reconcile applicants to the reductions' (*Report of the Unemployment Assistance Board for 1937*, 1937/38: p. 16).

The discretionary powers contained in the new regulations appeared similar to those in the earlier ones, but were now likely to be used more flexibly. They now explicitly referred to prolonged unemployment as a source of exceptional needs. The explanatory memorandum on the first set of regulations had stressed that needs such as clothing and household equipment should be met out of the ordinary scale of payment, but the new memorandum (*Memorandum on the draft Unemployment Assistance Regulations* 1936), in exemplifying situations in which exceptional needs payments might be made, stated that it might often be found that a household was in immediate distress due to want of adequate clothing, bedding or household equipment for which it could not reasonably have been expected to make provision. In fact the new form of the regulations rather than introducing change reflected a gradual clarification and liberalisation of the instructions to officers on the exercise of discretion carried out during the period of the 'standstill' (*Report of the Supplementary Benefits Commission for 1976*, 1977: paras C6–C16). The number of exceptional needs payments made increased considerably, for whilst in 1935 about 10,000 lump sum payments had been made, this figure more than doubled to 22,000 in 1936 and reached 23,229 in 1937. A similar development of explicit guidance together with actual liberalisation occurred in the instructions relating to the award of additions to allowances in special circumstances, and whilst in the third week of the scheme about 5 per cent of cases received such additions, this had increased to about 20 per cent by the end of 1936 (*Report of the Supplementary Benefits Commission for 1976*, 1977: paras C17–C22). In general terms the Board's report for 1937 stated that 'the powers of discretion which were contained in the old regulations were extended and made more explicit in certain directions in order to meet, with the greatest possible elasticity, the wide variety of circumstances which the individual cases disclose' (*Report of the Unemployment Assistance Board for 1937*, 1937/38: pp. 9–10), and according to one writer (Millett 1940: p. 211) 'to foster initiative in the use of discretionary powers the Board took several positive steps with the object of building up an *esprit de corps*, a morale, within the organisation favourable to the exercise of discretion'.

The events of the mid thirties are a particularly good example of the role of discretion in reducing the visibility of government policy. The problems of the transitional payments system made it inevitable that the Government would introduce a centralised system for the administration of unemployment assistance necessarily involving considerable reductions in allowances. At the same time it wanted to avoid opportunities for the political criticism of its actions, hence the establishment of an independent board. Initially the reductions to take place on the introduction of the new scheme were disguised by official statements pointing to the discretion to increase allowances. This was not successful in making the scheme acceptable because of the rigidity of actual administration during the initial period. By the time the new regulations were introduced in 1936 steps had been taken to ensure that the discretion was much more extensively exercised, and this together with the gradual phasing in of the reductions played an important part in legitimating the new scheme and in preventing open conflict or apparent hardship through it. Before I discuss the theoretical implications of this I would like to describe recent pressures for the development of rules within the SB system.

Welfare Rights and 'Social Assistance'

I am going to omit the bulk of the history of the scheme between 1936 and 1978 both for reasons of space and to highlight the two opposing pressures on the structure of the scheme which applied in the mid 1930s and in the late 1970s. It changed dramatically both in function and name, but much of the legal form retained considerable similarity to that developed in 1934. Thus the present discretionary powers are obviously derived from those in the original regulations.

The earlier part of this chapter described the political pressures contributing to the inclusion of wide discretionary powers within the initial scheme. However, there are opposing administrative pressures for the development of rules, particularly given the vast scale on which the scheme has to work, for in 1978 there were about 5.6 million claims for benefit (*Report of the Supplementary Benefits Commission for 1978*, 1979: p. 96). It would obviously be impossible to administer the scheme on the basis of an individual discretionary decision of whatever kind in every case. There are a few regulations but much more important is the administrative rule-making carried out by the Commission and embodied in unpublished codes including the famous A-Code, although general description of policy has been provided in the SB handbook (DHSS 1977b). The trend towards the confining of discretion by rules has now culminated in *Social Assistance* (DHSS 1978), the long-awaited review of the scheme by a team of DHSS officials (for background, see Bull 1980).

The trends affecting the scheme in the late 1960s and early 1970s were quite different from those envisaged in earlier years, particularly by the Beveridge Report with its plan for the scheme merely to be a 'safety-net' for those few not in work or provided for by National Insurance benefits. The load on SB has increased considerably, and there are now over five million people relying on it (including claimants' dependants). Moveover, the composition of the load has changed and there has been a decline in the proportion of pensioners, a group whose benefit is relatively simple to administer. At the same time, the proportion of unemployed claimants has increased dramatically. This has been accompanied by important changes in attitudes to the scheme by some claimants. From the late 1960s much activity has been undertaken by welfare rights groups and a particularly important tactic has been to attempt to use the theoretically wide powers of the tribunals to get around the provisions of the internal rules (see DHSS 1978: para 3.11). This has been particularly so with exceptional needs payments under section 3 of the Act, and between 1974 and 1977 the annual number of appeals heard in relation to such payments rose from 6206 to 28,705 and the proportion successful remained higher than in appeals on other matters (*Report of the Supplementary Benefits Commission for 1977,* 1978: table G1). Although the apparent breadth of the tribunals' power is often limited in practice by regard for Commission policy, the use of tribunals in this way has nevertheless been seen as a threat, at least by the office staff whose decisions are being overruled. As *Social Assistance* put it,

> the broad legal framework and wide discretionary powers in nearly every provision of the Act mean that the scheme can be stretched to cover practically any case if persuasive enough arguments can be found. This encourages resort to appeal tribunals, which can substitute their own discretion in individual cases, thereby sometimes creating further inequities particularly over exceptional needs payments. Already local office staff are often unsure whether the SBC's [the Commission's] policies can or should be adhered to in the face of pressures from claimants' groups and obviously different views adopted by their local appeal tribunal.
>
> (DHSS 1978: para 3.11)

The effects of rising numbers and greater activism have been drastic. As the Chairman of the Commission himself put it

> if we sit back and do nothing, allowing the volume and complexity of the work to increase year by year, it is simply a matter of time before the service collapses. Indeed there are signs that the collapse is already beginning in some of the more hard pressed offices.
>
> (Donnison 1978a: p. 17)

Social Assistance was an attempt to deal with the problems created by these pressures. In examining it one is conscious of a degree of irony. The review incorporated many of the demands made by welfare rights groups for a clearer legal structure and for the confining and structuring of discretionary powers by published rules. Yet such groups have (and, in my view, quite rightly) subjected the review to the severest criticism on the grounds that it would result in few substantive improvements for claimants and that some proposals would in practice be disastrous. The key to understanding this lies in certain initial assumptions made by the review team. The stress was claimed to be on the need to simplify the scheme for the sake of both claimants and staff. However, the team considered that 'it has not been within our remit to propose additions to benefit or staff costs' (DHSS 1978: para 1.4). The result of this no-cost approach to simplification produced the concept of 'rough justice', heavily criticised since the publication of the review. This was the view that in order for any improvement to take place, some claimants must be made worse off; there must be 'some losers as well as gainers' (DHSS 1978: para 1.15). Moreover, the review team decided at the outset that there was no prospect of reducing the numbers dependent on SB and said little about the adequacy of the basic scale rates of benefit. As Ruth Lister has put it, 'the review team's main concern is to rationalise the administration of the SB scheme. Little attention is paid to the needs of the five million people dependent on that scheme.' (Lister 1979a: p. 6).

I will now summarise briefly the proposals in *Social Assistance* most relevant to the study of the discretionary powers. The general theme was that such powers should only be used for truly exceptional cases, and this is reflected in the proposals for a new legal structure for the scheme. Rather than having a vague statute fleshed out mainly by administrative rule-making, the review team proposed that

> the Act and regulations should lay down at least the basic rules of entitlement in a more precise form than at present; where exceptions are necessary they should wherever possible be spelled out in the Act or regulations rather than being left to be dealt with under the umbrella heading of 'exceptional circumstances'.
>
> (DHSS 1978: para 3.12)

It was also proposed that many of the detailed rules should be given more formal status, either through being incorporated in regulations binding on the adjudicating authorities, or by incorporating the more detailed matters in a Code of Practice (DHSS 1978: para 3.14).

The review team also suggested a simplified system for dealing with short-term claims and the first few weeks of other claims, probably to cover only those who had recently been in employment. A key element in this was that no discretionary additions or lump-sum payments would be available in this period (DHSS 1978: Chapter 6). The same stress continues in discussion of the current powers to increase benefit. The vast majority of 'exceptional circumstances additions' are for heating, and most of these are paid to pensioners. In practice eligibility and rates of payment have been set out and limited to a considerable degree by the Commission's administrative rule-making. The review team suggested that some limited efforts to consolidate the additions into the scale rates could eliminate most heating additions now paid, but notes that this would be costly and proposed simplified criteria for their award instead (DHSS 1978: para 9.23–9.29). The second largest group of additions are those where a doctor has recommended an expensive diet for medical reasons. *Social Assistance* suggested that these should be completely abolished because 'the medical advice we have received is to the effect that special diets are not universally regarded as essential in the treatment of particular conditions; the point is that there is a body of opinion which sees no place for special diets at all' (DHSS 1978: para 9.34–9.35). Similarly, it was recommended that the other major form of addition, that for high laundry expenses, should be discontinued in almost all cases (DHSS 1978: para 9.36). Insofar as 'exceptional circumstances additions' continued the team proposed that they should be 'standard additions of fixed amounts for people with special needs and the amounts and qualifying conditions would be set out' in regulations or a published code (DHSS 1978: para 9.37). The proposals, then, were for an extension of the development which had occurred throughout the history of the scheme towards the replacement of 'officer discretion' by 'Commission discretion' implemented by administrative rules, the main difference being that the rules were to be in a more fully published form. As regards the power to reduce or withhold benefit in 'exceptional circumstances', it was also suggested that detailed conditions be set out in the regulations or code, though a residual discretion should be retained to 'allow flexibility' (DHSS 1978: paras 9.46 and 9.53).

The proposals in relation to 'exceptional needs payments' were in some ways similar. The review team noted that in practice these payments are not only made for expenses not covered by weekly benefit but also for items in theory provided for by the scale rates but which in practice cannot be met without an additional payment. It was accepted that such payments should continue for substantial items such as furniture, redecoration and removal expenses, and that eligibility for this should be set out in the code or regulations. In relation to other expenses the team proposed the automatic payment of lump sums at intervals of six months (DHSS 1978: paras 9.11, 9.38 and 9.40–3). Thus again the stress is on simplified administration and published rules. However, it was accepted that a residual power, perhaps structured by published guidance, should remain to deal with 'truly exceptional' expenses (DHSS 1978: para 9.48).

One other proposal relating to the discretionary powers was of the greatest practical importance. It was mentioned above that a very considerable increase in appeals concerning exceptional needs payments has taken place; in 1978 such appeals accounted for 45 per cent of all appeals heard (*Report of the Supplementary Benefits Commission for 1978*, 1979: para 8.13). *Social Assistance* proposed that no appeal should lie in relation to such a payment without leave of the tribunal chairman, which would only be given if an important point of principle was involved or the decision was clearly unreasonable (DHSS 1978: paras 9.51–9.52). The arguments used to support this were extremely weak (see Lister 1979a: pp. 82–5) and the consequences would be severe, particularly taking into account the important process of internal review triggered by an appeal and the importance of this type of appeal in everyday welfare rights work. It is perhaps this proposal which shows most clearly that the central theme behind *Social Assistance* was not improving the quality of the scheme for claimants but simplifying its administration and making life easier for staff.

Before examining the events subsequent to the publication of the review it will be useful to stand back and fit the recommendations into context. Some of the proposals, such as the stress on the publication of the rules of eligibility appeared pleasing from the viewpoint of openness and accountability. The substantive results of many of the suggested provisions seemed far less desirable. One view of this which has been put forward by Adler and Asquith (Chapter 1 above) is that it represents an attempt to give inexpensive 'procedural' rights whilst heading off pressure for costly 'substantive' rights to more cash, a particularly attractive means of pre-empting opposition in a period of public expenditure cuts. This may represent part of the function of the review, and indeed as will be seen, can be applied more strongly to recent government attempts to implement some of the proposals. However, the reasons for the team's suggestions must be sought within the internal needs of the administration of large-scale poverty relief. Lister has claimed that *Social Assistance* was the product of a review 'by civil servants for civil servants' (1979b: p. 146), and it has been suggested more generally that it represented an attempt to bring expenditure under control and to make the scheme simpler to administer, thus reducing the large increase in staff numbers which has occurred in recent years. I argued in the previous section that the discretionary powers in the scheme arose largely through external constraints such as the need to reduce expenditure without appearing to undertake direct cuts. The trend towards rule-making which has culminated in *Social Assistance* represents an opposing tendency internal to the administrative institution itself and emphasised by the recent pressures on the system. In addition to its role in 'opening up' administrative bodies, rule-making has long been associated with the development of large-scale bureaucratic administration, and however far SB administration may be from Weber's ideal type of bureaucracy, it is clear that for one of its central problems rules provide the solution. This is the characteristic that decisions have to be taken by relatively low-level staff who are largely untrained, yet the decisions involve the assessment of the complex personal and social factors which form the basis of concepts such as 'need'. It would be simplistic to assume that this is wholly undesirable (see Hill 1972: Chapter 4 for some of the compensating advantages), yet it is clear that administration by rule has certain advantages here. One that is currently of the utmost importance is that rules enable forward planning and effective restraint of expenditure. They permit the routinised handling of cases and, perhaps paradoxically in view of the stress often placed on rules as ensuring the accountability of administration, 'may provide an effective political shield behind which officials may hide, safe in the knowledge that in response to pressures they have a valid reply: "I'd like to help you, but I'm bound by this rule."' (Jowell 1975: p. 21). Moreover, rules in the form of regulations binding on appeal tribunals would prevent the use of appeals to undermine policy.

The publication of the review was followed by a process of consultation, including the holding of open meetings. The response to the substantive proposals was almost uniformly hostile (for an account of the process see Bull 1980). In particular, the Commission themselves totally rejected the idea of reform on a no-cost basis, and considered that the reduction of the reliance on discretionary payments would only be acceptable if provision was made to recompense claimants either by raising the scale rates or by providing automatic lump-sum payments. They opposed the ending of dietary additions and the short-term scheme in the form the review team had suggested, and rejected any proposal for the restriction of appeal rights. They also stressed that recommendations for reform were not suitable for selective or haphazard implementation but should be seen as closely related and interdependent packages. The proposed transformation of policies into published rules has, on the other hand, been widely welcomed (DHSS 1979; *Report of the Supplementary Benefits Commission for 1978*, 1979: Chapter 2).

Nevertheless, the government is at the time of writing implementing reform on a highly selective and 'no-cost' basis, and indeed it seems likely that the package of reforms will enable much stronger central control of expenditure. The proposals have been set out in a white paper (*Reform of the Supplementary Benefits Scheme* 1979) and are embodied in the Social Security Bill currently before Parliament. The effect of this will be to replace much of the 1976 Act with broad powers to make regulations that will be binding on both the administration and the appeal tribunals. It is stressed that the proposals 'will not increase the total cost of the scheme or the number of staff involved in administering it' (*Reform of the Supplementary Benefits Scheme* 1979: para 8), and indeed it is coupled in the Bill with changes in the index-linking of pensions designed to reduce costs. A central advantage for claimants of the new system is stressed as being that all the detailed rules of eligibility will be published as regulations and therefore 'all claimants will reap the benefit of the emphasis on legal entitlement and published rules' (*Reform of the Supplementary Benefits Scheme* 1979: para 8). However, it has since been admitted that the revised equivalent of the A-Code setting out instructions to officers administering the scheme will not be made publicly available (*Guardian* 16 January 1980). The Supplementary Benefits Commission will be abolished and responsibility for the formulation of policy will pass to the Minister. Other substantial changes will also be made.

Full assessment must await the publication of the regulations late in 1980, but the present likelihood is that the effect will be restrictive. An example to illustrate this will be the probable treatment of 'exceptional needs payments'. The grounds for which these will be awarded will be set out in the regulations, with a residual discretion in truly exceptional cases. However, such payments will apparently not be available to meet items covered in theory by the scale rates except in narrowly defined, fairly rare circumstances. Yet many such payments, it is now generally accepted, are necessary for the purchase of items supposedly covered by the scale, but in practice out of reach because of the low level of these rates. Important examples are worn out items of children's clothing. This problem has been recognised both by *Social Assistance* and by the Commission's response to it, and the solution has been seen as an increase in the scale rates or the payment of automatic lump sums in addition to normal benefits. Such lump sums are not included in the reforms, and the scale rates will in real terms be reduced. Appeal rights against exceptional needs payment decisions are retained, but will be of limited value in comparison with the present situation, for the regulations embodying policy will of course be binding on the tribunals and so it will be far more difficult to make use of appeal as a means to avoid harsh policy and gain generous treatment in particular cases.

I argued earlier that *Social Assistance* was an expression of administrative needs for the formulation of rules. However, with the election of a government determined to curb public expenditure the central element has become effective control of the system (for a brief discussion of the review reaching similar conclusions see Kincaid 1978). Rules will prevent the use of discretion as a means for extracting more from the system by the use of the broad powers of tribunals, and in substance can be seen as one more part of government attempts to restrain public expenditure. Yet a superficially liberal appearance can be maintained by claims that they represent an advance toward 'open government' and 'welfare rights'.

Some Conclusions

Theories of public law have tended to see discretion as a void surrounded by legal rules and principles. To borrow a metaphor from a rather different context, discretion is the 'hole in the doughnut' (Dworkin 1977: p. 31). Thus the approach usually adopted has been to ask whether filling in the void with rules is feasible and whether it will assist in the performance of the overt legislative purpose, the assumption being that there is such a purpose embodying a consensus on aims. Thus the transition from discretion to rules is seen as primarily a technical rather than a political problem, as devising efficient and fair administrative practices rather than choosing between political values. The events of the 1930s discussed in the first part of this chapter suggest that this is to view the role of discretion too simply: rather than existing because of a technical inability to frame rules it may perform the distinct and deliberate function of blurring political issues and disguising the necessity of choosing between different policies. Indeed in his seminal work on discretion, Davis recognises this (1971: pp. 46, 49, 95–6). It is in this respect that the theoretical work on power referred to in my introduction becomes important. Discretion, or the appearance of discretion, may confer power not simply through the overt opportunities for manipulation opened up but by preventing the choice of policy made from appearing as a distinct issue around which political debate can take place. This becomes particularly important given that conflict between ideologies is a central feature within welfare provision and many problems have been caused by failure to make explicit the real basis for policy-making (see George and Wilding 1976: Chapter 6).

Discretion, then, performs a similar function to the 'nondecisions' discussed earlier. The implication is that the development of rules in administration represents a process of political struggle rather than mere technical innovation. Moreover, it is implied that those seeking accountability of government should press for rules because open rules provide a basis for argument around policy and for criticism of administrative action. Thus Nonet (1969) in his study of California's Industrial Accident Commission described how this development changed the status of those receiving benefits from passive objects of welfare policy to citizens able to exert rights before the Commission, to hold it accountable to rules rather than being dependent on its assumptions as to their welfare. I have argued elsewhere that pressure for the transformation of administrative policies into rules is one of the justifications for the adoption of a test-case strategy in the absence of any direct potential of such a strategy for creating change (Prosser 1979). The adoption of this view involves a rejection of the separation of 'procedural' and 'substantive' rights made by Adler and Asquith (Chapter 1 of this volume). Their theme was that provision of the former would leave unaltered the position as regards the latter, and indeed might be a means of buying-off pressure for substantive reform. Yet demands for what are within their definition 'procedural' rights may include pressure for the crystallisation of policies into open rules providing a basis for criticism of policy and for conflict over it not available if the substantive issues are concealed within the exercise of discretion. Such 'procedural' rights are not necessarily ends in themselves but may be resources in a broader struggle, and indeed this has been the theme of the more sophisticated theoretical work on welfare rights. Thus Scheingold (1974) has suggested that the chief use of litigation to groups seeking change lies not in its ability to produce reform directly but in the forcing of issues and raising of awareness as a basis for political mobilisation.

However, it is easy to slip into an uncritical support for formal welfare rights as self-evidently desirable ends in themselves on the assumption that the development of open rules automatically provides advantages for the recipient of benefits. The second part of the chapter was an attempt to show that this view is too simplified. There are other reasons apart from the development of accountability which may push for the development of rules, and key examples are administrative efficiency and effective control of administration by government. The effect of such rules may be highly restrictive and may limit opportunities for taking advantage of discretion in unanticipated ways. However, given the present appeal of 'open government', such change can be made to appear as embodying liberal principles, as providing 'rights' rather than leaving claimants to the whim of closed, paternalistic discretion.

Any conclusion about the merits of rules or discretion must then be an ambiguous one. The crystallisation of policy into rules provides a basis for debate and conflict over its content, yet this need not automatically provide an advance for those dependent on it; it is merely part of a political process which may produce various results. It is important to examine, then, the broader political structures which will shape the outcome, and also the ways in which the rule-making procedure will reflect these. Formal welfare rights are not ends in themselves but may be resources to pressurise government, yet they may also permit government to effect its control more firmly.

8 From Rules to Discretion: the Housing Corporation
David Noble

Recently, access to and allocation of public housing has rightly attracted the attention of lawyers and sociologists (Lewis 1976; Lambert, Blackaby and Paris 1978). The focus of attention for lawyers has been the extensive discretion exercised by local authorities and their officers in the allocation of homes to both new applicants and transferring tenants. On this, Lewis has stated:

> In the field of council house allocation and transfer, a matter pressing on the very quality of life of large numbers of people, administrative discretion is normally subject to few controls outside the manifestly political, which are themselves capable of operating unfairly and arbitrarily. (1976, p. 147)

The extent of discretionary powers in the state housing system is widespread and has been shown to be open to abuse especially in the allocation of houses. To concentrate, therefore, on questions of procedural fairness in administrative systems does not imply, necessarily, that there is no need to consider the underlying inequalities in society which demand a public housing programme. Adler and Asquith (Chapter 1 in this volume) rightly state that 'enhancing procedural rules does not, of itself, enhance substantive rights' but that need not imply that all concern with the equitable distribution of benefits is inherently barren. Substantive redistribution may result from an alteration in the primary distribution of income (Winkler, Chapter 5 in this volume) or even from a move towards mass participatory democracy (Bankowski and Nelken, Chapter 12 in this volume). A concern with the procedures of distribution presently operated by the state does not necessarily ignore the wider social and political order. The emphasis of this chapter is upon the suitability of legal techniques to the resolution of problems of procedural justice in both the regulation of housing associations and the allocation by those associations of homes to would-be tenants. As such it is concerned with ensuring the equitable distribution of the available benefits and does not claim that a return to legality in administration will, of itself, resolve fundamental inequalities in contemporary society.

The effects of reductions in public expenditure on the voluntary housing movement and other areas of welfare demand that greater attention be paid to the procedures operated by these welfare agencies to ensure that whatever becomes available is fairly distributed. However, procedural fairness is relevant not only at a time of service reduction, it merely becomes more critical in such a period. A system of allocation applied at a time of expanding provision may incorporate many injustices which remain hidden by the general level of distribution. However, as the voluntary housing movement shows, systems of allocation, once adopted, tend to remain in force and inequalities become more obvious and acute as the service is contracted.

The Voluntary Housing Movement

In common with the Family Fund, the development of the voluntary housing movement after 1974 can be viewed as 'a small policy innovation' (Bradshaw, Chapter 6 in this volume), but it differs from the Fund in both its style and extent of development. The experience of the voluntary housing sector after the 1974 Housing Act is, arguably, one of the clearest examples of what Winkler has termed 'off-loading'. He suggests that delegated implementation of state welfare policy to private groups is one of the principal coping responses that government is taking in response to the excess of demand for services over the income from taxation. In the case of the voluntary housing movement, the 'co-optation' by the state was not inspired merely by a desire to off-load the cost of state provision onto private agencies. In fact the cost of implementing the 1974 legislation has been more than would have been incurred by expansion of the public sector by a similar amount.

The empowering legislation enjoyed all-party support in Parliament to an extent almost unique in housing policy. The incoming Labour administration did little more than resuscitate the Conservative Housing and Planning Bill which had fallen with the

Heath government. Anthony Crosland, then Secretary of State for Environment said, introducing the new Bill:

> Parts I to III relate to the voluntary housing movement and are substantially in the form proposed by our predecessors in their Housing and Planning Bill, and which we generally welcomed at the time. I have always been a firm supporter of the Voluntary Housing Movement more so, perhaps, than some people in my own party. I believe it would be intolerable if we reached a situation in which everyone either had to become a tenant of a local authority or had to buy his own house. Monopoly is as undesirable here as it is elsewhere. (Hansard 1974: col. 48)

To the Conservatives, voluntary housing was viewed as preferable to state provision and housing associations were seen as semi-private supplements to, covert competitors with, or even potential replacements for local authority housing. In the main, the Labour government saw the potential in the movement for the creation of a centrally controlled housing service in contrast to the relative autonomy of local authorities. Publicly the voluntary sector was applauded for providing diversity in both housing tenure and design. Subsequently the relative obscurity of the movement and its quasi-independent status have assisted in deflecting criticism of the limits placed on resources. Increasingly, decisions in the 'public' housing sector are not taken by state officials; instead it is a 'voluntary' agency official 'who exercises the mean spirited discretion which deprives the citizen of what he needs' (Winkler, Chapter 5 in this volume). The policy of incorporating the voluntary sector into the state provision of housing was not, as was the case with the Family Fund, a reflex answer to an immediate crisis but a long-developed concept with clearly stated objects.

The 1974 Housing Act is typical of the widely framed enabling statutes identified in other areas (Ganz 1974; Jowell 1975; Daintith 1979). The central government agency, a public corporation, one step removed from ministerial control, was charged with the general functions of promoting the development of housing associations whilst, at the same time, establishing and exercising a system of control over those same associations (see the Housing Act 1974, section 1). Such 'administrative schizophrenia' forms the basis for many of the subsequent developments in the implementation of the statute. On this type of dichotomy Hood (1976) has stated (p. 13):

'Clearly, it is administratively impossible effectively to pursue incompatible objects at the same time.' Much of the accommodative approach to the exercise of discretion by the Corporation is rooted in this dichotomy. The incorporation of the promotional role into the value systems (Vickers 1968) of the officers stems from it being the primary function of the Corporation in its ten year history prior to the 1974 legislation. .

The Duty to Register

The establishment of a duty to register was laid down in the Act and section 13 went so far as to specify some preconditions for securing registration (such as the need for the association to be of charitable status or a society under the Industrial and Provident Societies Act 1965). The Act also gave the Housing Corporation a wide discretion, beyond these technical requirements, to register as it saw fit. The only confines on this agency discretion were provided by a preliminary rule-making exercise performed by the Corporation in consultation with an advisory committee. The requirement to produce these rules, or criteria against which housing associations would be assessed in determining whether or not to register them is clearly one of the major methods of confining administrative discretion (Davis 1971: pp. 55–57). Such a process enables procedural justice in individual cases to be brought about by clearly stated rules rather than the exercise of discretion. Davis readily admits that discretion is necessary in the determination of rules but with the participation of those affected by registration (provided for by the 1974 Act, section 14) it seems that injustice in the formulation of the criteria is less likely than in the discretionary determination of individual cases.

The registration criteria produced took the form of either strictly framed objectively assessable rules or more subjective but nonetheless measurable standards. Three types of criteria can be discerned:

(1) Rules reinforced by statute such as the charitable status requirement (e.g. criterion 1);
(2) Unambiguous rules determined not by statute but by the agency which nevertheless eliminated or severely confined officer discretion (e.g. criterion 3(2)); and

(3) Generalised standards, applied to those areas where some judgement was necessary but where, nevertheless, discretion exercised by the evaluating officer could be structured (e.g. criterion 4).

The Corporation had, therefore, provided a basic matrix confining both its general discretion and that of individual officers involved with registration. The operation of registration, however, raises questions about the ability of such limits actually to confine the exercise of discretion in practice. What were the influences which encouraged the move from rules to discretion in the Corporation?

Registration in Action

The various criteria were applied first by regional officers of the Corporation in the initial 'sift' of applications from housing associations. In deciding what the rules embodied in the criteria meant, these officers exercised their judgement. This limited form of interpretational discretion was, itself, further restricted by guidelines and advice from the centre. This subsequent guidance served to structure some of the more nebulous and subjective standards in the criteria. Hence, the requirement that more than half the management committee of an association should have no financial interest in the association grew from the more vague criterion that there should be 'a sound management committee'. The discretion of field officers was, therefore, confined further by the structuring techniques established by the head office of the Corporation as part of its attempt to control the periphery of its organisation.

Following this initial processing, the applications were dispatched to the head office for re-examination. There, the senior registration officials exercised their judgement in interpreting and evaluating the comments appended by regional staff. Such an exercise is uncontroversial, an essential element in bureaucratic decision-making. However, what is questionable was the wide discretion enjoyed by these officials to exempt associations from the full force of the criteria with little or no justification. By such a wide and unpublicised, unstructured discretion many associations were registered although in breach of one or more criteria; for example, the rule requiring proof of financial viability.[1] This criterion had the appearance of being a strict, objectively assessed rule permitting of no flexibility.

Thus, an openly formulated and published rule was, in operation, evaded by the extensive and hidden use of discretion. It is quite possible that the reasons for relaxing the effect of the financial viability criterion were administratively valid but the mechanism adopted undermined the value of the criteria themselves.

This development within an administrative agency is the type of discretion with which Davis (1971), Jowell (1975) and Kagan (1978) have been concerned. If the objective of the registration process is taken to be 'to provide a body of associations to be trusted with public finance' (Housing Corporation 1974) and that the criteria were a translation of that objective into impersonal tests to be applied impartially, then the adoption of such an accommodative approach on one criterion alone prevented the achievement of that objective. If the criteria were to have meant what they were purported to mean, implementation of them should have been on a more rigorous basis. The decision to operate an accommodative rather than a rigorous approach to the application of the criteria to individual cases was made by the Corporation balancing the costs of the outcomes of each method. Registering more associations than fulfilled the criteria enabled the Corporation to have a sufficiently large number of associations and to be able to fulfil the development programme intended for the voluntary housing movement. The costs of such an accommodative approach were less clear than those of a rigorous approach where the development programme would be restricted by insufficient numbers of associations. The Corporation therefore employed what Kagan terms the 'expert model' of regulation in which experienced agency officials are free to formulate policies in response to changing environments: 'making intuitive judgements as to what result will maximise the public interest' (Kagan 1978: p. 14).

The dilemma was further compounded by the duality of functions invested in the Housing Corporation, for although regulation was its primary function, promotion was an already well established activity with considerable agency momentum behind it. Consequently an accommodative, expert model approach to registration was adopted rather than a more rigorous legal method. Thus, although possessing the external appearances of legalism the Corporation was in effect operating an extremely discretionary system, possibly beyond that authorised by the statute. Evasion of the established criteria was not envisaged by the 1974 legislation. As Kagan observed about this sort of development:

> The regulatory agency's dilemma however, stems equally from the risk of bending over too far in the direction of accommodation. Its *primary* duty after all is usually seen as implementation of a specific police mission and fidelity to the terms and intent of its authorising legislation.

Where the agency has been given dichotomous functions it is less clear than in Kagan's example of price–wage freeze agencies that regulation is the primary duty of the bureaucracy. Nevertheless, it is clear from the analysis of the Corporation's exercise of registration that it was unfaithful to the 'terms and intent' of the Housing Act.

What, then, are the reasons for this move from rules to discretion? It is possible to discern two strands of explanation, which are related to each other. First, the concept of agency history/philosophy and second, the assumptive worlds of the Corporation officials (Young, Chapter 2 in this volume). By 1974 the Housing Corporation had been operating for a decade as a sponsoring and financing body to a small, tightly-knit community of housing associations and societies producing cost-rent and co-ownership housing. The staff, especially in the regions, had worked in close contact with these societies and had enjoyed considerable autonomy from the head-quarters in their decisions as mortgagees and sponsors of schemes. During this period the agency's underlying philosophy, entrenched with time, was one of promotion of the voluntary movement. Consequently, the promotional funding and protecting parts of the 1974 Act were most easily assimilated by the organisation. The regulatory function in contrast was a departure from the normal role. Similarly, the 'assumptive worlds' of many of the Corporation's senior officials within which 'are integrated the values, beliefs, and perceptions the individual has of the world he acts upon' (Young, Chapter 2 of this volume) formed during this first period in the Corporation's life. Hence both the agency as a whole and individual actors approached registration with a disposition to accommodate.

This move away from a rule-structured process towards a more discretionary approach has continued, with less emphasis being placed upon the publicly stated criteria and more upon informally determined, internal objectives and negotiated settlements. An association that strictly fulfils the published criteria may, nevertheless, find it impossible to secure registration in the absence of a negotiated agreement with regional officials concerning, for example, an association's intended area of operation. Resource constraints also played a part in under-enforcement of the legislation. The Department of the Environment apparently required registration to be completed on a strict time-scale in order to facilitate early financing of associations to begin housing development. As the Permanent Secretary of the Department admitted at the Public Accounts Committee:

> We recognise that the first state [registration] imposed a heavy task on the Corporation, but it was thought desirable to apply what was called at the time, a coarse sieve. It was thought that there was some value in having associations registered, so that they could be monitored.
>
> (HC 327 1978/79: para 188)

Also the Corporation was limited by its existing personnel quota which further precluded a policy of full enforcement:

> For the Corporation, registration has involved a much greater amount of resources in terms of time and manpower pressures than could have been envisaged at the outset.
>
> (Housing Corporation 1976: p. 4)

Equally, the realisation by Corporation staff and Board members that registration had serious implications for the survival of individual associations may have encouraged the move to an accommodative, discretionary approach. It has also been suggested that the lack of an appeals procedure for associations failing to secure registration focused the attention of the Corporation too acutely on the finality of the process they were operating. Eventually, the establishment of a statutory register became an end in itself rather than a means to securing a 'body of housing associations in which the public can place their trust regarding their managerial ability and probity'. (Housing Corporation 1976: p. 1). As Pressman and Wildavsky (1973) have shown, confusion between complex ends and identifiable means can lead to 'goal transposition' during the implementation of a social programme.

The consequence of this general abandonment of rules in favour of discretion has been that the Corporation has experienced considerable difficulty in supervising the activities of those associations it has 'on its books'. Monitoring the performance and probity of the associations registered has proved to be an intractable problem further complicated by the deficiencies of registration (see, House of Commons 1978/79). In part, the intractability of the problem stems from the Corporation's 'quasi administrative limit' (Hood 1976) which results from the failure simultaneously to meet contradictory objectives. In this case, the existence of dual functions ensures administrative failure. Furthermore the adoption of a discretionary approach to the administration of registration has extended into other areas of Housing Corporation responsibility. Notably, the agency has not structured the discretion of regional chief officers to allocate funds for new housing development as they see fit. No guidelines have been produced on when to withhold finance from associations not in compliance with the criteria or on what would be an equitable distribution amongst the competing associations. This wide discretion to distribute financial support remains unstructured and unconfined; individual associations are at the whim of the officials of the Corporation. Moreover, this discretion to distribute reappears at the local level when associations come to allocate homes to would-be tenants.

The Allocation of Housing

On council housing Lewis (1976: p. 149) has said that 'the discretion given to local authorities as to their rules, if any, concerning allocation in the widest sense is extremely broad and is encumbered by the minimum of legal regulation'. The position in the voluntary sector is even less trammelled by legal rules. The decision-making processes regarding tenant selection, even if formalised in the structure of the housing association, are almost always invisible to the outsider. The scope for bargaining, collusion and even corruption in the determination of applications is greatly increased by this lack of publicity. Information on the criteria for selection, if such exist, is often unavailable publicly. Some policies are not determined by the policy-making voluntary management committee but stem from decisions of the lettings staff in a custom and practice fashion. Whether an applicant is interviewed and how much information is sought from him varies enormously from association to association.

In contrast to the local authority sector, most housing associations did not, at the time of the survey,[2] select house applicants on the basis of points gained following an evaluation of their housing needs. In the past, this deficiency has been explained away by the small stock and development programme of the voluntary housing movement. However, with the increasing scale of provision after 1974 and the presence of many associations with a stock of 2000 or more units, this argument is less persuasive. It has been said that 'where there is no such [points] scheme the degree of discretion is increased and the visibility of the decision-making process even less formal' (Lewis 1976: p. 149). Most often the ordering of applicants on the basis of housing need priority was done, if at all, by the 'judgement of the professional officer'. Such a merit scheme confers extensive discretion on the individual housing officer and in many associations this was exercised in the complete absence of guidelines or constraints from the governing committee. Niner (1979) considers such an approach in housing associations as 'no bad thing' in that it enables them to offer flexibility and variety in comparison with the often mechanistic local authority points model. Nevertheless, she only supports this type of merit scheme if 'the system is still accountable, if the rules are known, and if an appeals mechanism exists' (p. 25). Few associations operated within a rule-bounded merit system and where they did it was rare for the rules to be published. Only one association surveyed was found to operate an appeal from the decision of an employee of the association to the volunteer committee.

The response of the Housing Corporation to the growing significance of the voluntary sector in the housing system (producing 1 in 4 of public sector homes in 1979) has been limited. It has advised that

> One of the most important items of information which might be published in the annual report will therefore be a statement on the basis on which tenancies are allocated.
>
>   While the public is normally aware, at least in general terms, of the priorities governing local authority housing policies, this is not the case with housing associations.
>
> (Housing Corporation 1978)

Beyond the practical point that the annual report of individual associations is not the most suitable vehicle for communicating information to those most in need of it, lies the important discrepancy between rule-statement and rule-application. As with the Corporation's implementation of registration, rule-statement may be full and public but rule-application may prove partial, hidden and discretionary. For example, one housing association director whose organisation was 'avowedly commercial' published a needs-based lettings policy whilst at the individual case level paying most attention to the ability to pay the rent without the complications of rebates. Consequently, heavily subsidised housing (80 per cent of cost) was not allocated to those in the greatest housing need. The broad object of the voluntary housing movement after 1974 was therefore frustrated by an extensive and unchecked discretion at the field officer level. Mere publication of lettings criteria, where they existed, was obviously an insufficient check on arbitrary, inconsistent or unfair decisions. As part of its monitoring visits the Corporation does analyse the outcome of a sample of new lettings against its own criteria for tenant selection or those specified by the association. However, there appears to be no argument in favour of preserving the secrecy of such analyses. Such an exercise provides a valuable *post hoc* check on the exercise of discretion by individual lettings officers.

The legal method of implementation not only calls for formal methods of control and published rules to prevent arbitrary decisions but also requires an adjudicative solution to disputes. In the one example of such an approach (see above) both present tenants and applicants had the right of appeal on any housing management decision to a sub-committee of the housing association. It was clear that in other associations informal techniques, operated by those who knew the officers or 'the system', could produce *ad hoc* reviews of particular cases. Commenting on a similar development in the local authority sector Lewis stated 'that such a situation does violence to the most elementary canons of equity' (1976: p. 155). The establishment of a formalised appeals mechanism based upon published rules would ensure a greater degree of procedural justice than is apparent at present.

Accountability and Participation
At the point of tenant selection the problem of accountability becomes more acute. Accountability is a fundamental problem for

the voluntary housing movement. At the top, the relationship among the Housing Corporation, the Secretary of State and Parliament is both unclear and consequently unsatisfactory. At the local level the relationship between non-elected housing associations and local people, tenants and would-be tenants is becoming critical. In contrast with local authority housing departments, which are technically accountable through elected members to the electorate, housing associations are accountable to no one other than a self-selected committee and occasionally the Housing Corporation. Neither the Parliamentary Commissioner for Administration nor the Commission for Local Administration has jurisdiction over the agencies of the voluntary housing movement. In theory the management committee of an association is elected by the general membership but many committees of management are self-perpetuating oligarchies. The possibility of greater participation in the affairs of housing associations is seen as both a solution to the problem of accountability and a panacea for the problem of discretionary power. Certainly the Housing Corporation appears to be espousing greater public involvement. Circular 3/78 states:

> Some housing associations may benefit from a wider more representative and active membership which brings the community and interested groups into the constitution of an association.
>
> (Housing Corporation 1978)

The practicalities of participation are fraught with difficulties however, as experiences in town and country planning have shown. Dominance by any one group, present tenants, local people or whoever could easily frustrate the aims of the voluntary housing movement as espoused by the legislation. The possibility of excluding the valid claims of other groups such as would-be tenants has to be considered in managing 'participatory democracy' in housing. What remains clear however is that, with an increasing impact both at the local level and in national housing policy terms, housing associations must widen their membership and open their committees to more frequent changes of personnel. Neither is participation a complete solution for discretionary decision-making, since arbitrary and inconsistent decisions can still be made in the absence of limits and confines as some of the housing co-operatives have shown. In the absence of a *genuine* 'mass participatory democracy' (Bankowski and Nelken, Chapter 12 in this volume) there remains a need for a return to legality in the administration of voluntary housing.

Conclusion

Seeking a return to the legal method dependent upon rules, adjudication and judicial techniques at the distributive level of the voluntary movement may appear contradictory given the evidence of rule abandonment at the regulatory level. The contradiction is, however, merely superficial.

At the regulatory stage the move from rules to discretion was a product of the influences considered above, namely, agency philosophy, officer value systems, resource constraints and 'administrative schizophrenia'. It is essential therefore that the legislature clarifies the objectives of the policy programme (as occurred in this case), examines the suitability of the administrative agency invested with the task of implementing the policy and finally, monitors the progress of that policy. Quite obviously monitoring by Parliament and Ministers is not facilitated by the peculiar status of agencies such as the Housing Corporation. The surprised tone of the Public Accounts Committee report on the Corporation (House of Commons 1978/79) emphasised the need for a more frequent and effective 'holding to account' of such bodies. Although unauthorised discretion developed during the implementation of registration, this does not, of itself, devalue the need for rules and guidelines to structure the discretion at the stage of housing allocation. With, at present, no requirement to publish selection policies or the results of that selection and with only a request to consider increasing the membership of associations, it is clear that procedural rights to housing in the voluntary sector are virtually non-existent. An increase in participation and a greater constraint on the discretion of officials are necessary to redress the balance in the distribution of this particular form of welfare. As Jowell (1979) suggests, this return to legality may also improve the responsiveness of the administration:

> An open, consultative rule-making process may well act as an effective control on administrative discretion and may also provide the on-going process of scrutiny and criticism that Nonet and Selznick [1978] suggest will help render administrative responsiveness to affected interests.

The problem at both stages, regulation and allocation, is to establish procedures and values which will not permit arbitrary and inconsistent decisions but which, at the same time, will permit alterations in policy in specific cases or when the 'administrative climate' changes. External limits to the implementation of policy may have to be accepted, such as the pressure to register rapidly, but there is nothing inherent in a decision-taking system that prevents the structuring or confining of discretion to improve procedural fairness.

9 Some Aspects of Discretion in Criminal Justice
F. H. McClintock

In this chapter, a fairly ample view of the criminal justice system will be taken so as to cover the three interdependent segments of law-enforcement, criminal justice administration, and penal processes. All three comprise organised bodies of personnel with responsibility for dealing with those who do not conform to rules of behaviour recognised by the common law or made the subject of legislation. Their multifarious duties are regulated by several complex bureaucracies. In Great Britain, we maintain the separate corporateness of the police, the courts, the prison service, the probation and after-care service, and (in the case of Scotland) the independent prosecuting authorities. Central government is responsible for unifying the results and controlling the purposes of these diverse services but responsibility is divided between the Home Office, the Scottish Office, the Lord Chancellor's Department, the Crown Office in Scotland and the Director of Prosecutions for England and Wales. Each service has its own organisational structure and its distinct official aims, procedures and principles of accountability at the local, regional as well as at the national level. Accordingly, it is in the arrangement of this many-storied edifice that the use of discretion as delegated to a policeman, a judge, a probation officer, a social worker or a prosecuting counsel needs to be considered (see Sheehan 1975).

In recent years, the need for a sociology of crime control and of criminal justice has become more widely recognised (Baldwin and Bottomley 1978; Blumberg 1967; Black 1976), although its appropriate form and content are still being energetically debated. This is not the occasion to review developments in sociological approaches to crime control or related developments in criminological theory (see Cohen 1974; Downes and Rock 1979; Young 1980). However, it is important to note that there are many shades of opinion directing the course of these developments: some of them are coloured by traditional or consensus concerns and advocate the need for systematic and scientific study of specific mechanisms of control and the need for detailed study of the controllers, while others are more radical and rest upon the conviction that the definitions of criminal behaviour and the criminal justice processes are central to the debate about political power, the state and the well-being of citizens.

It can, however, be argued that most sociological writings today recognise, either implicitly or explicitly, that empirical research on and theoretical explanations of criminality and criminal justice processes have a political dimension (Bottomore 1979; Taylor, Walton and Young 1973 and 1975; Hall et al. 1978; Fine et al. 1979). It is noteworthy that several of the chapters in this book, in particular Adler and Asquith (Chapter 1) and Bankowski and Nelken (Chapter 12) deal with specific issues selected from the field of criminal justice as illustrative of a more general analysis of discretion and legality. It is suggested that the selection of themes from criminal justice by these writers and others is not accidental but a consequence of the central position of criminal justice in any consideration of political power and governmental administration. Clearly the subject of discretion in criminal justice is only raised above a discussion of technicalities about rules and accountability if it is examined in the wider sociological context of balancing individual freedom against state authority in a mixed political economy. In peacetime, the criminal justice processes constitute the largest area over which the servants of the state exercise direct and overt coercive power on a regular basis, and it is in this context that some aspects of discretion in criminal justice processes will be considered here.

Declining Confidence in the Criminal Justice System

In western industrial societies there is evidence of incipient dissatisfaction with the general administration of criminal justice, as well as with each major segment. Specific activities of the administrative personnel seem to evoke many more complaints than in the past, suggesting that confidence in the processes of control through parliamentary forms of democracy has been undermined, Some analyse the problem in terms of a crisis resulting from a sharp decline in the acceptance of the paternalistic rehabilitative ideal which has been part of the philosophy of penal reform since the end of the nineteenth century (Bottoms and Preston 1980). But the practically minded lay the blame upon the spectacular increase in the volume and seriousness of registered crime, so overloading the services that, without substantial renovation and reinforcement, there will be serious failure in the processes of crime control and criminal justice (Morris and Hawkins 1970; Wilson 1975). From a more radical standpoint, others arraign the legal and authoritative bankruptcy of the criminal justice system and its inability to resolve the contradictions which have visibly grown more threatening to society. Thus, the 'injustices' of criminal justice, such as the discriminatory enforcement of unpopular laws, the occurrence of political corruption, inordinate court delays and violence and brutality in prisons, are emphasised.

The kind of diagnosis pronounced upon the ills of the criminal justice processes determines the nature of the objections raised to the use of discretion. Those who see the central problem as resulting from the collapse of the rehabilitative ideology and advocate the need to re-establish the principle of legality in relation to a 'just deserts' model are inclined to be critical of discretion which was introduced and legitimised through the application of notions of paternalistic social welfare when rehabilitative dogma dominated, and of the many occasions on which discretion can be exercised in the present system (Asquith 1979a). However, those who consider the main cause of the contemporary crisis in criminal justice to be the gradual collapse of over-stretched resources among the services concerned with crime control tend to see the use of discretion as bound up with the question of 'diversion' from the avenues of criminal justice: they ask who should be responsible for deciding which cases are best dealt with outside the criminal justice system, what criteria should influence the decisions and what alternatives, if any, to criminal prosecution should be provided. The assumption governing their argument is that the criminal justice system should only be concerned with more serious crime and that it is impossible, inappropriate and too costly to attempt to prosecute all transgressions of the criminal law. Among the more radical criticisms a frequent objection is made that the use of discretion and the frank discussions about it serve, not only to disguise the contradictions within the present system, but also to shelve the basic issue that criminal justice can never be really 'just' while there are substantial social and economic injustices.

All these different views have one assumption in common, namely, that it is possible and desirable to develop a rational system of criminal justice, in which administrative personnel are properly controlled *and* able effectively to deal with the social problems of crime. This accords with traditional doctrines of criminal juris-prudence which assert that control of the functioning of the system is first effected by the legislature, and then by the judiciary in their interpretation and application of the law; subsequently, control passes into the hands of the prosecuting authorities, and then at a lower level to the police whose aim is crime prevention and the detection of offenders. Unfortunately this model is confirmed neither by first-hand knowledge, nor by empirical research. In fact, it would seem that the hierarchy of control in practice is almost the reverse of the hierarchy that is traditionally asserted. For instance, the police exercise a considerable negative control over all the other segments in the criminal justice process, as the selection of cases for investigation by the police is, in the main, discretionary and certainly does not conform strictly with the principle of legality. This state of affairs is principally a result of the widening gulf between the capacity of the system of criminal justice and the magnitude and complexity of the tasks with which it is expected to deal.

The Expansionist Response

Traditionalists, in their approach to penal philosophy, advocate ways of improving the criminal justice system within a given political economy in order to make it more effective and more just, and a great deal of attention is given by governmental administrators to discussion of public policy with respect to those two aspects of reform. As regards effectiveness, the results of research during the last twenty-five years overwhelmingly confirm that rehabilitative measures have not had any substantial differential impact on crime control. Furthermore, in tackling recidivism, there appears to be little difference between rehabilitative and punitive measures (Brody 1976). Now that adherence to the rehabilitative ideal has waned, the ineffectiveness of the criminal justice system is frequently attributed to the fact that the great majority of people who commit crimes are not detected, apprehended, tried, convicted or punished.

Traditionalists argue that if more were caught and punished then crime rates would be lower. It is not proposed to discuss in any detail the merits of their proposals here, but rather to note their implications in relation to the use of discretion. Until comparatively recently the expansionist approach to criminal justice control has taken into account neither economic nor social costs. Economic costs have been ignored on the ground that any lowering of registered crime rates is so desirable as an end that no justification of the costs is required. As regards social costs, adherents of an expansionist approach have given little attention to the inevitable extension of state power and to the degree of intervention acquired by the bureaucratic agencies that administer the criminal justice system. However, the consequences of such developments could have substantial adverse effects on the quality of life of ordinary citizens.

Advocacy of an expansionist approach is normally associated with proposals for a much stricter system of law enforcement as regards policing, trial and punishment so as to increase both individual and general deterrence. Within such a system of criminal justice, discretion is normally seen as undesirable: the principle of legality, it is claimed, should be strictly adhered to, social-welfare criteria should be eliminated from court deliberations, and, where there is choice in sentencing, this should be within closely defined guidelines (Thomas 1974 and 1979; Davis 1971; Radzinowicz and Hood 1979).

The expansionist approach to crime control is today very much tempered by financial considerations. It is recognised that implementation of a substantially expanded programme of law enforcement, and consequent increases in other departments of the criminal justice system, would be a very costly affair. Furthermore, because the relationship between the provision of additional resources and the outcome is far from clear, no accurate cost-benefit analysis can be made. It is not known whether the provision of additional resources, and the consequent intensification of activities by law-enforcement agencies, would actually produce more arrests, result in more convictions and harsher penalties, or have any appreciable effect on the volume of crime. However, even supposing that such a chain of reactions were to occur, there are few who would advocate such a course of action for all offences – from riding cycles at night without lights to murder. Clearly, the economic and social consequences of such a strategy make it, in terms of public policy, extremely unrealistic. The expansionist school tend therefore to restrict their attention to what are regarded by them as the 'more serious' crimes (Sellin and Wolfgang 1964), and to apply 'de-penalisation', 'diversion' and 'decriminalisation' to the less serious, thus introducing substantial areas where discretionary powers might flourish at what might be termed the 'gateway' to criminal justice procedures.

De-penalisation, Diversion and De-criminalisation

De-penalisation

De-penalisation, as part of the modification of the expansionists' early position, can have important consequences for the police's use of discretion. The police act as 'gatekeepers' to the criminal justice process in their decisions to record an offence and to bring a charge and in consultation with senior members of the service are accorded wide discretionary powers. Likewise, in the allocation of resources for the business of detection and in the expenditure of time for the preparation of cases for prosecution, the use of discretion is considerable. As a sequel, on the negative side, when they ignore trivial offences and when technically criminal conduct is left unrecorded, they are promoting the course of de-penalisation. Police action to de-penalise is, of course, more deliberate when offenders are dealt with by way of a caution (Williams 1974).

De-penalisation also has implications for the prosecutor's use of discretion. First of all, prosecutors may decide, on the given facts of the case, that prosecution is not worthwhile. For example, where the offence is regarded as too trivial, or the victim has contributed to his own discomfiture by having acted in a 'provocative' manner , or the punishment is seen to impose 'unwarranted' extra distress, the prosecution may either drop the case or issue a warning to the offender to watch his future conduct. Alternatively, if the offender has to be brought before the court, the prosecutor may reduce the charge to one of a less serious nature, with an eye to the attachable penalty or to avoid the expense of taking the case to a higher court, surmising that the accused would plead guilty to the lesser crime but would insist on a full trial on a more serious charge. The exercise of discretion in this way clearly departs from the principle of legality and tends to assert the principle of expediency, a saving of resources being the dominant concern.

De-penalisation is also closely related to the issue of 'structured discretion' in sentencing practice. It is suggested by those advocating this approach that while penal sanctions should match the seriousness of the crime and have due regard to their likely deterrent effect, decisions should also take into account costs and benefits in relation to possible alternatives. Given that penal institutions are overcrowded and costly to run, non-custodial measures, such as fines, community service, probation or compensation orders, are advocated wherever appropriate. In relation to structured discretion in sentencing the nature of the constraints which should be imposed on sentencers remains an open question, suggestions ranging from mere advice and formulated guidelines to rules and legislative restrictions. In the case of advice or guidelines, a considerable range of discretion could still be exercised by the sentencer albeit in a structured context: whereas the promulgation of rules or legislative restrictions would seriously curtail its use.

Diversion

Diversion from criminal justice, as an offshoot of the primary aim of the expansionist school, raises similar issues to de-penalisation. Diversion is, in reality, only another form of de-penalisation, in which some alternative action to the normal judicial disposal is taken on grounds of expediency. In accordance with expansionist ideas, diversionary measures are generally confined to what is considered as less serious criminal behaviour which does not require any element of positive deterrence and is amenable to the effect calculated to result from such measures. Diversion to de-toxification units for those convicted of aggravated drunken behaviour in public places is a current and successful example; other instances of diversion are provision of hostel accommodation and routine work-tasks for the socially inadequate who have become persistent petty offenders, and the practice of not proceeding against an offender who gives some indication of mental abnormality.

The conditions under which discretion is exercised by the police, prosecutors and others in relation to diversion to various other forms of social control are not usually clearly laid down, while the question of accountability has frequently been raised but not adequately dealt with. Where discretion, in relation to de-penalisation and diversion is exercised on a considerable scale, the importance of the invidious distinction between those who are brought into the criminal justice system and those diverted from it should receive more attention. For those who look upon justice as the most important element when improvements in the judicial system are being sought within the existing political economy, the important and complex question of the exercise of discretion is bound up with the protection of the rights of the accused on the one hand and the onus of accountability for the exercise of power and authority by the agencies of criminal justice on the other. One example is that of the abuse of their discretionary power by the police in holding a suspect before a charge is preferred. Some claim that because of the way in which discretion is currently exercised those of high social status are less likely to be arrested and charged than those of low social status, more likely to be granted bail, more likely to be acquitted if tried, and less likely to receive custodial penalties if convicted. Concern over these disparities has led to a discussion of the possibility of tighter control by explicit guidance and stricter rules of conduct, with suggestions for greater accountability through independent inspection, new appeal procedures and processes for investigating complaints. Even with these improvements, however, the question of the relationships between criminal justice and social injustice, as raised by the radical reformers, remains in the background, and the underprivileged are likely to remain in a disadvantaged position when caught up in the criminal justice processes (Fine et al. 1979).

De-criminalisation

De-criminalisation has also become a theme of discussion, testifying to an awareness of its importance in judicial administration (Council of Europe 1980b). The complex origins of this movement cannot be systematically examined in this chapter, but certainly include the decline of confidence in the effectiveness of the criminal justice system, the recognition that the criminal law rarely solves a social problem but often exacerbates it, the contemporary drain on resources created by crime-control tactics and the historically piecemeal development of the criminal law and penal sanctions. Some of the proposals for de-criminalisation, e.g. those referring to pornography, prostitution, incest, misuse of certain drugs, begging or vagrancy, would only produce marginal reduction in the total volume of criminal justice cases. However, other proposals go much further and would radically alter the structure of the criminal justice system, e.g. by de-criminalising theft from shops and supermarkets, and by employees from their workplaces.

De-criminalisation on a massive scale has its supporters, appearing in the writings of Lemert (1967) as the development of 'judicious non-intervention' and in Schur (1973) as 'radical non-intervention'. These writers claim that the cardinal rule of public policy should be a *laissez-faire* attitude to offenders wherever possible, since intervention often produces further criminality. In modern times, according to them, the state, particularly that part of it responsible for the criminal law, has intruded in a great variety of areas in which it does not really belong. They insist that the removal of stigma and the adverse consequences of illegality from behaviour is not the same as conferring approval on it, but only facilitates a more constructive approach to devising alternative ways of coping with undesirable social behaviour. They argue that although a substantial proportion of the population regard tobacco smoking and alcohol consumption as socially undesirable and deleterious to individual health, to prohibit such habits by criminalising them would only make the task of coping with concomitant problems more difficult, and pass from that to the logical corollary of legalising the smoking of marijuana.

When it is accepted that de-criminalisation on any extensive scale could only take place with the consent of the majority of the community and that the public would have to be assured that adequate facilities were available for dealing with undesirable behaviour, a shift is made to the minimalist's position, by stressing, as Cohen (1979) has done recently, that some minimal criminal justice system is necessary to constrain the few, i.e. those whose crimes are regarded as dangerous to the community. However, Hulsman (1978), taking up an extreme position in this debate, points out that criminal justice control is the problem of contemporary society rather than the social behaviour designated as criminal, and that the solution to the problem lies in the abolition of criminal justice, carrying with it a substantial reduction of state power, thereby getting rid of the whole of the discourse on discretionary power which is seen as providing legitimation and credibility to largely uncontrolled authority among the agencies of a basically repressive criminal justice system. It is suggested that solutions to problems arising from behaviour designated as criminal should be left to the helping services, to more direct participation by members of the local community, to technological innovations, and to fundamental changes in the social organisation of society. In connection with the question of discretionary powers, it is important to note that de-criminalisation which results in the reduction of discretion among the agencies of the criminal justice system, may merely result in a transfer of discretion to other social control systems, such as the medical or social services. By such a transfer, it is contended that the intrinsically negative use of power involving coercion will be reduced and will more easily become oriented to the needs of the clients. This, however, remains a debatable point.

The Minimalist Response

A number of writers have commented that in recent times criminal justice has become a major growth industry, they have pointed to the increase in financial resources, capital and technical equipment, the extension of legal powers and the expansion of manpower in all its major segments by way of illustration. Yet on examining the results of this investment one is properly surprised that such an expansion has persisted: more and more crimes continue to be registered, without any decrease in recidivism among the identified offenders. Thus, the possibility of radical alternatives to the present criminal justice processes is seriously mooted as a way of dealing with the social problems of crime. The search for radically opposed alternatives is rendered urgent by the fact that contrary to prevailing beliefs there is no coherent criminal justice system, no adequate participation in or information on criminal justice processes, and a lack of overall control of criminal justice processes.

In discussions of criminal justice it is often tacitly accepted that the criminal justice processes make up a rational system of control. The use of discretion, based upon acceptance of the principle of legality, is then stated to be, or very often assumed to be, one of the ways in which the formal system can function more or less smoothly. However, it is clear that this model of criminal justice is a faulty one.

This view was forcefully expressed in a United Nations working paper prepared for the World Congress on the Prevention of Crime, held in Geneva in 1975:

> One of the problems is that it is taken for granted that such a complex structure [the criminal justice system] indeed works as a system, that the several sub-systems share a set of common goals, that they relate to each other in a consistent manner and that the interrelationships constitute the particular structure of the system, enabling it to function as a whole with a certain degree of continuity and within certain limitations. However, in countries where researchers and policy-makers have undertaken a criticial examination of the structure of their criminal justice systems, they have found that there are few common aims, that there is considerable diffusion of duties and responsibilities and little or no coordination between the sub-systems, and that there are often differing views regarding the role of each part of the system. Yet, when people talk about the criminal justice system as a whole they implicitly or explicitly assume that the system functions well and is effectively controlled. They also assume that it is a system oriented towards goals that are designed to meet the needs of the community. (Quoted in United Nations 1975, p. 16.)

If this is accepted as a satisfactory description of criminal justice processes, it follows that a great deal of the research into the use of discretion is based upon false assumptions and that in most instances one should be discussing 'expedient adjustment' rather than 'policy implementation'.

In urban and industrialised societies a small proportion of the population are caught up, to varying degrees, in the criminal justice processes. For the majority of citizens there is very little, and at most only spasmodic contact of a direct sort. Direct and regular participation in the system occurs, however, for the personnel employed in the agencies of control: it is entailed in the daily duties of the police, the prosecutors, the judiciary, the correctional personnel, and social agencies, but is limited for the majority of them to only one part of the system. It is not surprising therefore that most of these groups see their role and the practice of discretion from a rather narrow and specialised viewpoint. Accountability has been developed in these restricted segments in relation to rules, guidelines and special tribunals; but nobody, not even a group of persons, occupies a position of overall responsibility for control.

The possibility of controlling criminal justice processes involves a feedback of accurate and adequate information pertaining to them. In addition, control also implies knowing where one wants to go, as well as the ability to adapt the objectives, and the means of achieving them, in the light of reliable information. Such conditions are clearly not met for criminal justice processes, and consequently there is no prospect of authentic control. Information coming from face-to-face contacts and intimate participation is generally lacking in the formal criminal law system. The majority of citizens feel lost as well as helpless when confronted with criminal justice machinery; their attitudes show the need for the introduction of guidelines and other related processes of accountability into the existing system as a means of overcoming what Bankowski and Nelken (Chapter 12 of this volume) have described as 'the difficulty of trusting people with power'. Under the present structure of criminal justice, the overall effect would be a tightening of control through the extension of the state's managerial power rather than a reduction or redistribution of such power. Moreover, as Bankowski and Nelken point out, there has been little critical discussion of the role of experts and professionals in relation to discretion and control of the criminal justice processes. Almost the only exception is Nils Christie (1977) who has discussed this issue in terms of experts monopolising the means for solving conflicts, as (in the author's words) 'stealing' them from ordinary citizens, thereby excluding them from direct participation.

As a result of such criticisms of the criminal justice system there has been a serious search for alternatives to it. A number of such proposals have in common the basic assumption that, in its present form, the criminal justice control system should be drastically curtailed along with the discretionary powers of the personnel of the various control agencies (Cohen 1979). Thus, a majority of minimalists support a 'just deserts' model as a viable alternative to the discredited 'correctional model'. While the expansionists see just deserts and deterrence as the twin objectives of criminal justice, the minimalists see just deserts as the only basis for criminal justice intervention, and qualify this by the stipulation that it should be the minimal application of this principle compatible with maintaining the confidence of the community that the quality of their lives is being safeguarded. 'Just deserts' is thus a relativistic principle.

The Separation of Criminal Law and Social Welfare

It is well known that by a process of legitimation through welfare ideology a greater degree of coercive control of citizens has been brought about, in the present century, by the agents of the state responsible for criminal justice control. Statutory and voluntary agencies have been co-opted by the criminal justice services to provide, under the cloak of assistance to clients, a means of crime control and prevention under the 'correctional' model, and helping agencies have in fact become controlling agencies against crime. Thus, much of the tension that has arisen is a consequence of the fact that the exercise of discretion by the helping agencies takes place in the course of criminal justice control. A return to a 'just deserts' model in criminal justice would provide a way of restricting judicial processes to a purely punishment system based solely on the notion of relative retribution, and without attempting to correct the social injustices in society generally. This trend may be regarded as aiming at the separation of powers; helping agencies provide services to 'clients' while the criminal justice agencies punish 'offenders'. Where services are provided within the penal system they would be based on humanitarian grounds and on individual rights and not informed by a correctional ideology which emphasises the effectiveness of intervention. It is suggested that through a procedural reform there could be a significant change in the circumstances in which services are provided. Paternalism and the role of the professional would still raise issues in social welfare but not as part of the criminal justice processes. Discretion would remain (at least for the time being) but would be much less widespread and complex, being confined to the standards and goals of the penal system. This can be illustrated from a modified version of the diagrammatic table of control processes developed by Black (1976) and illustrated in the table. Using the modified Black models the proposal of the minimalists is that all criminal justice modes of intervention must be restricted to category A, and in so far as they have extended to categories B, C and D, they should be eliminated from the criminal justice process. This does not mean, of course, that services under these categories should cease to exist but that they should be independent of criminal justice control and should be client-oriented.

As a result of these shifts in direction certain fundamental changes have begun to manifest themselves in other countries. For example,

Model of Social Control*

	A Penal criminal justice	B Therapeutic (+ social work)	C Educational (+ social work)	D Compensatory (civil or criminal law)	E Conciliatory (civil, criminal or social)
(1) Standard	Prohibition	Normality	Educated	Obligation	Harmony
(2) Problem	Guilty	Need	Ignorance/incompetence	Debt	Conflict
(3) Initiation of action	(i) agency of community (police)	(i) agency of community	(i) agency of community	(i) agency of community	(i) agency of group
	(ii) victim	(ii) deviant	(ii) student	(ii) victim	(ii) disputants
(4) Identity of deviant/or 'problem' individual	Offender	Patient/client	Ignorant, uneducated or incompetent person	Debtor	Disputant
(5) Solution/or goal	Punishment	Help/treatment	Standard, certification or recognition of competence	Payment (in cash or kind)	Resolution of conflict

* Adapted and modified from Black (1976).

in Sweden helping agencies no longer contribute to the criminal justice process, social-welfare agencies have ceased to be answerable to the courts or to parole boards for the management of offenders returned to the community, while the probation order is to be withdrawn from penal measures. Similarly, in the Netherlands, the probation service is to become entirely client-oriented, having already shed most of its responsibilities to the courts for the subsequent behaviour of offenders. In Sweden and the Netherlands, the role of the prosecutor has extended beyond that of a mere lawyer applying the principle of legality; he is now very actively and extensively involved in informally arranging help from the social and medical services, as an alternative to prosecution and with the agreement of those involved. This could be seen as a corollary to other positive initiatives, although on their own they may give rise to the dangers described earlier.

The extent to which the 'just deserts' model of those advocating minimal state intervention in crime control may develop in Britain in the future, in conjunction with different forms of help and intervention of a non-penal nature, is hard to foretell. However, it is probably much more realistic to expect that in the immediate future the expansionist school of thought will prevail.

10 Social Change and the Shifting Boundaries of Discretion in Medicine
Tom McGlew and Alex Robertson

Whatever the yardstick one employs, doctors must without doubt be regarded as a highly successful occupational group. They have status, prestige and social influence. They are free to control their own training, numbers and – to a large extent – working conditions. They enjoy autonomy in the regulation of incompetence and abuses within their own ranks. And there is widespread public acceptance of the notion that these privileges are exercised through, and justified by, a body of scientific knowledge and an ethical code which stresses the good of the patient. Above all, of course, doctors have the authority – only minimally impinged upon by 'fringe' practitioners – to differentiate between 'health' and 'illness', and to prescribe appropriate forms of treatment with reasonable certainty that their injunctions will be followed. Such attributes have for long identified medical practitioners in many people's minds as the example *par excellence* of a 'profession', and the model for aspiring professions (such as social work) to follow.

To describe medicine in the above terms is to present a set of points and observations with which most sociologists would find it hard to disagree. Equally, however, it is in our opinion also to assume altogether too static (and homogeneous) a view of the current position of the medical profession. For whatever reasons, doctors do enjoy both dominance and legitimacy in dealing with health-related problems. The sources of that dominance will form part of our subsequent analysis. But important changes are taking place at present both in medicine itself and in a number of areas relevant to medical practice; and whilst we would not go so far as certain authors who claim that we are witnessing a major and widespread 'erosion' of professional authority (see, for example, Haug 1976), it is our contention that these changes are in turn transforming the work of doctors, and producing shifts in the kinds of contacts and relationships they have with each other, with patients, and with 'paramedical' and other ancillary staff.

We propose to examine these changes and their implications for the exercise of discretion among doctors. We intend to approach this analysis by way of a preliminary examination of models of professionalism and their relevance for medicine. Although our discussion will cover trends which we feel to be universal to medical practice in all developed countries, these will be considered within the particular context of the British National Health Service. One could point to several current trends with some potential significance for the exercise of medical discretion. For reasons of space our analysis will, however, be restricted to only a certain limited number of these and we shall have to ignore, for example, such factors as the intoduction of new drugs (Dunlop 1973; Coleman 1977, Chapters II and III) and technologies (Mechanic 1977) in medicine; trade union organisation and militancy (Elston 1977); and the changes brought about by the administrative reorganisation of the NHS.

Professionalism, Authority and Medicine

Doctors probably make less use of the word 'discretion' than of terms such as professional judgement and the exercise of clinical freedom. In Chapter 12 of this volume, Bankowski and Nelken draw attention to Dworkin's (1977: pp. 31–9) distinction between 'strong' and 'weak' discretion. Dworkin avers that:

> The concept of discretion is at home in only one sort of context; when someone is in general charged with making decisions subject to standards set by a particular authority. (1977, p. 31)

Whether or not, under this definition, one could say that doctors are exercising 'strong' discretion is at least an interesting question, because the 'authority' under which doctors (and other professionals) are working refers to relationships with peers, rather than with hierarchical superiors; and 'standards' would relate to such notions as recognised 'good professional practice', rather than to discrete rules. To this extent, there may be something in the distinction drawn by

Adler and Asquith (Chapter 1 in this volume) between 'professional' and 'administrative' discretion, although we find ourselves in greater sympathy with Young (Chapter 2) and Smith (Chapter 3) in their arguments that the distinction between 'discretionary' and other kinds of decisions is a relatively tenuous one; and that it may therefore be more useful to concentrate on the context within which decisions are taken, rather than on the construction of *a priori* classifications of different types of decision.

For present purposes, perhaps the most useful way of under-standing professions – and in particular the medical profession – is in terms of the role of knowledge in society. As knowledge has expanded, so of course has there been a tendency for specialisation to take place and for role-specialisms to develop around particular areas of knowledge. Certain types of knowledge have in consequence come to be regarded as the province of particular groups, with only those who share in a specific body of knowledge being seen as having the authority to act on it. This tendency towards exclusiveness is strengthened – as Johnson (1972), for example, has observed – by the kind of technical terminology which is attached to professionals' work and training and by the fact that professionals are usually members of a socially distinct group. Insofar as this occurs, questions arise as to how one decides which types of knowledge are appropriate for dealing with particular issues; and how the people who possess that knowledge are to be controlled. How, in other words, is the independent use of knowledge made compatible with the public interest?

Given this starting point, there would seem to be two basic extant approaches to the study of professionalism. The first is contained in functionalist theory, of which the work of Talcott Parsons (1951) is probably the best-known and most influential example. In common with most other writers on the subject, Parsons sees the growth of professions as an outcome of specialisation and increasing division of labour within industrial society. Greater occupational differentiation has meant, in Parsons's view, that the basic 'functional requirements' of a society can be more adequately and efficiently met than is the case in undifferentiated social systems, because it permits the application of more rational and informed approaches to the solution of problems. Professionalism develops to ensure that the power and capacity for control which knowledge entails are used to further collective, rather than personal, ends. Parsons thus sees the emergence of professions as necessary, because they are part of an 'automatic' unfolding of the division of labour in advanced industrial societies, and desirable, because they enable control of the environment and of social problems to be effected within a framework which protects the public interest.

These general assumptions serve as a background in Parsons's analysis of the medical profession (Parsons 1949; 1964). His theory of professionalism in medicine is founded on the postulates that illness gives rise to a situation in which certain psychological tensions exist for both patient and doctor and that a body of social norms has been devised to govern this relationship and so reduce these tensions. These norms are in addition geared towards the optimal performance of socially useful tasks, thus ensuring the continued smooth functioning of the social system. For Parsons, illness is socially dysfunctional: it prevents individuals from performing their social roles effectively. It is, moreover, construed in social, rather than purely biological, terms – as a socially legitimised state which exempts the individual from having to fulfil social responsibilities. The sick person thus has an obligation to seek competent help and to cooperate with attempts to make him better (Parsons 1952: pp. 436–9; see also Bloor and Horobin 1975: p. 272).

From the patient's point of view, the tensions inherent in the medical encounter relate to such factors as his lack of knowledge to judge the technical competence of the physician; and his own emotional involvement, which impairs his capacity for assessing his case objectively. The patient is therefore vulnerable and open to exploitation. For the doctor, tensions are created by the fact that there is always an element of uncertainty about whether and what kind of technical knowledge will help in specific cases; by the distress he may feel when confronted by the particular facts of an illness; and by the need to overcome inhibitions the patient may have in cooperating over physical examination or a specific aspect of treatment. The way to resolve these tensions has been for patient and physician to adopt problem-solving roles. The sick person must be able to enter a role which entitles him to acceptable help and Parsons's theory is accordingly centred on the (institutionalised) practices which render medical services more attractive to the patient. Briefly, and sparing the reader the language of the 'pattern variables', this is achieved by a system in which doctors practise and are recruited on the basis of ability, rather than social origins; rely on generally accepted scientific standards; restrict their work to medical objectives; remain emotionally neutral towards patients; and put the patient's interests above their own. These emphasise technical competence on the doctor's part, separate the medical encounter from the context and connotations of other social relationships, and reassure the patient that trust and privileged information will not be abused. To the extent that they have succeeded in making services more acceptable, so have these practices legitimated the authority of the doctor and motivated people to seek medical assistance.

Parsons's explanation is thus couched in terms of the need for certain norms to facilitate the attainment of medicine's 'functional task' of enabling individuals to perform their social role competently by minimising illness. There are several problems with this analysis. First, and although Parsons places his analysis within an overall historical context (see, for example, Parsons 1952: pp. 332–3), his treatment of the medical profession is ultimately profoundly ahistorical, taking the form of an *a priori* application of the pattern variables to the occupational situation of doctors, without looking at the evidence on the actual development of the medical profession in the course of the nineteenth and twentieth centuries. We follow such writers as Freidson (1970a), Jewson (1974), Berlant (1975) and Parry and Parry (1976) to believe that the historical evidence suggests a rather different pattern of development in the professionalisation of medicine. Professionalisation and professionalism can be better understood as the outcome of conflicts of power and self-interest, than of the automatic unfolding of the technical exigencies of industrial society. Second, and as Berlant (1975, Chapter 1; see also Freidson, 1970a: pp. 159–60) has observed, the object of Parsons's account is not the behaviour, but the belief-structure of individuals in the medical profession. As such, it presents

> a moral analysis which does not undertake a description of the actual condition of the medical profession and its relationship to patients but which wishes to draft into being a set of moral rules that would bring about certain desired effects if adhered to. (Berlant 1975: pp. 15–16)

Parsons's analysis is accordingly more of a prescriptive statement than a framework for explaining the behaviour of the medical profession. It discounts the possibility that that behaviour will not always conform to these prescriptions – less because breaches of the norms *do not* occur, than because they *should not* occur. Parsons (1952: p. 455) himself draws attention to the fact that Pasteur's work was initially repudiated by the medical profession because its author was 'only' a chemist; but then comments that this is now 'rightly' regarded as 'a very unfortunate aberration' from the profession's commitment to scientific knowledge, whatever its source. The effect is to paint and embellish a rather 'conservative' picture of the medical profession, taking it again at its own valuation. By assuming that this system of beliefs works (ultimately) in the interests of the community, Parsons ignores the possibility that these norms serve professionals as much as clients; and that they may indeed at times benefit professionals at the cost of clients.

Finally, although he starts his analysis from the dynamic stand-point of a potentially unstable (clinical) relationship, Parsons's explanatory emphasis on the factors which are held to create an equilibrium within that relationship ultimately means that the account he presents is somewhat fixed and static. This tendency is reinforced by his underlying assumption that professions are an inevitable consequence of the progressive specialisation that takes place within the labour force of industrial societies, and is further compounded by his belief that both the trend towards occupational differentiation in industrial societies and the existence of the norms that he believes govern the professional relationship in medicine are socially useful and desirable. It is therefore rather difficult to account for change, or incorporate it into one's analysis with this model.

The second major perspective on professionalism in medicine is reflected in the work of Freidson (1970a; 1970b), Berlant (1975), Illich (1975) and Parry and Parry (1976; see also Johnson, 1972). Contrary to the functionalist emphasis on the (implicit) rationality of professionalisation and the altruism of professionals, these authors concentrate on power relationships and on the organisational structure which permits an occupation to control the content and the forms of its own work. Within this perspective, professionalism, according to Johnson (1972, p. 45):

becomes redefined as a particular type of occupational control rather than an expression of the inherent nature of particular occupations. A profession is not, then, an occupation, but a means of controlling an occupation. Likewise, professionalisation is a historically specific process which some occupations have undergone at a particular time, rather than a process which certain occupations may always be expected to undergo because of their 'essential' qualities.

In his important book on the *Profession of Medicine* Freidson (1970a) argues that medicine has in part achieved its dominant position by successfully establishing claims to specialist knowledge and competence ('expertise') and a concern with the service of humanity ('ethicality'). Making a further distinction between 'autonomy' (which relates to the claim to expertise) and 'self-regulation' (whose referent is ethicality), Freidson concludes, on the basis of an analysis of the social organisation of medicine in the USA, England and Wales and the USSR, that the only significant attribute that distinguishes professions from other occupations is autonomy – or more specifically, the legal right to control the content of their own work. He further observes that autonomy is granted as a result of political negotiation with the state. The importance of the medical profession is thus a consequence of the fact that it has established a negotiated order which protects 'insiders' from competition, evaluation or direction from others. Nurses will never succeed in being recognised as a 'profession' because they remain dominated by doctors. For Freidson, therefore, there is nothing 'inherent' in medicine to explain its autonomy: that autonomy is the outcome of a political process, rather than an intrinsic occupational characteristic. Berlant (1975) also argues that ethics have basically served as a tool to enable doctors to exercise a monopolistic control over the field within which they work.

Freidson makes a further distinction between the *content* and the *terms* of work – between the tasks the professional performs and the conditions, circumstances and organisational forms under which those tasks are carried out. Whilst the former, and the knowledge on which it is based, may in most cases be said to be such as to justify protection against lay interference, the latter are neither systematic, codified nor objective. Rather than some special expertise deserving of autonomy, they reflect simply the social power and pre-eminence of the medical profession. In his related discussion of *Professional Dominance*, Freidson (1970b) argues persuasively that the internal sanctions and structure of the medical profession have far more influence on the nature of medical care (in the USA at any rate) than either the good intentions (and skill) of individual members of the profession or the economic and administrative arrangements by which men have attempted to provide or improve care. He concludes that the medical profession should enjoy far less discretionary authority and prerogatives than are currently accorded it.

Whilst the somewhat polemical nature of Freidson's second mentioned book, and his tendency to presume a professional encounter involving an autonomous doctor and dependent patient do introduce certain weaknesses into his account, we find ourselves in considerable sympathy with Freidson's overall argument and approach. Insofar as it is accepted to be operative, any distinction between 'professional' and other types of work will be seen as reflecting a political rather than an occupational reality; as a manifestation of an order negotiated by occupational groups working on unequal terms and the assumptions imposed on the thinking of individuals by that negotiated order. In his discussion of the distinction between bureaucratic authority and the authority of expertise, for example, Freidson (1970b: p. 130) states that it is erroneous to assume that:

> technical expertise unlike 'arbitrary' administrative authority is in some way neutrally functional.

and observes:

> that the authority of expertise is in fact problematic, requiring in its pure functional form the time-consuming and not always successful effort of persuading others that its 'orders' are appropriate.

Freidson asserts that, as a result of the concern in the extant literature with identifying the 'essence' of a profession, little attention has been given to the crucial factor of the organisation of practice and the division of labour among professionals.

With reference to our present purposes, a particular merit of Freidson's approach is that, by construing the phenomena of professionalisation and professionalism in terms of vested interest and the interplay of power relationships, it provides a framework for understanding the field of medicine in dynamic and processive terms. The reasons why we believe this to be important will, we hope, become apparent in the remainder of this chapter. We do, however, also feel it necessary to extend and somewhat modify the kind of analysis Freidson presents. We will argue that a number of changes are at present taking place in medicine, which have the potential for effecting changes in the traditional position and dominance of the medical profession. Although this argument is to a great extent implicit in Freidson's approach, his emphasis on professional dominance has perhaps also meant that he has tended to overlook the possibility that inroads may be made into that dominance. Consistent with the Freidsonian thesis, however, these threats to its established position will in many cases elicit defensive responses from the medical profession, and we shall point to certain of these. The situation we are describing may therefore be more appropriately characterised as one of 'flux', rather than of professional 'erosion'.

Medical Autonomy and Illness Trends

The twentieth century has seen a major and universal shift in the problems confronting medicine in developed industrial societies. These changes have been the result of two basic (and related) trends: changes in the causes of sickness and death and shifts in the age-structure of the population. With regard to the former, the main change has been in the decline of infectious diseases; a decline, incidentally, which can largely be attributed to improvements in living standards, rather than to medical intervention, either preventive or curative (McKeown and Record 1962; McKeown 1965, 1976; Powles 1973; Illich 1975; Smith 1979). As the acute, infectious diseases have diminished, so has infant mortality in particular declined and the proportion of the population surviving into middle and old age increased. Medicine now has increasingly to cope with the degenerative conditions of old age. Cancer, bronchitis, arthritis and heart disease – not to mention mental disorders – have replaced TB, typhoid and diphtheria as the pre-eminent problems of the medical calendar (McKeown 1965: part 1; Lalonde 1975; Parry 1977).

The history of (Western) medicine has shown a constant tension between 'essentialist' and 'nominalist' conceptions of disease; that is to say, between the notion that disease-conditions are real and universal entities which can be identified according to a set of definite criteria and the view that diseases are no more than arbitrary categories imposed by human beings on basically unrelated phenomena. The development of 'scientific' medicine in the course of the nineteenth century saw a gradual but progressive shift towards models of the 'essentialist' type. Thus, the popularisation by Morgagni and Bichat in the latter half of the eighteenth century, of post-mortem dissection as a routine procedure meant that disease began to be identified with a characteristic morbid or pathological feature observed in the cadaver. Following the development of powerful microscopes, Virchow was able to extend into medicine the work on plant and animal cells of such men as Schwann and Schleiden and to propound the view that cellular derangements are the basis of disease. The roughly contemporaneous work of Koch and Pasteur led to the emergence of 'germ' theory – probably still the single most influential model of disease – in which morbidity is attributed to the invasion of a host by a specific agent of disease (see, for example, Garrison 1929: Chapter 10; Haagensen and Lloyd 1943: Chapters 12–15; Singer and Underwood 1962: Chapters 6 and 7; Youngson 1979: Chapters 4 and 5). The main point to be noted here is that these models were developed within, and helped further to reinforce, an authoritarian tradition of medical practice, in which a knowledgeable doctor imposes remedies on a passive patient.

'Germ' theory was of course spectacularly successful in explaining and developing appropriate therapies for infectious diseases. As these have become proportionately less urgent problems, however, so medical practice has found itself lacking in effective models to construe and deal with the kinds of diseases which increasingly confront it. As opposed to the relatively brief and normally well-defined (acute) disease-process of infectious illness, degenerative diseases are chronic in their duration, insidious in their onset, irregular and episodic in their manifestation of symptoms (Wadsworth et al. 1971) and multi-factorial in their aetiology (Oldham et al. 1960; Morris 1967). Degenerative diseases are, in short, much more ambiguous and ill-defined entities and doctors have a much less secure mandate of expertise for dealing with them. The development of 'statistical' models of illness – in which 'health' and 'illness' are seen as more or less arbitrarily separated points on a continuum,

rather than as discrete states (Oldham et al. 1960) – and the introduction of notions such as 'stress' into the armoury of aetiological
agents (see, for example, Rahe et al. 1974; Rabkin and Struenig
1976; Cox 1978) has rendered the position even more complex. As
one of the problem-types currently falling within the purview of the
medical profession, psychiatric disorders – whatever the validity of
including them in the category of 'illness' – perhaps epitomise this
fact.

Several consequences flow from this trend. First, and while a large
part of the GP's work is, for example, taken up with consultations for
influenza, headaches, back pains and other minor afflictions
(Wadsworth et al. 1971) for which 'mechanical' remedies are readily
available (though certain of these ailments may, of course, be
symptomatic of a more insidious condition), we would argue that
the increasing need to deal with chronic and degenerative states has
profound implications for the doctor–patient relationship.

In their discussion of the clinical relationship between patient and
physician, Szasz and Hollander (1956) distinguish between three
models of that relationship. In the 'active–passive' model, the doctor
'does things' to an inert or at best passively-recipient patient. In the
'guidance–cooperation' type, the doctor tells the patient what to do,
and the patient obeys. In the 'mutual participation' model, the
patient is viewed as one side in a 'partnership', using expert help, in
which the physician 'helps the patient to help himself' (Szasz and
Hollander 1956: p. 586; see also Freidson 1970a: p. 134). As Szasz
and Hollander point out, the exercise of power is a major differ-
entiating variable between these three models. The first two models
clearly correspond to what we above called the 'authoritarian'
tradition of medical practice. As the common disease-types change
to ones about which medical knowledge may be judged irrelevant or
at best uncertain, so does the 'mutual participation' model become
the most appropriate pattern on which to base the clinical relationship. And in contrast to the other two, the mutual participation
model 'requires a more complex social and psychological organisation on the part of both participants' (Szasz and Hollander 1956:
p. 587).

Zola and Miller (1975) have also suggested that a shift is taking
place in the 'balance of power' within the therapeutic relationship.
They point out, for example, that 'success' in treating chronic condi-

tions tends to be judged by relative rather than absolute criteria. 'Improvement' rather than complete cure is the target of medical intervention. For the doctor, the problem is not only that of convincing the patient that his condition is susceptible to medical intervention, but also that of maintaining a continuous motivation to co-operate and actively participate in treatment. Szasz and Hollander (1956) use the example of diabetes mellitus. Here, the patient's own experiences provide important clues for therapy. Moreover, the treatment programme itself is carried out for the most part by the patient. Essentially, the doctor helps the patient to help himself. In such situations, 'treatment' cannot therefore be said to occur unless both participants address themselves to the problems of the case. The traditional notions of 'disease' and 'health' lose most of their relevance in this context: the notions of 'adaptation' and of behaviour which are more or less 'successful' (given the context in which the patient has to act) take the place of earlier, more categorical, concepts. Treatment goals and evaluations of the success of treatment depend on judgements made by patient and physician in collaboration (see also, Davis and Strong 1976). This last process is made more complicated, as Szasz and Hollander (1956: p. 590) point out, by the fact that its elements may change in the course of treatment. The physician accordingly has to engage in consultation and negotiation in clinical contacts with his patients. His autonomy and scope for making discretionary decisions *vis-à-vis* those patients are correspondingly reduced.

Haug's comparison (1976) of medical practice in Great Britain, the USA and the USSR develops this point somewhat further. Her data lead her to argue that a trend is emerging in the West, whereby:

> Clients, with greater or lesser knowledge of the tasks [the medical profession] performs, negotiate a course of action designed to accomplish some individually or socially desired end. The underlying model is one of expert and consumer, without the moral and evaluative overtones of the professional model.
>
> (1976, p. 105)

Within the National Health Service, the 'bargaining' or negotiation aspect of this relationship is augmented by such tasks and requirements as signing certificates to validate sick leave. Haug suggests that the trend toward a less acquiescent attitude to the physician is most marked amongst younger people, and those who have spent longer in full-time education. She argues that the growth of a popular lay literature on health has further contributed to the move towards 'consumerism' in medical matters and a greater willingness to challenge the judgements and authority of doctors. One's reaction to Haug's data should perhaps be tempered by the fact that they were gathered from interviews with physicians, although the fact that doctors perceive and report such changes to be taking place is probably revealing in itself.

Some support for Haug's argument may be contained in the common observation/complaint that modern GPs work on 'recipe' knowledge, with a relatively limited range of (chemical) remedies for common ailments. (Indeed, some medical mavericks – see, for example, Cargill 1967 – have suggested that a number of antibiotics and other drugs could be removed from the prescribed list and made available commercially, with clear instructions as to the symptoms of the conditions for which they should be used, and what should be done if they do not have the desired effect.) This factor works in conjunction with the 'six-minute rule' – the convention operative in many NHS surgeries that 'average' patients get six minutes of the doctor's time in any appointment (Balint and Norel 1973; see also, Foster 1979) – to render patients cynical about the expertise possessed by the doctor and his, to use Freidson's term, 'ethicality'. In this connection, and following the argument presented by Smith elsewhere in this volume, the discretionary powers exercised by doctors' receptionists in deciding who merits being seen by the doctor would constitute a very fruitful area for research (see also, Foster 1979).

A further outcome of the change in disease patterns has been the increased pressure it has generated in favour of particular kinds of preventive programme (Lalonde 1975; McKeown 1976, Chapters 6 and 7; DHSS 1976a; Ringen 1979; see also Dubos 1960). Perhaps the most radical statement of this view is to be found in the working document produced in 1975 by the Minister of National Health and Welfare in the Canadian government (Lalonde 1975). This proposes a shift in perspective and commitment in health policy away from the organisation and provision of medical and hospital services and towards a focus on the causes of health and illness and on positive health-promotion programmes. The document argues that medical services are relatively ineffective in treating chronic diseases. Its main message is that further improvement in the health of Canadians will depend as much (or more) on a better knowledge of human biology, on quality of environment, and on individual lifestyle, as on the increased efficiency with which personal health care is provided by health professionals and hospitals. It is proposed that the proportion of GNP spent on health services should be frozen at its existing level, and that any improvements in those services should be financed out of the savings made on reducing 'preventable' illness, through concentrating on environmental improvements and in particular through changes effected in the 'lifestyles' of individuals. To that end, a set of strategies are outlined (Lalonde 1975: Chapter 12) and 'Operation Lifestyle' was launched about four years ago (see also, Gellman et al. 1977). A more cautious statement of similar points is made in the DHSS (1976a) document on *Prevention and Health*, and a modest start has been made to health education programmes in this country. In Norway a nutrition and food policy has been introduced, prompted mainly by health considerations (Ringen 1979).

To the extent that future policies would therefore seem to be moving in the direction of encouraging individuals to view health as a personal responsibility, so is the authority of the medical profession over health matters likely to be set further under siege. Although the criticisms of such writers as Illich et al. (1977) of the *Disabling Professions* seem unlikely to gain widespread credence, a preventive policy – with its possible consequential emphases on advertising, programmes of exercise, legislation against certain forms of behaviour (as on the compulsory wearing of seat-belts or crash helmets, or the ban on smoking in schools and hospitals in Norway) and uses of fiscal measures, with taxes on 'harmful' products or (more radically) subsidies for non-noxious ones, particularly foodstuffs (McKeown 1975) – may help to spread the perceived responsibility for health and so remove at least part of that responsibility from the ambit of the profession of medicine.

This relates to one final point. Both the introduction of preventive policies of this nature and the need to deal with chronic illnesses when they present themselves at a clinical level have in many cases led to the introduction of health visitors and a number of ancillary workers into general practices. While experience suggests that doctors remain dominant within these 'teams', factors such as the fragmentation of responsibility for patients and the need to consult colleagues to check the progress of particular cases may again be expected to impinge on the autonomy of the general practitioner. Suggestions for the introduction of 'nurse-practitioners', in which community-trained nurses take over certain of the functions of general practitioners, may be viewed as illustrative of this trend.

The points made in the last paragraph do of course relate to a wider current issue. General practice emerged in the early nineteenth century in response to social requirements and developing medical knowledge to meet the needs of a rapidly expanding industrial and commercial middle class. A large part of the popular perception and esteem for medicine may in fact be connected with the nineteenth century concept of 'family doctoring'. As medical (and largely hospital-based) specialisms have expanded (to deal increasingly with chronic conditions), so has general practice

> tended to be the undefined and residual legatee of the medical care estate. Positive definition has tended to be reserved for the things which it shall not do, perhaps without sufficient regard for the coherence, purpose and requirements of what is left behind.
>
> (Brotherston 1971: p. 88)

The Medical Profession's Response

The picture we have presented so far is one of potential decline in medical autonomy and authority, in the face of changes in the characteristics and treatment requirements of the diseases with which doctors have to cope. We shall conclude this part of our argument by pointing briefly to one or two of the possible responses by the medical profession to such encroachments.

First, one may expect attempts on the part of physicians to colonise the field of preventive policies because of greater expertise about the most relevant targets for, for example, health education programmes. This may extend to a demand for a dominant stake in the actual conduct of such programmes. The recommendations in the Todd Report (Report of the Royal Commission on Medical Education 1968: paras 27, 119, 133 and 280–2) for a greater emphasis on preventive and community medicine in the medical school curriculum may provide the vehicle for such claims because they are linked with a stress on the doctor's potential role in primary care. The likelihood, from the profession's point of view, of continued dominance by the doctor in the general practice setting is also reflected in the Todd Report's recommendation (ibid.: 33) that staff be introduced to perform the 'trivial or routine jobs which do not require the knowledge and skill of a fully-qualified doctor' (Report of the Royal Commission of Medical Education: p. 33).

A variety of interpersonal strategies exist for handling the problem of the therapeutic relationship in chronic disease. West (1976), for example, in his study of the interaction between doctors and the parents of epileptic children, suggests that physicians are trained to recognise a symptom in the context of a biological syndrome rather than of a patient's whole life. They also lack the time and skill to recognise the significance of illness for the patient. They therefore tend to give non-committal answers to questions because they do not want to have their competence challenged should they be proved wrong. Other essays in the same volume (Wadsworth and Robinson 1976) indicate that physicians rarely give patients alternatives from which to choose and so exclude them from participating in decisions about treatment and management. Whether this is ultimately a wise tactic is, of course, open to question. The frustrations and disenchantment patients suffer seem more designed to undermine than to enhance the physician's authority and credibility (see also, Freidson 1970b: pp. 140–2).

Physicians who feel uncomfortable in the 'mutual participation' relationship may attempt to redefine the clinical encounter in medically more traditional and hierarchical terms. To use more or less 'heroic' techniques (from organ transplantation, to the prescription of drugs for 'nervousness') in dealing with non-acute conditions is to construe and to attempt to deal with a problem in terms of the unilateral use of expertise.

Professional Self-regulation

As Freidson argues, the medical profession's claim to relative freedom from outside control rests explicitly on three grounds: that non-professionals are simply not equipped to assess the technical aspects of medical practice; that professionals themselves may be trusted to perform responsibly in the absence of external supervision; and that the profession itself may be trusted to regulate the conduct of members if the need arises. Professional autonomy, then, is justified on the promise of effective professional self-regulation (Freidson 1970a).

Freidson, of course, is personally identified with the now familiar argument that, in the United States at least, this implicit promise of self-regulation is rarely upheld. Formal review procedures were until recently uncommon in most American medical settings: they exist rarely in office practices and are found commonly only in those hospitals accredited for postgraduate training, that is university teaching hospitals.* Nor is the absence of formal review machinery balanced by the existence of *ad hoc*, informal methods of regulation and control, techniques potentially of great significance occurring, in Alvin Gouldner's phrase, 'below the waterline of public visibility'. Informal control mechanisms are again found most commonly only in teaching hospitals, and there apparently in the form of Mary Goss's 'advisory bureaucracy', a system of relations involving senior and junior staff in which senior doctors assume the right to review cases delegated to subordinates and to offer unsolicited advice about clinical practice. Junior doctors acquiesce to this breach of their clinical autonomy and disregard advice only when they are satisfied that, in the event of a challenge, they would be supported unambiguously by the facts of the case. Thus, although Freidson finds little evidence of formal hierarchical (and control) relations in American hospitals, like many other observers he does acknowledge the presence of a tacit hierarchy of 'skill and judgement', at least in certain teaching centres (Goss 1963; see also Perrow 1965: p. 958).

'Advisory' relations are made possible because senior practitioners possess the right to review systematically medical case records produced by subordinate staff. The medical record becomes, in this relatively special instance, a means by which the clinical judgement of peers is made visible, a means by which the performance of peers is laid open for assessment. Medical decisions in this context acquire a uniquely 'public' character – the individual doctor practises in the certain knowledge that his decisions are available for scrutiny by colleagues (Freidson 1970a: p. 154).

According to Freidson, this informal system of peer regulation is

*Freidson's discussion may be amended to a certain extent in the light of recent events. Since 1972, as a result of Congressional legislation, the Professional Standards Review Organisation network has evolved to monitor federally financed medical schemes such as Medicare and Medicaid.

virtually unknown in American office practice. Many doctors maintain single-handed practices, and this simply precludes the possibility of peer control. Group practice or partnership arrangements typically linking colleagues representing complementary specialties, normally 'share' neither patients nor medical records in the way described by Goss. Indeed, American 'groups' are perhaps properly described as loose confederations of solo practitioners assembled to spread overhead expenses and to rationalise referral arrangements. Group affiliation does not impinge on the individual doctor's claim to clinical autonomy (Freidson 1970a: pp. 91ff).

Of course doctors, like all independent professionals, are able to obtain some information bearing on the competence of colleagues. In a large, university affiliated clinic studied by Freidson, doctors acquired information about one another by 'tapping the paramedical grapevine', by direct observation of gross violations of clinic rules (such as missing appointments or permitting large queues to form), or, infrequently, by gossip about individuals. Some estimate of technical competence was made possible by referral relations, although the medical division of labour itself insured that knowledge of specialist groupings was disproportionately distributed. Practitioners in surgery and internal medicine, two specialties central to the medical division of labour, were well known; practitioners in ophthalmology, on the other hand, proved more difficult to evaluate. The process, in any event, was haphazard and based on untrustworthy forms of evidence: medical records become a source of evidence only in the aftermath of a crisis of some sort (Freidson and Rhea 1963).

The weight of evidence, then, for the United States indicates clearly that self-regulation is weakly developed because practitioners are not routinely able to make competent judgements about the quality of each other's clinical work. However the greatest caution must be exercised in transferring this kind of argument about professional autonomy from the United States to Britain. There have been *a priori* grounds, at any time since 1948, for seeking to distinguish conditions of service between the two countries. We shall suggest that recent developments in British medical practice have made trans-Atlantic generalisation all the more hazardous. And yet it may be that British researchers have adopted Freidson's case, apposite though it is for America, with rather more enthusiasm than would appear warranted. This has coloured the British literature on the profession of medicine; it has also directed attention away from elements of British practice which perhaps do encourage self-regulation. British medicine, with its distinctive hospital and general practice arrangements, at the very least provides an interesting test of Freidson's specific argument that the observability of clinical decisions creates an essential precondition for professional self-regulation.

The relations between British hospital consultants and junior hospital doctors, for instance, are unambiguously hierarchical. Rowbottom, reporting on the Brunel Health Services Organisation Project, argues that the consultant is 'accountable for the work of his juniors in all its aspects, he may prescribe that work, and he provides formal assessments of the capability of the junior' (Rowbottom 1973: p. 87). These relations, he says, are 'much stronger' than those described in the American literature. A substantial majority of British hospital doctors, then, are lodged in a work situation – indeed this is the case for many a career structure – in which formal procedures for delegation and control function as a matter of course.

There is, moreover, nothing in the United States comparable to the structure of British general practice. Almost 80 per cent of American practitioners are specialists; American consumers are typically not 'fed' into specialist services by general practitioners but rather contact specialists directly (or are referred by other specialists). There is, in a word, no American equivalent of the multi-handed general practice partnership (or health centre) forming a first line of contact for consumers seeking primary care or specialist referral. The table presents information revealing the trend in Britain recently towards larger practice units. Almost 40 per cent of British GPs practise in groups of four or more partners; only one in six GPs remain in single-handed practice (although almost half of all Scottish GPs were 'solo' practitioners as recently as the early 1950s.

It is difficult to assess the implications of the development of large, segmented practice units for informal self-regulation. On the one hand, the consolidating of GPs may have no effect on the individual partner's historical freedom from clinical interference. In this case, GP group practices, whatever their advantages, will have proved no more conducive to the creation of self-regulatory mechanisms than the group specialist teams evolving in America.

Distribution of British general practitioners by type of practice (%)

Type of practice	England and Wales		Scotland	
	1960	1976	1960	1976
Single-handed	30	17	32	15
Partnership of				
2 principals	35	20	36	20
3 principals	21	24	20	27
4 principals	9	18	8	19
5 or more principals	5	20	4	20
Total	100	100	100	100
	(19,847)	(20,546)	(2628)	(2820)

Source: *Scottish Health Statistics*, 1963 and 1976
    Health and Personal Social Service Statistics, 1977
    Digest of Health Statistics for England and Wales, 1969

On the other hand, research in progress by one of the present authors suggests that certain aspects of medical practice in health centres may produce, albeit in a limited way, Freidson's essential precondition for regulation, the observability of clinical decisions.

In the two Scottish health centres under study, each housing six or more partners with supporting paramedical and administrative staff, patients (and their records) are routinely 'shared' by cooperating GPs. Thus, all six principals in one centre operate a 'pairing' system in which two doctors combine to offer cover for each other's patients during specified sessions (usually on two half-days a week). These 'pairs' are relatively stable and afford GPs the opportunity to hold part-time attachments at a neighbouring district hospital. Similarly, night cover is provided in both health centres by partners on a rota basis (in cooperation, in one case, with GPs from group practices in the same Health Division), and holiday cover arrangements are standardised among partners in each centre. In the Health Centre without formal 'pairing' arrangements, half-day cover (again to pursue attachment work) is organised by rota.

In the case of 'pairs', there is a formalised mechanism by means of which GPs cannot but help to be put in contact with clinical decisions made by colleagues. Patient records in this practice are clearly the product of more than one practitioner; indeed, typed entries in a given file must be initialled in order to establish the identity of the doctor producing the note. Patient sharing in the other practice, although less developed, also results in record-sharing and joint annotation. Again, even in this setting, decisions made by individual GPs are relatively 'visible'; the file containing the record of any given decision is extremely likely to be seen by one or more colleagues.

GPs in both practices are fully aware of the novelty of these arrangements, but they consider them a fair trade-off against reduced patient loads and the opportunity to accept specialist hospital appointments (or, in one case, to do research). Record-sharing does not actually make individual decisions as observable as one might in theory expect: not all participants, for instance, take notes for all visits and some participants produce notes that are too sketchy to be useful in reconstructing episodes. Also notes recording visits involving the diagnosis and treatment of physical complaints tend to be detailed and precise; visits arising from psychiatric or social problems are sometimes not recorded or recorded partially ('had a helpful chat').

Efforts are also made to mitigate some effects of the system. GPs in the 'pairing' practice scrupulously observe a rule forbidding partners to alter a course of treatment until its conclusion ('the rule' having arisen in response to attempts by 'shared' patients to play-off one member of the practice against another). 'Pairing' relations are not constructed randomly: partners seek suitable colleagues with whom to 'pair'.

Information of two kinds, each relating to a different professional audience, is stored in medical records. The record, of course, contains a running chronicle of patient contacts and actions made in response to those contacts. The record also contains, in many practices, correspondence occurring between GPs, acting as 'feeders' into the specialist system, and hospital consultants. GP/consultant correspondence involves requests from GPs for opinions or investigations, sometimes accompanied by detailed resumes of the case in question, and replies from consultants, occasionally making recommendations for treatment.

The GP as referral agent has no structural counterpart in American medicine, in part because of self-referral patterns and in part because American specialty services, viewed as a resource, simply are not scarce. But the British GP, acting as gatekeeper to the hospital services and obliged to justify his claim for specialist resources, must therefore routinely expose his judgement to consultant scrutiny. In the practices under study, the GP's referral decisions are exposed not merely to consultant scrutiny (as happens universally in Britain), but, indirectly, to the probable scrutiny of partners in 'pair' or covering arrangements as well.

Now GP/consultant correspondence files are a significant source of observable evidence on professional competence precisely because GPs in these practices appear to value the opinion of hospital consultants. GPs wish to be evaluated favourably by consultants; errors of judgement exposed by consultants can be a source of acute embarrassment. GPs motivated in this way may be normally expected to exercise some care in managing clinical exchanges with hospital consultants. And GPs, for whom a written record of such exchanges is potentially open to colleagues' inspection, may be expected to approach consultant relations with particular caution.

In both practices under investigation, the issue of GP consultant relations is additionally complicated by the fact that several partners hold specialist appointments and thus actually function as consultants within their own health centres. Cases suitable for referral in psychiatry, paediatrics and obstetrics and gynaecology are simply routed within each practice to the appropriate partner. But, again, a clinical argument must be put forward to justify the referral and a résumé of the case is usually also prepared. Moreover, the correspondence arising between partners concerning the referral is stored in the patient's medical record. Relations, further, tend to be relatively symmetrical in that partners receiving referrals as specialists in one field may simultaneously be referring other patients to colleagues in a different field.

Here, the GP's clinical behaviour is made uniquely observable, both directly to partners linked in the referral relationship and indirectly to other partners linked in patient 'sharing' relationships. Inasmuch as the GP seeks to be favourably assessed by consultant–partners, with whom he must interact daily and whose judgement will contribute to his own professional self-esteem, he will be inclined to observe the ordinary canons of good professional conduct. He will be constrained, in everyday practice, to maintain the standards of clinical performance articulated in principle by his immediate colleagues. Paradoxically, in a setting involving significant numbers of partners with specialist qualifications, the net effect of this kind of process may be to establish as normative the clinical standards of the consultant–physician. In one practice, for instance, a majority of partners have agreed to participate in a medical auditing scheme in which diagnostic and prescribing behaviour are monitored and reported. The results are circulated in the form of computer output and 'deviant' partners, perhaps, GPs whose prescription profile for psychotropic drugs is exceptional in some respect, are readily identifiable.

We have sought to establish that, however much clinical decisions may be screened from colleague surveillance in American medicine, various elements of British medical organisation make virtually inevitable some measure of observability. Many more British than American physicians practise in relatively large, segmented general practice partnerships. GPs, independently of practice circumstances, are expected to justify in clinical terms their decision to refer a patient to specialist services. GPs in practices housing specialist colleagues are likely to experience a distinctive kind of peer-pressure to maintain clinical respectability. GPs in practices with well elaborated 'pairing' or covering arrangements possess, in the form of medical records, a strategic source of information about one another's clinical performance.

If, as Freidson argues, observability of performance is a necessary precondition for professional self-regulation then, at the very least, that precondition is apparently more firmly established in Britain than in America. It is difficult to know, however, precisely how widely arrangements giving rise to observability are actually distributed. Multi-handed practice settings may not always conduce towards increased visibility. 'Pairing' arrangements are probably relatively unusual in GP partnerships and, indeed, they may never become widely accepted. Joint attachment schemes, linking GPs and part-time consultants within partnerships, may prove to be only an unusual feature of selected health centres.

Further, these mechanisms, even assuming their widespread appearance, do not in themselves guarantee the emergence in turn of effective self-regulatory machinery. Their existence merely simplifies the detection of unacceptable conduct and makes conduct by practitioners in conformity with group expectations more probable. The limits to tolerable behaviour would in all likelihood be indulgently set; it is hard to imagine attempts within practice units to standardise clinical behaviour. Sanctions would be employed only with the greatest reluctance. These sanctions would be oblique, perhaps proceeding to the social isolation of the offending practitioner. They would not probably arise from an explicit or coordinated group decision; they would certainly not put the doctor at risk of lay opprobrium. And thus they would rest squarely for their effectiveness upon the value attached by individuals to the esteem and companionship of their colleagues.

Whether this apparently fragile standard will prove sufficient to form a reliable basis for self-regulation is now a matter merely for speculation. It is worth nothing, however, that Freidson himself adopts a surprisingly optimistic position concerning informal control mechanisms: they are, he says, not only significant but can be 'under some circumstances, both necessary and sufficient for the optimal regulation of performance'.

Resource Rationing

If changes in medical organisation have the consequence of constraining the scope for action of individual GPs, then resource allocation proposals set before recent governments may carry implications for the freedom of manoeuvre of the profession at large, and of hospital doctors in particular. One recommendation associated with these proposals – the establishment of health education programmes at central government and regional levels – has already been mentioned. We wish now to consider the background to these proposals and to outline some additional recommendations arising from them.

Following hard upon the 'rediscovery of poverty' in Britain in the 1960s, the last decade has seen a remarkable concentration of attention, both scholarly and polemical, on inequalities in health and health care provision. Work by Howe (1970), Townsend (1974), Backett (1977) and Brotherston (1977) establishes beyond doubt that substantial disparities by social class and region, the two not being unconnected, continue to characterise British morbidity and mortality experience. England and Wales, for instance, divide neatly on a North–South axis defined by regional standardised mortality ratios: the North and North West regions experience mortality 10 to 13 per cent above the national average; certain of the home counties experience mortality 10 to 15 per cent below the national average. Strong regional variations continue to persist in mortality attributable to specific diseases such as ischaemic heart disease, cerebrovascular disease (or 'stroke'), lung cancer and chronic bronchitis (Howe 1970).

Social class differentials in mortality have actually expanded across the past half century (Brotherston 1977), despite major gains in mortality reduction for the population as a whole. Social class differences among men in mortality caused by stomach cancer and a variety of chest diseases remain particularly marked. The *General Household Survey*, produced only since 1972, has provided a rich (if difficult to validate) source of epidemiological information on social class variations in acute and chronic illness: again, for each year of the series, a clear gradient by class – i.e. better off persons reporting better health – emerges for both measures. Further, Britain's disappointing inability to keep pace with other European societies, particularly Scandinavian, in reducing perinatal and infant mortality (both subject to sharp class and regional variations) has been widely reported and publicised.

Criticism of the NHS itself was summarised succinctly in the form of Tudor-Hart's 'inverse care law' – actually less a 'law' than an effective slogan – which asserts that 'the availability of good medical care tends to vary inversely with the need of the population served' (Tudor-Hart 1975). Thus, an embarrassing variety of regional discrepancies exist in health care provision (such as *per capita* spending, GP list size, hospital doctors per head of population); and the provision of certain medical services varies not only between but within regions (see Buxton and Klein 1975), recreating locally the absence of fit between need and provision characterising the nation as a whole. A recurrent theme developed in the same context is the relative plight of staff and patients in the geriatric and psychiatric services, expenditure in neither case having adjusted to growing demand.

National Health Service reorganisation was, of course, addressed in part to the goal of reducing regional inequalities (Levitt 1976: p. 51), and the newly created Area Health Authorities were empowered to consider resource imbalances within their own boundaries. But their efforts have been made difficult, if not impossible, because national resource distribution policies tend to reflect –

in the language of one official task-force – 'the inertia built into the system by history' (DHSS 1976b: p. 7). These policies tend to increment established financial allocation commitments; they tend as well to respond only grudgingly to changes either in population composition or in morbidity patterns. Historic decisions concerning the disposition of money and manpower continue, even within the reorganised NHS, to influence current expenditure planning.

These issues have been made explicitly political through the appearance, dating from the mid-1970s, of a series of official policy documents. Regional imbalances (and implicitly, one assumes, social class disparities) are examined at length in the Report of the Resource Allocation Working Party (DHSS 1976b; see also Royal Commission on the National Health Service 1978). The redistribution of resources amongst services within the NHS is proposed in two consultative documents, one prepared by Barbara Castle, the other by David Ennals, as well as in Mrs Castle's 1976 statement on preventive health care (DHSS 1976a; DHSS 1976b; DHSS 1977a).

The Resource Allocation Working Party calls for rapid national progress towards 'equal opportunity of access to health care for people at equal risk' (DHSS 1977a: p. 7), a principle designed in practical terms to produce parity in financial allocation defined by need both between and within regions. Need at regional level would be measured by means of a set of indicators such as aggregate population, mortality in the form of SMRs (standardised mortality rates), population composition, estimates of cross-boundary patient flow and a London weighting factor. The speed with which a relatively deprived region would be brought towards its revenue target would be determined by its distance from that target. No region would fall below nor rise above certain arbitrarily defined minimum and maximum rates of growth. Regions in the North of England would benefit relatively by this scheme; the relative advantages now enjoyed by regions surrounding Metropolitan London would be systematically reduced.

What we may be charting is a decisive shift in emphasis from policies permitting 'implicit rationing' of resources (to use David Mechanic's terminology) by the medical profession itself to a state directed system of 'explicit rationing' (Mechanic 1977). The distinction is potentially crucial in its implications for professional autonomy (particularly in the hospital services). Resources are rationed implicitly when barriers to service use (queueing, bureaucratic obstacles, limiting sites of care, reducing contact time per patient) are determined in a fundamentally *laissez-faire* way by the activities of professionals themselves (Mechanic 1977; Rees 1972; Cooper 1975). It is perhaps inevitable under conditions in which resource allocation occurs partly as a by-product of clinical practice that allocation outcomes tend to reflect substantially the values and priorities of the more powerful sections of the profession. Thus, hospital doctors have traditionally managed to secure a flow of funds towards hospital medicine, particularly high technology medicine as practised in major teaching centres.

A system of explicit rationing, however, alters decisively the frame of reference within which allocative decisions are made. A new emphasis is placed on forward planning. An attempt is made to specify precise planning objectives, and to derive rules to guide the actual disposition of resources. Resource allocation becomes the proper object of rational deliberation; this is a system in which is precluded neither the articulation of new ideas nor the formation of new interest groupings.

As we have tried to suggest, recent policy proposals proceed quite unapologetically from premises couched in the language of social reform. Indeed appeals for change in the name of the socially deprived, the elderly and the mentally handicapped have probably not been registered with such effect since the debate surrounding the creation of the NHS three decades ago. Reorganisation, on the other hand, has almost certainly increased the ability of administrators, representing their own priorities for the use of resources, to influence decisions about allocation. The challenge to the medical profession arises therefore across a series of closely related developments: a move towards explicit rationing has served to alter the criteria by which decisions about resources are made, and rival interests – political, administrative, consumer – have emerged to claim a voice in debates concerning resource disposition, rival interests whose influence upon allocative decisions is no longer insignificant.

More interestingly, all these proposals involve in some measure a special challenge to the clinical autonomy of hospital doctors. Some acute departments will be run down (or will close); other departments will be obliged to pool beds (creating a need for more coordination between consultants); demand in excess of available bed space may be rationed by a medically qualified admissions officer (a person, that is, designated to adjudicate claims lodged by competing consultants). The more rational use of hospital bed space may be achieved by reducing the average length of stay for patients, by the development of surgical day care units, and by rationing more stringently the availability of certain surgical procedures. Criteria for the admission of patients to intensive care units may be revised. 'Unnecessary and often costly' investigations involving radiology and pathology may be controlled (see DHSS 1977a, for a summary of recommendations affecting the hospitals service).

These measures fall short of a full-blown system of explicit rationing which, according to Mechanic, would include the total exclusion of some procedures, the determination of fixed limits for the performance of other procedures, and the development of formal pre-review machinery (that is, machinery obliging the doctor to justify in advance his petition to use resources). They do, however, apear to suggest a movement in the direction of explicit rationing, and they do, at the very least, represent a challenge of some importance to the professional autonomy of hospital doctors.

Conclusions

We have attempted in this chapter to describe a number of developments which carry implications for the traditional position and dominance of the British medical profession. Following Freidson, we have argued that professional dominance is secured, not because of qualities inherent in the profession or its activities, but rather as the product of continuing transactions between the profession and its publics, most notably the state. This is to say, simply, that the unique privileges associated with the practice of medicine must be seen as subject to challenge, as properly the object of political debate, and, ultimately, as contingent upon the success of these transactions. Professional dominance, once won, can – at least in theory – be again lost.

Changes in morbidity and gains in human life expectancy, for instance, have affected doctor–patient relationships, the treatment of degenerative or chronic illnesses being a relatively 'participative' process, and resulted increasingly in the development of preventive strategies. Preventive schemes, as we have suggested, have the effect of shifting responsibility for health away from medical professionals and towards the individual. Further, both the care of chronic illness and the development of preventive policies have the consequence of increasing the relative importance of paramedical personnel and technical support staff. The individual practitioner, in this case, must surrender at least some measure of autonomy for the sake of maintaining effective team relations.

Recent trends in general practice organisation may also function to limit the freedom of action available to individual doctors. The observability of clinical decision-making, certainly more a feature of British medicine than American, is, as Freidson would submit, a condition for the development of informal mechanisms of professional self-regulation. Circumstances conducive to observability may well become more common than they already are; indeed, attempts by the state to rationalise primary care, particularly through the promotion of health centres, would seem to have precisely this effect.

Finally, current debates about the direction of health policy may foreshadow an historic shift in emphasis by the state from a programme of 'implicit' to 'explicit' resource rationing. Again, at the very least, the very terms in which these debates have come to be conducted suggests a new kind of challenge to the ability of professionals, particularly hospital physicians, to control the disposition of resources.

11 Discretion, Moral Judgement and Integration*
David Watson

In this chapter I shall eventually be concerned with the effect of discretion, at certain points in the administration of social policy, upon social relations. In Chapter 1 in this volume, Adler and Asquith rightly make the point that 'an adequate analysis of the actual exercise of discretion must be informed by an understanding of the structural position of welfare institutions and their relationship to the broader social, political and economic framework of society'. In what follows I shall present a theoretical and, in parts, normative account of social policies and their relationship to the broader social framework of human society. I go on to defend a particular kind of discretion as a feature of certain social policies within that social framework. At least at that point, I suppose, the political framework of society is also in question, because my defence of the discretion I discuss presupposes a redistribution of power.

Discussions of 'discretion in social policy' very often occur in a context in which a particular distinction is exlicitly or implicity accepted. The distinction I have in mind is neatly named as that between legalism and discretion. Broadly following Jones et al. (1978: p. 140), legalism involves the allocation of benefits and burdens on the basis of legal rules and precedent, discretion involves the allocation of benefits or burdens on the basis of individual judgements. It seems to me that this distinction is by no means as sharp as all its users imply, but here I want to develop just one of my reasons for taking this view. To quote more of Adler and Asquith's phrases, the discussion to follow is of 'lay ideologies', and is concerned with 'conceptions of social reality' which do indeed 'contribute to the

* I should like to thank the editors of this volume and various friends at Bristol, particularly Joe Ryant and Noelle Whiteside, for critical and helpful comments on an earlier draft of this chapter.

maintenance of social order'. But the exercise of discretion with which I shall be concerned, informed by lay ideologies, in an important sense is *not* to be contrasted to decision-making guided by rules but exemplifies it: such decision-making may be contrasted to that guided by a rule-book but exemplifies that guided by rules learned by growing up in a particular society. Discretionary judgements not based upon legal rules and precedent are not thereby arbitrary. On the contrary, such judgements may still be characterised as purposive and rule-following, though the rules are of a distinct and socially fundamental kind (see Peters 1958; Winch 1958). Lay ideologies incorporate, perhaps just are, views of social relations which may be analysed as governed by rules. These rules primarily facilitate the intelligibility of judgements and behaviour in a context in which decision-makers, and others, are conceived of as having purposes that make certain decisions and behaviour rational, in the sense of 'intelligible'. Such rules in a sense permit or describe our identities as agents in society. In addition, our purposes and choice of means to achieve them are further subject to appraisal in the light of moral rules. Discretionary judgements not based upon legal rules and precedent are not arbitrary: they follow rules of action governing intelligibility for agents in a particular society and moral rules accepted by the decision-maker (on the latter, see Rees 1978; Giller and Morris, Chapter 4 in this volume). As we shall see, rules of action and moral rules may be the basis of decisions about an individual's future social relations, and it is with discretion in the context of such decisions, based in such rules, that I shall be concerned.

The effects and value of discretion for social relations are usually discussed in terms of the status-enhancing and stigmatising propensities of, say, social service systems (see Titmuss 1968: Chapter 1 and Pinker 1971: Chapter 4). I shall discuss discretion and social relations at the next higher level of generality. Talk of the status-enhancing and stigmatising propensities of social policies presupposes criteria of identity for social relationships and some conception of social policy which ties it firmly to the promotion of such social relationships. First in my discussion comes the outline of a general and normative theory of distinctively human social relations, and then the related conception of social policy. Together, these views provide a conceptual framework within which a certain kind of discretion may be seen as a useful component of attempts to sustain and direct forms of social integration by means of social policy. I then go on to illustrate a context in which such discretion is exercised. The context is Part III of the Social Work (Scotland) Act, 1968 (Chapter 49) and the discretion there granted to members of Children's Hearings.

Theory

The outline of a general and normative theory of distinctively human social relations, which I now present, has two sources, each inspired by a third. I begin with the views of John Benson, as presented in his article 'The Concept of Community' (1976), and Peter Winch, as presented in 'Nature and Convention (1972). Benson and Winch develop a line of thought suggested, in the usual fertile hints, by Wittgenstein (1958).

Benson notes three necessary conditions of *any* animals being correctly said to have a social life. First, their collective existence must involve differentiation of function and interdependence of individuals performing different functions. Second, individuals must form groups that have some degree of continuity. Third, the individuals must be dependent on others in some identifiable group in a reasonably high proportion of their activities, and for some substantial portion of their lifespan. For the *human* form of social life, Benson argues that in addition it is necessary that the distribution and performance of functions should be not merely *de facto*, but should be governed by rules or norms. He points out that:

> It can be illuminating to think of society as a network of roles, institutionalised and non-institutionalised, of many different kinds, each regulated, indeed constituted, by a set of rules. Each person's conception of his society consists in the knowledge that he has of the network of roles he occupies and what to expect of others in theirs.
>
> (1976: p. 241)

As Benson illustrates at the beginning of his article, we use the word 'society' in a variety of ways. But the use just outlined is the one that is central to the conception of distinctively human social relations to be described.

Human social life cannot be adequately understood simply, or in a complicated way, as a matter of automatically responding to a stimulus. Distinctive of human social life, and necessary for understanding it *in terms intelligible to the participants,* is the notion of acting in a way appropriate to one's social identity. Our social roles, and the circumstances in which we find ourselves, provide a reason for our behaviour, making it intelligible as a particular action. As Benson says, the rules or norms that govern the distribution and performance of roles determine what is expected and recognised. Social roles of this sort are a crucial part of the context in which individual behaviour can be a particular purposive action because of its appropriateness for an individual in that role, given the rules governing the role. If he is in that role he must or may act in certain ways: He's a Private Detective – so that's what he's up to! Or again, in my social role as 'friend', or any other of my friends, a request for five pounds, may be a request for a gift or a loan, but is not an act of begging. And we recognise this because we have learned the rules governing friendship. My behaviour is recognised as the act it is, by participants and observers, when we know not only that there's a hole in my pocket, but also who I am in relation to the person making the request.

Incidentally, it is important not to be misled by the word 'govern'. Rules of the sort in question are not all rules that require; some are rules that permit. To take an example from Benson, a father must feed and clothe his children, and may, or may not, send them to public school if he is relatively rich, or encourage them to follow in his trade, if he has one. Further, to repeat a point I made earlier, and as the illustrations so far employed suggest, rules of the sort in question need not be made explicit in law or in religious or moral codes. They may be learned at one's mother's knee and all those other knees to which one pays attention, learning what is worthy of pursuit, and by what means it can be pursued.

Before enlarging upon the sense in which rules governing social roles determine the 'appropriateness' of behaviour, and in particular the relation between appropriateness and intelligibility, I would like briefly to mention the implications of the view of human society outlined so far for the notion of 'social integration'.

Benson presents an account of human society as distinguished from that of other animals by the appropriateness of individuals' purposes and actions in the context of the network of rule-governed social roles which make up that society. Social integration, then, for a society, may be thought of as relative to the understanding its members have of the rules governing roles within the network, or, to put it another way, as relative to the appropriateness of members' actions in relationship with each other. For an individual, social integration is relative to his understanding of the same rules, relative to the appropriateness of his and others' actions in relationships with him.

Since the rules governing social roles are sustained by our following them, social distintegration, on this account, may begin where there is a failure to follow rules as a result of not having grasped them. If there were widespread failure of this kind in respect of the rules governing a particular social role, that role would cease to be within the network making up that society. To that extent the society with which we began has disintegrated, or we might prefer to say, simply, that it has changed, depending on our criteria of identity, but in either case it is true to say that it is no longer society as we knew it.

Social disintegration may also begin where there is, what we might call, the *abuse* of rules governing social roles, if it is widespread, and also where there is *refusal* to follow such rules. And in these cases the rules are fully grasped. When, for example, friends 'borrow' not intending to return, or when children reject any responsibility for their parents in old age, at least a part of each of these roles, and so of these relationships, has been abandoned. Social integration may be promoted by attempts of various kinds to avoid all three sources of distintegration. When we turn to the conception of social policy which I want to introduce, I shall argue that social policy is to be distinguished from economic policy by its promotion of forms of social integration.

This is perhaps an appropriate point at which to introduce two disclaimers. First, I am not committed by the account so far to the view that all forms of social integration are morally desirable. On the account so far, the form of social integration in any society is no more than the network of roles making a limited range of social relations intelligible to members of that society. Thus I am not saying that social integration must be cosy. One may understand one's place and what one may therefore do or suffer as a slave, and still resent one's slavery. This point, together with recognition of the decline of certain forms of social integration, no doubt to be replaced by others, leads into the second disclaimer. On the account so far I am not committed to any suggestion that the rules governing roles result from the parties' consent. Some may indeed be imposed by one party to a social relationship upon the other. Consent is not necessary for intelligibility. Even in the context of lack of agreement we may talk of rules governing the relationship, making the acts of each party intelligible to both. As we shall see in more detail below, a particular form of social integration may not be welcomed equally by all paricipants, for all its intelligibility, and rule-abuse or refusal may be the result.

However, I want now to say a little more about the relation between appropriateness and intelligibility, as regards rules governing social roles, in order to clarify the relation between grasping the rules governing a role, and abusing the rules or refusing to follow them. I shall go on to draw out the relevant moral implications, too, because these are significant for the conception of social policy I wish to develop.

Benson draws a distinction between 'rules of action' and 'rules of meaning'. He calls 'rules of action' the rules that govern the appropriateness of some behaviour, and make it the action it is, in relation to a particular social role. We need the distinction between rules of action and rules of meaning, he argues, because failures to follow rules of action can be socially meaningful.

> Because of this it is possible to 'say' things with actions, and particularly to say unusual, unconventional, and even defiant and revolutionary things, and be understood. It is because a description of society in terms of roles involves reference to rules of this kind that such a description does not imply that the behaviour of social beings is sterotyped and invariable, but rather lays bare a framework within which both conventional behaviour and innovation become intelligible.
>
> (1976: p. 247)

What I have referred to as rule-abuse and refusal to follow the rules governing a social role are examples of unconventional and innovative behaviour. A number of years ago someone posing as a conductor employed by Blackpool Corporation collected a small fortune by boarding trams on the promenade. In the busiest periods the Corporation employs 'locum' conductors to assist those 'attached' to particular trams. The man wore an appropriately coloured uniform, issued tickets, rang the bell, left people behind, and, of course, collected fares. Thus following the rules governing occupation of that role, he was taken to *be* a Blackpool Corporation conductor. But he wasn't. The man fully grasped the rules governing the role – hence his success. I call this rule-abuse because it is a deception, and one possible only because there are rules of action governing performance in social roles.

An example of refusal to follow rules governing a social role, fully grasped, in the area of social policy, is supplied by Corrigan and Leonard (1978: Chapter 5) in their account of a Marxist approach to social work practice under capitalism. Corrigan and Leonard describe a series of cases in which, as they themselves put it 'social workers struggle against their roles as members of the ideological state apparatus' confronting stigmatising definitions. In the case in question the stigmatising to be confronted is in relation to one-parent families. On a conventional conception of the social worker's role in working with a one-parent family, Corrigan and Leonard suggest, the social worker panders to the idea of the family as the only way of bringing up children: fighting to sustain the family unit in the face of disconnection of the electricity supply, social security's reluctance to pay certain extra monies for furniture, and the lack of support from the client's own mother. The conventional role requires the social worker to patch up these problems to avoid whisking the children into care, and confirms the view that the family (one or two-parented) is the only way to bring up children. It also confirms the client's view of herself as a failure if she cannot cope with five children in the impossible situation she is in.

Having acquired 'an overall analysis of the position of one-parent families' the social worker should, however, refuse to follow the conventional rules governing the role of social worker and begin to put new rules into practice. The practice recommended in this case may be summed up as helping the client 'to develop her consciousness of her position in the reproduction of social relationships', which can actually be said with a straight face once the full details of Corrigan and Leonard's account have been read. I recommend it.

Even so, I don't think we need the distinction between rules of action and rules of meaning to explain the continued significance of unconventional or revolutionary behaviour. It seems to me that rules of action, which govern appropriateness, thereby entirely govern intelligibility in terms understood by participants, and that unconventional and revolutionary behaviour does continue to be meaningful if and only if it can be brought under the rules of action for some modified or quite different social role. The behaviour of our man on the promenade was misunderstood under the rules of action for being a conductor, but once the deception was exposed, his behaviour remained meaningful because it was appropriate under the rules of action for being a petty thief.

Consider our position if we could not bring his behaviour under other rules of action. Would his behaviour remain meaningful? I think not. Suppose he issues tickets and takes no money. If we do not know what role he occupies and acts in, then his behaviour is not intelligible as fulfilling requirements or permissions of that role. And at that point we might well seek intelligibility not in terms understood by the participant but in others, perhaps, for example, by seeking medical advice. In the same way, failures to grasp rules of action yield behaviour lacking significance in terms understood by the participants, though we may investigate such cases to determine that they are not significant unconventional or significant revolutionary acts. Perhaps the conductor not collecting fares works undercover for a company making private cars, hoping to destroy public transport. Again, the Marxist social worker's behaviour cannot be understood as an action rather than an aberration until her new role is clarified: 'Giving low priority to defence of family units and high priority to improvements in residential care in her area – what on earth is she up to?' The behaviour can then be understood as an action of a sort appropriate for someone in that role.

Let me now turn to the implications of this conception of human social relations for our moral relations with each other. Benson makes a point of saying that it would be a misinterpretation to suppose that rules of action all embody moral requirements. I think this is correct, but that he makes a mistake when he enlarges the scope of his claim by going on to say:

> By and large such rules do not prescribe what the occupant of a role must do on pain of being immoral.
>
> (1976: p. 242)

I say that the initial claim is correct for two reasons. First, because rules of action include both requirements and permissions, as we have seen, and to 'fail' in the latter is merely not to do what one is free not to do: except where the role itself is morally condemned, doing what one is free to do can hardly be morally condemned. Second, it is not true that in all cases the requirements of a role prescribe morally right actions, because, of course, some roles ought morally not to be occupied.

However, I baulk at the stronger claim made by Benson, that by and large we are under no moral obligation to follow rules of action. My grounds are to be found in Winch (1972). The argument draws upon a distinction, which may be drawn in respect of words and deeds, between what the words or deeds mean and what people mean by their words or deeds. In respect of words Winch says:

> People can only say something and mean it if they use words that mean something; and it belongs to the kind of meaning that words have that they can be used by people in statements that they [the people] mean. But this is only possible in a society where people are so related that for one person to say something is for him to commit himself with others; and an important part of such a relation is that there should be a common respect for truthfulness.
>
> (1972: pp. 65–6)

Except for cases in which we or the circumstances make it clear that we are not committed to the truth of what we say, we are committed to its truth and morally obliged to stand by it. This fact about commitment is what makes it possible to lie. We are committed by our words, and are taken to be committed, but we do not intend to stand by what we say.

In respect of deeds, Winch suggests that we talk of the commitment implied as a matter of integrity.

> To lack integrity is to act with the appearance of fulfilling a certain role but without the intention of shouldering the responsibilities to which the role commits one. If that, *per absurdum*, were to become the rule, the whole concept of a social role would thereby collapse.
>
> (1972: p. 70)

As we saw on the promenade, individuals lacking in integrity may unexpectedly let us down, to their own advantage, and this is precisely because they are committed by their deeds, and are taken to be committed to future acts prescribed by the rules of action for the role in question, such as paying-in fares collected, which they do not intend to carry out. And such lack of integrity may not always be motivated by self-interest. A probation officer, committed by word and deed to reporting his client's breaches of the probation order, may not intend to do so where the breach advantages his client but does not seriously disadvantage others.

To intend not to stand by what our words commit us to, or to lack integrity in a role, except where we make our intentions clear, is to exploit the context in which words and deeds have significance, misleading other language-users or members of our society. And so I would say that by and large we are under a moral obligation to stand by our words and to fulfil the requirements of rules of action governing the roles we occupy. Which is not to say that such obligations may not be overriden by stronger moral obligations in some circumstances.

The cases in question are, of course, what I earlier called examples of 'rule-abuse'. To use Benson's phrase, we indulge in rule-abuse 'on pain of being immoral'. But immorality of this sort does not occur where not following the rules stems from not grasping the requirements of a role, even though the failure to grasp the rules might be the result of negligence. Nor does it occur where not following the rules stems from partial or complete rejection of a role. There may, of course, be cases in which rejection of a role, or the new role occupied, is morally condemned, but in general revolutionaries make their intentions clear.

In any case, I have now paved the way for the conception of social policy I want to introduce. As I said earlier, I shall argue that social policy is to be distinguished from economic policy by its promotion of forms of social integration, and, in practice, by its promotion of forms of social relations held morally desirable (which is not to discuss by whom) in the society in question. Social policy will therefore inevitably concern itself with individuals not following rules of action, whether as a result of a failure to grasp those rules, rule-abuse or rejection of those rules.

Starting out from the views of Kenneth Boulding (1967) and Richard Titmuss (1968 and 1970), I have argued elsewhere (1980, Chapter 1), that we may distinguish social policy, in a narrow sense of the expression 'social policy', from economic policy, by the form of its appropriate justification: social policy, unlike economic policy, is justified by some kind of appeal to a moral status or identity or community. The same point may be expressed as a distinction between policy objectives: social policy, in contrast to economic policy, aims to create moral relationships between individuals, giving them moral status, or a moral identity in relation to others, relating them as members of a moral community. The distinction turns on arguments to the effect that economic policy promotes egoistic relationships, and that egoism is a non-moral motive, arguments which I cannot go into here (but see Williams 1973). In the present context, policies promoting fulfilment of the requirements of the rules of action of the role an individual occupies would be classified 'social' because of the moral commitment role-occupancy confers.

The view put forward, then, is that social policy may be distinguished from economic policy by the fact that its justification is moral in type; that is, moral as opposed to non-moral, rather than immoral. Of course, actual policies of this sort usually also aim to create relationships which are held morally desirable. And, of course, policies called 'social' in our society sometimes turn out to be merely 'so-called social policies' if we adopt this conception. Many policies we call 'social' turn out on this analysis to include elements which are economic (think of income-maintenance policies based on the insurance principle, for example, and their element of self-protection). I don't think this is a weakness. On the contrary, the theoretical distinction I adopt reveals a direction for critical appraisal of actual policies.

We might now compare social policies, as defined or so-called, by reference to the moral relationships they promote. Titmuss does just this in *The Gift Relationship*, urging us to consider, in relation to any social policy:

> whether these instruments or institutions positively create areas of moral conflict for society by providing and extending opportunities for altruism in opposition to the possessive egoism of the market-place.
>
> (1970: p. 13)

In that book, this is precisely the question Titmuss raises about social policies for obtaining blood for medical purposes, arguing that in this case a voluntary system fosters altruism while a commercial system stifles fellow-feeling (for further discussion of this claim see

Arrow 1972; Singer 1973). And in general this is the kind of question we raise in assessing social policies as status-enhancing or stigmatising, or in debating the implications of discretionary elements in those policies for levels of benefit needed or deserved by individuals.

To sum up this outline of my conception of social policy, let me simply record my general agreement with Boulding and Titmuss that the institutions with which social policy is especially concerned all reflect degrees of integration or community, that social policies promote different types of moral transaction to bring about and maintain social and community relations.

Our attempts to 'bring about and maintain social and community relations' through social policy are attempts to sustain and direct social integration. And in those attempts, as I said earlier, we must concern ourselves with individuals not following rules of action, for whatever reason. Social policy, that is, policy promoting forms of social integration, may now be seen more clearly as an instrument available in the defence of our society, defending the network of roles and relations which constitutes our society by maintaining rule-following, but, in addition, as an instrument available for the development of our society, allowing rule-following to lapse where we think it appropriate. Failure to follow particular rules, as a result of their not being grasped, rule-abuse, or role-rejection, might be tolerated or even encouraged in consciously modifying or eliminating roles within the network and thus changing our society.

At long last we are in a position to outline the positive contribution discretion can make in social policy. The discretion that I have in mind is what Ronald Dworkin (1977) calls discretion 'in the strong sense'. In this sense the individual, or tribunal, or whatever, is not bound by any standards set by the authority granting discretion. Though, as Dworkin hastens to add, this is not licence. Standards of rationality, fairness and effectiveness still apply, and permit criticism of decisions, but otherwise the decision-maker is free to act as he sees fit.

Discretion of this kind above all may be responsive to changes in the values prevailing in society, and if we regard this as desirable, such discretion may be commended as a suitable component in social policy. It seems to me that such discretion would best facilitate what is called 'creative' or 'individualised' justice, giving a system 'the capacity to respond to the special needs and circumstances of each individual' (Jones et al. 1978: pp. 143–4). It certainly seems to me to be desirable, *but only* where it is set in a context in which citizen participation and intelligibility to the parties feature strongly. It seems most suited where social policy is concerned with decisions about the prevention, tolerance or encouragement of failures to follow rules of action. On the account of human social relations given, social roles, and relations in which we occupy them, are sustained by our following the appropriate rules of action. Except where failures in rule-following are failures in grasping the rules, not to fulfil the requirements of a role we occupy is not to fulfil a moral obligation based in the expectations created by our occupancy of the role. In a society in which moral values are changing, we may wish to change the requirements of a particular role and welcome an opportunity to tolerate or encourage failures to fulfil the requirements in question. Discretion, in the strong sense, at the relevant point of decision, gives us such an opportunity.

Further, since social roles are sustained by our following them, and occupancy of a role may be described as a commitment to other members of our society to act according to the rules of action of the role in our society, it seems most appropriate if the discretion in question is granted to those to whom we are committed – our fellow members, or their representatives, or a representative group of them. It is the society in which they participate, society as they know it, which is challenged in the cases in question. In addition, because the rules to be followed are necessarily of a kind intelligible to participants in social action, failure may be identified and classified by laymen. No special knowledge is required for this, nor in decision-making, except in cases where rules have not been grasped, for what is to be decided is whether the challenge should be resisted, tolerated or encouraged. This question is to be answered by reference to our moral values, rather than to special knowledge. And all of us are, as laymen, fellow participants.

Indeed, as Giller and Morris argue (Chapter 4 in this volume) following Rees (1978), even where assessment is dominated by professional rather than lay participants, the focus is often upon what may be called 'the search for moral character'. Professional expertise may be necessary for the allocation of responsibility or its causal explanation, but neither the social worker nor anyone else has special expertise in the identification of behaviour as problematic. Granting the discretion in question to laymen is not a sufficient, but is a necessary, condition of a redistribution of power in social policy.

Finally, discretion in the strong sense, at the point in question in social policy, will allow us to identify more effectively the kind of failure in rule-following in any particular case, and better enable us to determine the future activities of the individual concerned if that individual himself participates fully in the decision-making. This is simply because the roles in question, and the rules governing them, are a construction explaining the behaviour of social beings in terms intelligible to them. Full participation helps all participants grasp the rules to be followed, bring into the open the role in which the individual encountered sees himself as acting, for criticism or encouragement, or helps bring into the open his demands for changes in his role and his own defence of his substantive rights. All of this assists fellow participants to express their decision in terms which describe a role the individual may occupy in future, because its rules are intelligible to him. But now my illustration is beginning to show, so I turn to it at once.

Illustration

I conclude with some comments on the system of Children's Hearings established under Part III of the Social Work (Scotland) Act 1968. I shall not describe the system in detail (see Martin and Murray, 1976), but draw attention to some of its features because it is a policy which aims to sustain and promote forms of social integration, and is therefore, on the conception earlier outlined, a social policy, promoting moral relations. In addition, it is a system in which discretion in the strong sense is granted to members of the Children's Panel, three of whom are the decision-makers, on any particular occasion, at what is called a 'Hearing'.

Let me illustrate this last point. Panel members, at a Hearing, have jurisdiction over a child who, with his parent, accepts that some 'ground of referral' is satisfied in respect of the child. And in every case, even if such grounds are accepted, and no matter which of the possible grounds are accepted, panel members may dispose of the case either by discharge or 'in accordance with such conditions as they may impose' (sections 43, 44 of the Act).

It is, further, a system in which the decision-makers, exercising this discretion, are lay (see Schedule 3 to the Act), and in which there is a requirement that, so far as panel members are able to achieve it, the individual required to attend a Hearing participate in the Hearing. Rule 17 of the Children's Hearings (Scotland) Rules 1971 (no. 492(S60)), requires discussion of the case with the child, parent and any representative attending, including taking steps to inform the child and his parents of 'the substance of any reports, documents and information if it appears material to the manner in which the case of the child should be disposed of and that its disclosure would not be detrimental to the interests of the child'. The decision, and reasons for it, must be stated at the time, and child and parent have a right to the statement in writing.

Finally, as one would expect of such a social policy, it is a system which concerns itself with individuals failing to follow rules of action not having grasped them; others lacking the integrity mentioned, and still others rejecting the social roles they occupy and the related requirements.

Children seen as sons, daughters, or just as 'children', are asked to make their being 'beyond parental control' intelligible. 'You've been told that obedience is a requirement. Don't you understand? or realise it's for the best?' Or, 'Do you think you can come home, let your mum get your tea, and then just go off and do as you please?' Or, 'What do you think you'll be like if you carry on as you are?'

Children who have 'failed to attend school regularly without reasonable excuse' and those who have 'committed an offence' are asked to do likewise. And, in discussion, panel members have discretion in the strong sense, because of the wording of the grounds, to suggest roles alternative to those presently occupied and in terms of which present behaviour is intelligible. Throughout such discussions, from the way in which children are encouraged to make their acts intelligible, or grasp what their acts suggest about themselves, to the 'compulsory measures of care' aimed at a return to neglected rule-following or intended to offer new relationships to individuals themselves neglected, the social values of participants are central. Without recourse to such values we could not determine, for example, how much control a parent should have over his child, and the point at which loss of control occurs and is a problem.

My illustration is not chosen in order to suggest that the system of

Children's Hearings is beyond reproach (see Brown and Bloomfield 1979); it is chosen as an example of a social policy based on the conception outlined above and centrally concerned with the issues one would expect. Further, it is an example of social policy incorporating discretion in the strong sense, at a point which makes the system a powerful instrument available in the defence or development of our society. And, finally, it illustrates such discretion in the hands of laymen, and the opportunity this gives for those subject to it to be criticised, tolerated or encouraged in their failures in rule-following, in terms intelligible to them as participants in our network of social roles.

Perhaps I need to stress that the system of Children's Hearings is not presented as typical of tribunals in social policy in the opportunities it offers for the defence or development of our society. Rather I would suggest it as a piece of social administration which indicates a direction for policy development if, to use the words of Bankowski and Nelken (Chapter 12 in this volume) we wish to move towards 'the type of society in which people can be trusted with power because they find themselves in positions which allow them to act according to the genuine emergent consensus of those communities that they serve and of which they are a part'.

My illustration, and support for discretion in the strong sense in the context of lay control and intelligible expectations, should not be taken to imply support for such discretion outside such a context. It would, of course, be absurd to claim that incorporation of discretion in the strong sense, regardless of opportunities for participation in discussion of failures in rule-following, will give us decisions on action intelligible to all concerned. Consider, for example, the discretion granted to professional social workers in their meetings with potential and actual clients, in decisions about acceptance of a referral, and, thereafter, their own commitment of time and other resources. In a recent study of client and worker perceptions of their meetings Rees (1978) concludes that 'the *social workers*' interpretations of people and their problems as worthy or unworthy were the criteria determining the outcome of negotiations' (p. 106, emphasis added). In this context, discretion in the strong sense allows professional social workers to express their moral values in decisions about the support they will give to clients in particular social roles and relations. However, Rees's study strongly suggests that the relative ignorance of the nature of social work among clients and referral agents seriously undermines participation and intelligibility to both parties to client–social-worker meetings. In such a setting, discretion in the strong sense is not responsive, but a one-sided and blunt component of social policy promoting social integration.

Granting discretion in the strong sense to decision-makers can yield decisions intelligible to all concerned only if participation is unimpeded by intimidation, withholding of relevant information, inexperience of participation in the form required in discussion of matters of the sort in question, *and so on:* there are many ways of reducing participation to public relations (see Jones et al. 1978: Chapter 6). And of course, even in Children's Hearings, actual participation is often weak for reasons of this kind. Further, as we have noted, an intelligible decision is not necessarily an agreed decision. We may understand each other's actions and not agree on what is right. It is of course sometimes necessary to enforce decisions taken by tribunals on matters relating to juvenile justice, income-maintenance, rents, and so on. Even so, it seems to me premature to regard participation of the sort described as unachievable, and so premature to regard intelligibility to all participants and even agreement and compromise among participants as beyond reach. We have begun to identify obstacles to participation, and so to intelligibility and agreement.[1] Of course, granting discretion in the strong sense to decision-makers in itself carries no implication for the promotion of participation. However, discretion in the strong sense, set in the context of the form of participation described, does make explicit the ideological character of decisions taken and opens up the possibility of sensitivity to changes in or conflicting social values, and the negotiation of a fair compromise.

Finally, I should like to say something further about the nature of our moral commitment in our social relations. I have said that the social roles we occupy (by our actions) entail moral obligations. In acting in a social role we acquire an obligation to fulfil its requirements, and a moral one at that, since our social identity raises particular expectations in others about our future actions. However, I also say that such obligations may be overridden by stronger moral obligations.

What I now add is that I am in no way suggesting that what morally ought to be done, in any particular circumstances, can be settled simply by reference to the rules of action of the particular society of which we are a member. Social acceptance of these rules does I think provide a moral reason for conventional behaviour, but not one that is conclusive. This is important because, if conventionality were conclusive in the matter of how one should behave, the idea of moral commitment itself would collapse. This is because there would be no moral agents. A moral agent is precisely someone who behaves as he does because he has reason to believe it is right, and who can reject behaviour which is conventional when it is in conflict with what is right. A moral agent may thus initiate change in what is conventional, and I have tried to characterise social policy incorporating discretion in the strong sense at key points as able to accommodate moral agents acting in this way – refusing to fulfil conventional role-requirements.

But what is right? Well, we come to our answers to this question through moral training and life with other members of the communities to which we belong as moral agents, learning its morally justifying or normatively cogent reasons, which yield actions maintaining its moral order. And this is not to say that 'morality is behaving as you were brought up to behave', nor is it a piece of sociology, such as the claim that what we call moral obligations are the pressures of society upon its members, generalised as rules of good behaviour and internalised through social training. Such a sociological claim, if true, which it is not, would leave no room for the concept of moral agency, for it would leave no room for such moral questions as 'why should I conform to the pressures of society?'. Such a claim leaves no room for a man to do something because it's right (cf. Murphy 1965).

12 Discretion as a Social Problem
Zenon Bankowski and David Nelken

Practical and theoretical concern over discretion is best seen, not as an invitation to study a particular area of decision-making, but as an index to anxiety over the possibilities of unregulated decision-making. Concern over discretion constitutes a social problem. It is part of the larger problem of the distrust of power endemic in western capitalist societies because of their relatively partial, open but ultimately unjustifiable hierarchies (Unger 1976). Suspicion of those who exercise power over others is partly allayed by the existence of legitimating institutions, practices and ideologies, of which the most important are those surrounding professionalism, science and law. The distrust of power, however, periodically re-emerges in a variety of particular contexts and, as with most social problems, the proposed solutions are often more inextricably tied up with the problems than their advocates realise. In this chapter we are concerned above all to engage with those formulations of the problems of discretion which assume that the application of rules, with the consequent benefit of accountability, can and should provide the solution to anxiety over the exercise of power. Much of what we say, however, should be of some relevance to those concerned with the adequacy of other existing institutionalised solutions to the problems of power.

We discuss first the meaning of discretion and argue that rules are not enough to deal with the problems posed by discretion and that they may sometimes be too much. In developing our argument we suggest that it is almost always useful to ask for whom discretion constitutes a problem. This is true, not only in so far as some groups stand to gain or lose in each situation where the reduction of discretion is proposed, but also in the secondary sense that those groups who are concerned about discretion construct the problem in the light of their material and ideal interests.

Next we consider the question of when discretion becomes a problem and claim that the present call for the return of the rule of law may be understood, more generally, as an aspect of the changing legitimations of authority in society. Such calls use the notion of the rule of law as a dependable resource at a time of fundamental change in the administrative direction of society. We then argue that there is, in the last resort, no escape from the problem of discretion through the use of rules because the distinction drawn between rules and discretion is so often untenable.

We conclude by arguing that, insofar as these points are persuasive independently and cumulatively, the problem of discretion will not be seen as that of finding the best methods of managing the managers of society. It is more that of creating the type of society in which people can be trusted with power because they find themselves in positions which allow them to act according to the genuine emergent consensus of those communities that they serve and of which they are a part. We do not mean this paper to be exhaustive but rather see it as a proposal for the reconstruction of discretion as a topic of research.

The Meaning of Discretion

The dictionary provides two meanings for discretion. The first is a complimentary character trait, as in 'a man of discretion' or even 'a man who uses discretion'; the second refers to the exercise of choice amongst alternatives, through which an appropriate solution is distinguished. Both senses of the word came into English usage in the fourteenth century, so that discretion (like the related term discrimination) was used to mean both 'the liberty or power of deciding' and also 'sound judgement'. Since there are pejorative overtones in some contemporary discussions of the best methods of controlling and reducing discretion, it is as well to recollect this more positive and approving way of talking about the same phenomenon. It suggests, as will be seen shortly, that discussions of discretion fundamentally entail moral assessments of other people's exercise of practical prudential reasoning. Because the existence and use of discretion is not, *per se*, reprehensible, it is important to enquire when, why and for whom discretion is a 'problem'.

Other ways in which it has become conventional to talk about discretion also affect any subsequent interrogations of its properties and proprieties. In particular, discretion in the sense of the exercise of choice is usually taken to refer to the way decisions are made by delegated authorities (Davis 1971; Chambliss and Seidman 1971). This is an understandable usage in legal contexts where discretion has to be defined in terms of normative rules, but it may be misleading in the case of other situations such as that of decision-making by professionals using their 'clinical' or 'scientific' judgement. Even where legal decisions are concerned, however, it can be important to distinguish, as Dworkin (1977) does, various meanings.

(1) A weak sense of the word where someone has to use their judgement but they are bound by the standards laid down by a higher authority. An order to the sergeant to select five experienced men would be such an example. The sergeant is bound by the notion of 'experienced' but has to use his judgement to decide what that is.

(2) A sense of weak discretion which really means that the person has the final authoritative interpretation of the rules – thus the football referee has the final say, during the game, as to whether or not something was against the rules. That is not to say, however, that he has a choice. This underlines the argument that talk of discretion is about the difficulty, in a liberal society, of trusting people with power. The proliferation of appeal tribunals with no real justification apart from an unwillingness to let the buck stop is an example of discretion in this sense.

(3) Discretion in the strong sense is when someone is simply not bound by standards set by the authority in question. The sergeant has this discretion when told to select any five men. 'We use this sense', Dworkin says, 'not to comment on the vagueness or difficulty of the standards, or on who has the final word in applying them, but on their range and the decisions they purport to control.' (p. 32).

For Dworkin, discretion in sense (1) and (2) is not arbitrary and in sense (3) it does not figure in the law (we deal with this point later). Inattention to the special features of these different situations can lead to errors, for example to sociological recommendations for the curbing of what is wrongly assumed to be the legitimate exercise of strong discretion where the issue is rather that of the practicality of legally limiting the improper abuse of weak discretion.

The restrictive concentration on decision-making by delegated authorities often has the indirect consequence of insulating from consideration the decisions and purposes of the higher authorities who charge them with their decision-making, even when it is assumed to be their objectives (such as the increasing interventionist role of the state) which are contributing to the problem of discretion. As will be seen, discussions of the problem of discretion often become confusing because of the unexamined and yet apparently unchallengable assumption that there needs to be more and more discretion which requires more and more control. Even where the discussion of the problem of discretion does attempt to embrace the role of the state and governments, it is not without awkwardness. If discretion is used as in legal contexts it raises the problem whether the best way to examine government action is to presuppose that it works within a framework of rules: if discretion is used in any other way it seems to merge into a discussion of choices, power, authority and the 'limits' of 'the state'. Discretion may then not be the best way of talking about these issues because it carries a behavioural referent which can obscure the significance of the political choices (the nondecisions) that never get into the agenda as possible options over which to exercise discretion (Lukes 1974).

Yet, paradoxically, it was precisely the problem of the discretion available to kings and aristocracies as higher authorities which was, in one form or another, at the centre of the European bourgeois revolutions (Neumann 1957). The problem of their arbitrary power was reduced through institutions concerned with achieving a separation and balance of powers and achieving the subservience of men to rules of law. It is these solutions which are reproduced now by those who, for reasons of their own, are worried about the extent and abuse of power by those occupying lower-levels of decision-making. It is a solution based squarely on a utilitarian–liberal conception of the nature and role of man and the state. On this view, the best society is that which allows maximum freedom to individuals to pursue their individual ends, compatible with the same freedom being allowed to others. In the same way as the market makes objective and rational the pursuit of individual self interest, so the law is the rational and universal way of choosing between men's arbitrary and particular preferences (Hegel 1976). No man can know another's best interests, yet there must be some authority to guarantee the order in which this competition takes place. But on this view of man's nature all power corrupts (absolutely) and it cannot safely be entrusted to men without some means of checking or reviewing its exercise. It follows therefore that a resort to rules is the major solution to the ever present dilemma of the arbitrary use of power.

Let us now look at the implications of this for the Dworkinian distinctions that we introduced earlier. It is difficult to distinguish between discretion in senses (1) and (2) and discretion in sense (3), for in both cases the sergeant is limited, for example, by the order to fetch 'men'. If the distinction is to make sense, then Dworkin must mean the following: that in (1) and (2) the decisions are limited by authority and come within the 'hole in the doughnut' and in (3) they do not. But sense (3) decisions, though outside the doughnut and thus not 'limited' are nevertheless liable to criticism by 'certain standards of rationality, fairness and effectiveness' (Dworkin 1977: p. 33) which is why these decisions are not tantamount to licence (see also Watson, Chapter 11 in this volume). But this implies that sense (3) decisions come within the 'doughnut' because they are subject to certain standards. If that is the case then the difference between weak and strong discretion is that in weak discretion the 'doughnut' is legality.

Strong discretion, or the problem of arbitrary power, cannot produce this justificatory context and so legality is seen as the solution. But we shall argue that legality fails as a satisfactory context and so the problem re-appears again not as 'How do the rules determine the decision?' but as 'How can decisions be justified by certain standards e.g. of rationality?', which is precisely the problem of strong discretion. This then is the problem: how to be wise and by prudential reasoning justify our actions. Thus, discretion as a general issue concerns power and the problem of how a society is to be organised justly and rationally. But, because it appears to be connected with rules it is used in a narrow sense where it is viewed either as a problem of legality or as the lack of a rule-bound solution.

This way of seeing it forecloses other determinations of the problem of arbitrary power – how peoples' particular choices are to be made rational. We will go into this in our conclusion but we briefly note here that there is another way of determining that choice and that is to conceive of a society where more, rather than less, people take part in decisions that determine their own lives, a society where formal rules, in the way that we talk of them, will not need to play such a part because the universal element in them is realised by everyone taking part in the decision. In such cases, it might be argued, discretion, in the broad sense that we isolated, will be solved in such a way as to get rid of the problem of discretion in the narrow sense which is how it appears in our society today.

Liberal political thought (e.g. in the work of J. S. Mill) also developed the germs of this other solution to the problem, based on the moral value of an individual's direct participation in the making of decisions that affected his interests – even though, at the time, it represented little more than an ideal. 'Give us participatory democracy – but not yet.' We discuss later why liberalism cannot implement this ideal fully and why the attempt can lead to horrifying consequences. But, for all the dangers, there is more to be gained by looking at the question of discretion in the light of this conception of democracy than by tamely accepting recent re-definitions of democracy which presuppose the permanent coexistence of an apathetic (and ignorant) populace managed by an official technocratic caste (Lukes 1977).

Why is Discretion a Problem?

Discussions of discretion, whether in general or with regard to specific contexts of legal administrative decision-making, are rarely 'innocent' of practical implications because they concern, and are part of, struggles for power. No simple equation can be made between more rules and more justice without enquiring who gains and who loses under the proposed changed arrangements. These points are not new; Adler and Asquith (Chapter 1 in this volume) rightly discuss discretion in relation to power, even if they sometimes seem to share the conventional wisdom that discretion is a source of power and only hint at the equally important possibility that rules may, on other occasions, be an even more potent source of power for those who lay them down. But there is room for further illustration of what is lost when the problem of discretion, in particular settings and in general, is detached from the wider social issues in which it is embedded.

We start from the specific: take, for example, the question whether it is a good thing to have diversion schemes which avoid subjecting first offenders to prosecution. This criterion has the merit of involving only a limited increase in official discretion. But what if this leads to the police 'letting off' middle-class, rather than working-class, offenders because the latter tend to have more delinquency convictions? If an alternative scheme avoided this outcome, but entailed more discretion, would the price be worth paying? (See Walker 1974; Nelken 1976).

When discretion is looked at as part of a larger picture the issues that are raised are not only whether it would be good to increase or reduce its ambit, but also how far it is feasible to do so. By this we do not mean merely the familiar difficulty of checking on checks or guarding the guardians, but the problem that the social circumstances that nourish and sometimes mandate the use of discretion do not disappear when the opportunity to exercise it is curtailed. Officials charged with the regulation of powerful groups often carry out their tasks in ways that make extensive use of innovatory discretion – both of the legitimate, weak variety and the strong illegitimate sort. One of us studied the records of the private hearings of Family Practitioner Committees which deal, *inter alia*, with dentists who are suspected of having given their patients unnecessary fillings. Those that are found 'guilty' of what is euphemistically termed a breach of their contracts suffer a small reduction of their NHS payments. The discretionary decision-making which directs cases to these hearings, as well as the manner in which cases such as the above are handled, testify to the delicate symbiosis of interests involved in the management of an independent profession working under conditions of state sponsorship (see Johnson 1972). There can be no simple solution to the exercise of this discretion which would not risk the benefits of such a hard-worn compromise. Even if some new arrangement was developed, it might be expected to reflect somewhere these same troublesome elements of relative power.

The point becomes even clearer when applied to the reverse situation. For discretion can be used, sometimes, to insulate the relatively powerless from the full force of legal or administrative action at their expense. Officials can use their position to provide a buffer against the effects of legislative or administrative action when this is, at best, misconceived, and, at worst, designed to punish politically insignificant groups in the service of other ends. An example is provided by the activities of those local authority officials who are responsible for enforcing the criminal, anti-harassment provisions of the 1965 Rent Act. Observation of their work in London reveals that they find themselves dealing almost entirely with poor, and often confused, resident immigrant landlords rather than with the Rachmanite business-types depicted in public descriptions of the legislation and its impact. Although most harassment officers (who are usually ex-policemen) nonetheless endeavour to produce at least a small regular supply of criminal prosecutions, a few take it upon themselves to treat the whole problem of harassment as one which necessitates a sort of social work approach to the difficulties of both landlords and tenants. They therefore use their discretion to avoid preparing cases for prosecution. To insist on the abolition of this discretion might provide feedback for the legislators to enable them to improve the efficiency of the legislation, although this could also worsen the outcome for some of those affected by it. For it can be argued that the present system at least allows some officials to avoid further and needless criminalisation of a marginal group in society – something they could not do if discretion were abolished (Nelken 1981).

We do not suggest that in practice the presence of discretion always represents such a potential for benefiting the underprivileged. On the contrary, it is to be expected that, on the whole, officials will use their discretion to ease their tasks by directing their unpleasing attentions at those who cannot fight back. But we do argue that it is this potential which must stand as the main criterion of our own evaluation of discretion in any particular case, rather than a commit-ment for or against discretion in the abstract. It further follows that an increase in discretion is generally to be favoured when it allows for greater lay participation in administration. We do not make light of the difficulties of avoiding co-option by 'experts' or officials under such circumstances, but, again, it is this which worries us rather than the pure fact of an increase in discretionary decision-making.

In the general debate over discretion it is obvious that what is really required is a sociology of the growth of concern over discretion as a social problem. A full account cannot be provided here but such an analysis would surely point, *inter alia*, to the interests of the legal profession in colonising the area of tribunals and other welfare-state agencies (see Bankowski and Mungham 1978). In addition, it would include the practical concerns of those administrators (and their academic advisers) engaged in achieving specific effects through their social engineering programmes. It must also be noted that the libertarian critique of front-line officialdom which was the hallmark of the sociology of law and deviance in the 1960s also bears an indirect relationship to the latter interests. As Gouldner (1968) unkindly remarked, it was an approach which allowed the sociologist to feel radical while remaining well-heeled as a result of central government research sponsorship.

The interests that animated concern over discretion (and still do) necessarily impose their own boundaries on the way the problem is conceived and tackled. The lawyer's concern with formal justice and accountability leads him to be worried about the possible abuse of rights consequent on leaving important decisions to bureaucrats, or even worse, to laymen (as in the critique of Scottish Children's Panels). It does not, strangely, give rise to the same anxiety about the exercise of sentencing discretion by judges. On the other hand the interests of 'social engineers' (whether politicians or academics) drives them to try to understand, and curb, both extensive legitimate weak discretion and the abuse of discretion. It is because the practical implications are the same that they find there is little point in distinguishing the two cases.

One interesting demonstration of the redirection of intellectual interest as such immediately practical concerns are left behind may be provided by a brief account of recent developments in the study of the so-called 'gap' problem in the sociology of law. Many early studies of the discrepancies between legal norms and legal behaviour, between 'law in books' and 'law in action', tended to assume, in accordance with social engineering concerns, that 'the problem' consisted of why judicial decisions, legislative programmes, or administrative regulations were refracted or redefined by the officials who implemented them. This type of research was soon criticised for building into its starting point implausible, and often normative, presuppositions about the way in which law might be expected to affect behaviour (see Abel 1973; Black 1972; Galanter 1977; Friedman and Macaulay 1977: pp. 21–7).

The findings of studies cast in this mode also tended towards the sociological commonplace; the re-discovery of informal alongside formal organisation, the realisation that law jobs were, after all, also jobs, and were subject to the same organisational and personal constraints and objectives found in the study of other work settings.

From a social-engineering viewpoint, and also in many ways from a legal and moral standpoint, the practical problems posed by these findings ensure that they will continue to be the centre of attention even when their intellectual surprise-value is long exhausted. But there are serious objections to the assumption that closing 'the gap' is simply a matter of altering the conditions and circumstances of those who materialise it in their practice. Thus, some studies into the gap problem, both before and after these criticisms were levelled, were less struck with the evidence of divergence as such and more interested in using such findings as an index of the relationship between law and society. Most of these studies drew on an ill-defined sociological 'conflict' perspective (varying from pluralist to *soi-disant* Marxist), which supposed that 'society' was best understood as an unstable concoction of competing interest and status groups (or else classes). The passage and operation of law was taken to reflect the relative power of these competing groups, and the exercise of discretion was understood to be one means of preserving the appearance that law treated all like cases justly by covertly adjusting the law in practice to the realities of power. Despite the attractiveness and wide applicability of these studies there is a great deal that they left unexplained. Power was nothing more complicated than the flexing of economic, political or ideological muscle; law, and traditions and values, were instruments or resources to be deployed at will; social groups engaged in Darwinian struggle in the social jungle were both the beginning and the end-point of the analysis of social structure.

Most of the recent considerations of the law–society relationship (often still on the theoretical drawing-board) have abandoned the straightforward instrumentalism of 'conflict' studies, to develop and return to conceptions of society which see the form and content of law as an aspect of the structure and culture of the social totality (see Nelken 1980a). The concern here is with the way that law helps to transform power into authority, on the limits imposed on it by the social relations in the society and which it imposes in turn on subordinate groups (classes) and, to some extent, also on those who rule. The significance of discretion can be located in a number of areas within the theoretical space opened by this approach. Often, as in the case of the value of discretion for legitimation, this will be no more than a new variation on an old tune. But this will not always be so. In particular there is one way of discussing discretion, in terms other than its advantages as an instrument for social groups, which is worth considering separately.

When is Discretion a Problem?

We again make no claim to originality in advancing the view than an appeal to rules and procedures may have more to do with changes and movements in ideas rather than in material resources. Adler and Asquith (Chapter 1 of this volume), for example, point to the way in which the drive for procedural equality can distract our attention from the failure to provide substantive equality. The difficulty lies in finding the appropriate terms with which to talk about this subject. Exactly what ideological claims are being made by (or for) the law? Is substantive equality itself a coherent concept? Is the provision of equality an empirical possibility? Is it desirable? Is it something that has ever been claimed for the law? (and who speaks for the law?) Is ideology necessarily a matter of converting people through persuasive claims, or is it more a matter of preventing the formulation of alternative understandings or even simply, or not so simply, the reproduction of existing social relations of production? Part of the difficulty here arises from the unsatisfactory conception of ideology as 'mere' appearance.

Another set of issues concerns who (or what) produces ideological claims. Discussing these processes in terms borrowed from the conflict perspective can lend an air of implausibility to the whole argument. For example, does the government really call for an increase in concern over procedural legality each time it sees in the offing the need for financial cut-backs in welfare provisions? As this suggests, it is also important to be able to explain when such ideological issues became significant. In short, why is discretion now seen as a problem?

There is no way in which we could attempt to do justice to these issues here, but there are some valuable and particularly relevant suggestions in the analysis of the politics of welfare–capitalist states in the work of members of the Frankfurt School of Sociologists such as Claus Offe and Jurgen Habermas (see Offe 1976 and Habermas 1976a and 1976b). The crux of their argument is, as Offe puts it, that on the one hand 'unconditional technocratic rationality can only flourish in the shadow of ideological postulates' (1976, p. 419), whilst, on the other hand, key legitimating themes of these same societies 'reflect' the standards and values of an earlier bourgeois order. The growth of the interventionist state with its increasing directly productive and administrative rules leads to a weakening of these traditional values, without their being replaced by any stable set of alternative (plausible) standards. They give several examples of this:

(1) The ideology of an earlier period of capitalism made much of the principle that social compensation should be distributed by the market, according to individual achievement. This has now, substantially, been replaced by a more technocratic principle that the yardstick of reward should be professional training and skill. This justification of reward has not been fully accepted.

(2) The values of possessive individualism presuppose that maximum wealth will be guaranteed by a process in which each individual has the maximum opportunity to pursue his interests. But there is now only a constricted area in which this principle can still make sense, because except for the often artificially-stimulated competition for consumer goods, conditions of life in society have come to depend more and more on the creation and maintenance, by the state, of a collective economic and welfare infrastructure.

(3) There are increasing sections of the population, and even greater areas of social activity, which are no longer oriented to the exchange values of traditional bourgeois society. But there is no satisfactory, in the sense of officially recognised, legitimating rationalisation of these areas.

There are therefore a number of ambiguities or incoherences (which for Habermas constitutes a crisis) in the fit between the traditional legitimations which still influence the form of human motivations and the somewhat different requirements of late capitalist societies, which cannot (at least as yet) be legitimated as such. These ambiguities are reproduced through determinants which apply at a number of levels. The state, in late capitalist societies, pursues the goal of economic growth in ways that entail continuing reliance on private market institutions of investment and production, both for the satisfaction of those needs that the market finds profitable to satisfy and to provide the surplus from which collective social goals are pursued. At another level, the factors that influence all economic decision-making are supposedly technical–rational ones which can have little reference to public opinion and choice, though this is the legitimation of the democratic state. For these reasons neither the bourgeois ethos that justifies reliance on the market, nor the 'scientific' ethos that justifies administrative decision-making can be dispensed with, and both exist in uneasy cooperation.

The point which emerges from this discussion is that legitimations do not exist simply so that political manipulation can continue undisturbed by popular discussion. What needs to be understood is that there are objective limits to the extent to which the cultural realm can be manipulated, in any effort to make up the weakening of traditional legitimations. As Habermas notes

> The cultural system has a peculiarly resistant attitude to administrative control. There can be no *administrative creation of meaning*, only ideological retailing of cultural values. The creation of legitimation is self-destructive as soon as the mode of 'creation' is seen through. A systematic limit to efforts to make up for deficits in legitimation by attempted manipulation thus consists in the structural dissimilarity between the areas of administrative action and cultural tradition.
>
> (1976a: p. 377, emphasis in original)

Seen in this light, the debate over discretion as a symptom of administrative tyranny appears as a sign of the deepening ambiguity between old and new cultural themes in a period of transition.

Some commentators on discretion may therefore be seen as in fact preparing the way for a whole-hearted embrace of technocratic rationality as the justification of administrative decisions – even whilst they appear to be warning of what will be lost by the move to bureaucratic–administrative law. They do this by exaggerating the extent to which the latter is essentially different and subject to different methods of technical evaluation in comparison with all that has preceded it (cf Tay and Kamenka 1975; Tay, Kamenka and Brown 1978; Nelken 1980b). For a somewhat different analysis see Winkler (1975 and Chapter 5 in this volume). Other authors pursue very similar arguments in which it is usually assumed that the problem is a new one. It is claimed that rules cannot be expected to govern the process of creating and managing resources and benefits (now the prominent role of the state) in the same way or with the same methods that were successfully employed in the past to restrict the role of the 'Law and Order State', when the greatest fear was of unlawful expropriation (see Aubert 1978).

On the other side, writers such as Hayek, with even less desire for the growth of the planned welfare state, reach a similar conclusion about the inapplicability of governing it by rules by insisting that law can be used to adjudicate over claims to rights but not as a basis for judging policy determinations. It seems, in sum, that the problem of discretion now is precisely that it can no longer be resolved in traditional ways, and this will bring us, eventually, to our concluding comments.

Naturally enough, however, not all writers are so pessimistic about the capacities of rules to continue to supply the answer to the problem of power in society. In the next section we turn therefore to a consideration of recent contributions to the debate over the actual and ideal modes of legal reasoning to be followed under contemporary conditions.

Discretion and the Problem of Adjudication

As we have said, in liberal society, the problem of unjustified power becomes something which is solved by law so that power becomes rule bound and not arbitrary. Now this solution to the problem of order and freedom has many problems and philosophers from Kant to Rawls have exercised themselves with trying to justify the law. It is not our intention, in this paper, to go into the success or failure of these attempts but rather to look to the problem when it hits at the concrete point of rules, that is the application of these general rules to discrete instances. This is important because the 'legal' solution necessarily implies adjudication. It is here that the problem of arbitrary power again appears – for how are individual decisions made under the general rules to be justified. And so the problem of discretion, which we saw was at base a very general one about the organisation of power in civil society, reappears as a problem of the solution to that problem. That is why, here, we link the problem of discretion with the problem of adjudication. Because of this, attempts to solve the latter solely in the terms that it presents itself will fail because it stems from and is caused by conditions that go to the very root of liberal society itself.

Why is the problem of adjudication, which is closely bound up with discretion, a problem? The main answer is simply that formal justice – seen in very simplistic terms – cannot work because general rules cannot determine all individual outcomes. Put simply, the Blackstonian picture of the legal universe where judges discover and do not create the common law is not true. There cannot then always be a 'right answer' that the judges have to pronounce. The formalist mode of legal justice cannot be true because rules do not have an essential meaning which allows them to subsume all instances of their application clearly and without doubt. As Hart (1961: pp. 123–5) says, 'there is a limit, inherent in the nature of language, to the guidance which general language can provide'. Law may sometimes be indeterminate because of its 'open texture'. Moreover, according to Hart, our 'relative ignorance of fact' and 'relative indeterminacy of aim' in framing general rules in advance makes it necessary and desirable to exercise choice in subsequent applications of the rules. It is here that discretion appears as the problem of the gap wherein our choices are arbitrary and unjustified.

What is to be done about these cases and how is the gap to be closed and the problem of discretion solved? The standard way out of this conundrum has been to adopt forms of what can be described as purposive legal reasoning. But this retreat from formalism creates more problems than it solves and seems in the end to show the bankruptcy of the solution of the broad problem of discretion by law. Why is this so? Purposive legal reasoning recognises that there can be no essential meaning to a statute and that all meanings are to some extent conventional. When therefore problems of meaning and application of general laws arise they cannot be solved by attention to a timeless meaning of the statute. Rather one has to look to the purposes and intention of the legislators. Thus we look to the point of the statute rather than its meaning, to why the statute was passed, what mischief it wanted to prevent, etc. In this way then we can get some non-arbitrary choice because what we are trying to do is to put into effect the purpose of the Act and the desires and intentions of those who legislated for it. Now the problem of sorting out legislative intention is enormous and has been the subject of numerous works (cf Twining and Miers 1976). What we are interested in here is not so much the details but the style of this particular form of reasoning. What we find distinctive here is the concentration of purpose and effect in relation to the consequences that individual decisions will have for general cases. But this attempt to objectify the arbitrariness and indeterminacy of decision-making has devastating effects for a system of general rules. For if statutes can have many purposes and functions, then what we need is a criterion for deciding which purposes and which policies the judges are to claim as adhering to any particular statute. That becomes the great stumbling block of this form of reasoning and, in attempted solutions, appeals to 'reasonableness' and 'rationality' abound in situations where the problems (of discretion) have been caused precisely by a lack of any acceptable criterion of what is 'the reasonable decision' or 'the rational choice'.

The problem lies deeper than this. For this mode of reasoning subverts the idea of law as a solution to the problem of power and thus of discretion in the broad sense in which we have characterised it. For when, in our reasoning, we have to look to purposes and effects to make sense of the rules, then that implies that the rules themselves cannot be prescriptive as they are claimed to be in the legal solution. Rather they are themselves liable to be interpreted or ignored by the adjudicator. The ultimate question when deciding upon the application of a rule to a particular case is whether the ends of the legal rule in particular and the legal order in general are served by this particular judgement. Therefore that rule can never be final. It will always be a judgement of instrumental rationality as to whether or not the rule should be applied in a particular way. If that is the case then that rule cannot, as in a regime of legal justice it ought to, stand prescriptive and before the decision. One can try and escape this dilemma in three ways.

Firstly, it can be insisted that certain rules are to be sacrosanct. But that raises two problems. First, what criteria will there be to decide which laws are to be sacrosanct or thus 'entrenched'? History has shown that that decision is not an immediately obvious one and has often been severely contested. Second, even if a solution can be found to the first problem, the issue of formalism reappears with respect to these entrenched provisions.

Secondly, one can attempt to solve the problems presented by the first solution by saying that the only decisions and laws that should *not* be sacrosanct are those that are hard cases. Or to put it in terms of the 'golden' rule of statutory interpretation: apply the plain meaning of the statutes when that is obvious and when it is not, look to the intentions and purposes, etc., of parliament. The problem with this second solution stems from the notion that the only problem with a 'hard case' is how to solve it. That is not true – for one of the great difficulties in the notion of a 'hard case' is to define precisely what is meant by that, and how it is to be distinguished from a 'simple case'. For how are we to define the 'obvious' or literal meaning of a statute. The problem then is not to say when something is 'hard' but to say when something can be simple. To appeal to literal English is, in the end, not enough because that will always be coloured by the context in which that literalness is to be understood. Thus 'obvious' is how the lawyers see it – and if that is the case then of course we cannot be said to have a 'simple' answer to what is a simple case. Cases that deal with statutes embodying strict liability are a good example. Thus a statute that makes it an offence to allow a dwelling to be used for the smoking of marijuana might seem obvious and have a plain sense but some judges felt that it could only have such a sense if the word 'knowingly' was read into the statute (Sweet v Parsley [1969] 2 WLR 470).

Thirdly, there is the argument that the constraint here could be that of formal justice; like cases ought to be decided alike. There are two problems here, first, it is not at all obvious that 'like' is as clear as it seems. Thus, to take a Leibnitzian view, if two things were in fact identical then one could not distinguish them and they would be one thing. What is important, then, is to classify something as the same in certain respects and the problem is to find which respects are relevant to this process. Second, even if the case is held to be relevantly similar then one has to decide the further question of whether or not the principle under which that categorisation has been made is to be applied and thus extended to the instant case (Rondel v. Worsley (1969) 1 A.C. 161).

Neil MacCormick's (1978) account is perhaps the most incisive and rigorous plea for a form of purposive legal reasoning. His solution to these problems relies on an appeal to what he calls consequentialism. The process that he recommends is to test competing legal rules by seeing what their universalisable consequences are within the context of the coherency of the legal system as a whole. Consequentialism generates a procedure for testing but the process of generating the hypotheses and the ultimate guarantee of the rationality of decision-making stand upon their coherence and 'fit' within the legal system itself. This way of looking at legal reasoning has, as MacCormick admits, remarkable similarities with Karl Popper's theory of 'scientific method'. The process is one where the scientist makes a hypothesis (universal general legal rule) that rationalises facts in the world and then tests it by constructing experiments which are likely to falsify it. The more times that it is not falsified the more likely it is to be true. There remains a problem, however, about how the hypotheses are to be generated. Since the non-falsified hypothesis is our guarantee of fit with the world then there must necessarily be some procedure of selection – otherwise we could pick any crazy hypothesis we like and that, if not falsified but logically able to be, would have as much truth-value as any other one. The guarantee of fit that Popper in fact uses is its acceptability as a coherent hypothesis within the community of science. MacCormick says much the same thing in his account of legal reasoning. The generation of the rules and their ultimate guarantee of fit rests upon their having a 'legal warrant' – his term for coherence and consistency. When unpacked this comes down to precedent, statutes and the like which are themselves to be looked at and justified in terms of consequentialism. So what emerges finally from his project is a system which turns in on itself and gains whatever objectivity it has from the reflexive equilibrium that the judges construct. If this is the case it follows that the legal system that the judges are bound by is binding only because they agree to be bound by it. Just as science is ultimately, in Popper's theory, what scientists do, so law is what judges do and its guarantee of objectivity, or 'fit' in Popper's terms, is that they are a caste who have for centuries been socialised in a particular way (cf Simpson 1973).

We will have more to say of this notion, which can be seen as demonstrating the significance of shared values, when we come to discuss our alternative solution to the problems with which we began our paper. We now turn to the way our analysis of MacCormick's work enables us to see the faults in some of the ways that the problem of discretion is presented to us. What our analysis has shown is that the prior rules necessary to legal justice cannot be objectively entrenched, and what that shows is that 'government of law and not men' is really and strictly 'government of some men'.

This has one particularly important implication. Many commentators see the problems posed by discretion for a theory of adjudication as something that stems from what Tay and Kemenka (1975) have called the bureaucratic–administrative mode of law as against *gesellschaft* law which is taken to be the expression of legal justice. Thus Adler and Asquith (Chapter 1 in this volume), drawing on Tay and Kamenka make the following distinction:

> '*Gesellschaft* law' . . . arises out of, and is based on, atomic individualism and private interests. Each person stands before the law as a holder of rights and duties, as a legal person and not someone trailing status and history after him. The emphasis is on formal procedure, impartiality and adjudicative justice. The model for all law is contract and the *quid pro quo* : this is achieved by the fact that all persons are regarded as equal before the law. A distinction is made between law and administration, and between the legal, the political and the moral. This type of law is most clearly expressed in individualistic *laissez-faire* society where there is a sharp distinction between the public and the private but where the public or state interest is defined as just another, sometimes overriding private interest.
>
> In 'bureaucratic–administrative law' the concern is not . . . with a *laissez-faire* society composed of private individuals but rather with the pursuit of public policy in which individuals are seen as agents rather than holders of rights and duties as they were under '*gesellschaft* law'. The point of this type of law is to provide for the regulation of an activity rather than adjudicate disputes between individuals. It predominates in a managerial directive type of society. Tay and Kamenka see it as most fully developed in Eastern Europe socialist states but it clearly exists wherever the state assumes a regulatory role over the economy and within society and a concern with promoting the 'public interest' and the 'general good'. 'Bureaucratic–administrative law', they claim, elevates the socio-technical norm against the private right of the *gesellschaft* . . .'

Although there is a distinction in what the modes of law address themselves to, it is not necessary to see discretion as something inherent in bureaucratic–administrative law. We have argued that legal justice or *gesellschaft* law also cannot solve the problem of discretion. If we look to the reasoning involved in the bureaucratic–administrative system we see that it is characteristically composed of broad general rules which the bureaucrats have to apply to get the system working efficiently and see that the purposes of the system get fulfilled. Put this way this does not appear all that different to the theoretical end-point that we came to in our analysis of purposive legal reasoning. Indeed MacCormick's book could easily be used as a textbook for bureaucrats. And lawyers of a more formalist bent have always seen this type of theorising as really 'legal' theory for managers (cf Fuller 1969).

However, since on this argument the extensive use of purposive reasoning is always required by the logic of the judicial process, there is no real theoretical distinction between the two modes of law. Thus the choice of either rules or discretion is not one which can be theoretically justified. Adler and Asquith sometimes seem to assume that discretion is something that is inherent in bureaucratic–administrtive systems and that a call for a return to legality is wrong because the policy goals of bureaucratic–administrative systems are not amenable to judicial control. Our suggestion is that they are as amenable to control as the *gesellschaft* system's own basic principles, but that these are necessarily also an object of arbitrary power which substitute the guarantee of one set of people for another. Going back to legality is frequently a waste of time, at that level, precisely because it does not change this aspect of the situation. But if it does not make a difference in these terms does it follow that it does not matter which type of law is in operation and how far decisions are supposedly made subject to rules?

We claim that offering a solution in terms of rules does make some difference because it prevents attempts at a broader solution to the problem of power. We now go on to look at the range of alternative solutions to the problem of power and the road which we find most attractive.

Conclusion

We live in a changing society, increasingly technical and technocratic, in which the sort of rank hierarchies secured by a 'government of laws and not men' are no longer authoritative. The solution of law, which seemed to contain the problem of the unjustified exercise of power, is no longer now even seen as doing so. It is within this context – that of the breaking down of the old certainties – that we must ask 'Where do we go from here and what are the possibilities of any alternative conception?' Let us then look at where the possibilities take us.

To recapitulate our argument: if we take the road of legality and rules we are taking a backward road because the growing interventionist state is making it impossible to maintain that as an objective and justified solution. We showed how the government of law always becomes, in reality, the government of man because it is forced to rely on an institutional consensus. Because of this, and notwithstanding its ideology of freedom, law remains an institution which is not susceptible to popular control. Put a different way, the more it is subject to popular control, the more it is subject to genuine shared values and then the reason for its existence as a solution disappears. If people were really in agreement there would be no need for the legal solution. Thus the pull of the legal solution is always to the rule of the few and the legal solution is the enemy of full participatory democracy.

The bureaucratic solution, on the other hand, is to make the choice fit under the ideology of scientific rationality – the answer to arbitrary choice is provided by the scientific ideologies of workers and the like. But there is a difference. For when the point is to redistribute and look more closely at the taken for granted hierarchies, then science is not enough and democratisation seems to force its way in. The idea that choices can be made objective by people participating in and controlling decisions about them – the idea of shared values – must play a part. Indeed the tension in those areas is between scientific ideologies and community power. This provides the setting in which we might see possibilities of ways forward, in which the problem of discretion, that is of arbitrary power, can be solved if we all agree to and take part in, the making of choices (cf Watson, Chapter 11 in this volume).

But the idea of shared values, or 'community' is redolent with pitfalls. There is the problem that 'community' might be used, as Winkler (Chapter 5 in this volume) points out, as an ideological device to co-opt groups and make them manage themselves for state purposes. Also, in a liberal society in which people are believed to have logically subjective values, the idea of objective shared values is always precarious or contingent. It is assumed that 'community' will mean not the genuine community of all but rather the community of a few, and we readily concede that appeals to the symbol of community have served to cover the most horrifying abuses of power (cf Bankowski and Mungham 1978; Bankowski 1979).

But to say that this actually happens is not to say that that is all there can be. The point of this paper has not been to anticipate utopia but to look at, and try to understand, present-day movements. Our point is that one cannot understand the problems that are the topic of this book in terms of a simple minded distinction between rules and discretion or, to be more theoretical, between *gesellschaft* and bureaucratic–administrative systems. Both these models try objectively to rationalise and justify the use of power. Both ultimately depend for this, as we have shown, on the institutionalised consensus of the few. This can lead to abuses of power which often present themselves as the problem of discretion.

We believe that, in the long term, these problems can only be solved by letting more and more people have power. This being so, we cannot solve the problem by adopting one or the other model. Rather we must work towards our goal by using the opportunities and safeguards that both offer.

Notes on Contributors

Michael Adler: Lecturer in Social Administration at the University of Edinburgh. He is currently engaged in research on statutory debt enforcement. With A. W. Bradley, he is co-editor of *Justice, Discretion and Poverty* (1975), a critical assessment of Supplementary Benefit Appeal Tribunals.

Stewart Asquith: Lecturer in Social Administration at the University of Edinburgh. His main research interests are in the areas of juvenile justice and social philosophy.

Zenon Bankowski: Lecturer in Jurisprudence at the University of Edinburgh. He is author (with G. Mungham) of *Images of Law* (1976) and several articles on law and politics, and editor (also with G. Mungham) of *Essays in Law and Society* (1980).

Jonathan Bradshaw: Director of the Social Policy Research Unit in the Department of Social Administration and Social Work at the University of York. His publications include (with K. Jones and J. Brown) *Issues in Social Policy* (1979), *The Family Fund: An Initiative in Social Policy* (1980) and (with D. Piachaud) *Child Support in the European Community* (1980).

Henri Giller: Lecturer in Law at the University of Keele. He was formerly research assistant in the Institute of Criminology at Cambridge, where he wrote numerous articles on juvenile justice with Allison Morris, and also with her co-authored *Justice for Children* and *Care and Discretion*.

F. H. McClintock: Professor of Criminology and Director of the School of Criminology and Forensic Studies at the University of Edinburgh. Amongst his publications are *Attendance Centres* (1961), *Robbery in London* (1961), *Crimes of Violence* (1963), (with N. H. Avison) *Crime in England and Wales* (1968), and (with A. E. Bottoms) *Criminals Coming of Age* (1973).

Tom McGlew: Lecturer in Sociology and Director of the Social Demography Research Unit at Edinburgh University. His research interests are in the areas of demography and medical sociology.

Allison Morris: Lecturer, Institute of Criminology at Cambridge. She has written extensively in the field of juvenile justice and her publications include (with M. McIsaac) *Juvenile Justice?* (1978), (with Henri Giller, Elizabeth Szwed and Hugh Geach) *Justice for Children* (1980) and (with Henri Giller) *Care and Discretion (1980)*.

David Nelken: Lecturer in Sociology of Law in the Department of Jurisprudence at the University of Edinburgh. His publications *include Landlords, Law and Crime* (1981), and several articles on the sociology of law and criminology.

David Noble: Research Assistant in the Faculty of Laws, University College, London. He has conducted research into the voluntary housing movement and has written on the 1974 Housing Act.

Tony Prosser: Lecturer in Law and member of the Centre for Criminological and Socio-legal Studies at the University of Sheffield. His research interests are in the sociology of law and he has written several articles on welfare law.

Alex Robertson: Lecturer in the Department of Social Administration at the University of Edinburgh. Author of a number of articles on mental disorder, penal policy, and current trends in welfare policy, he is also Director of a research project investigating the experiences of men released from Scottish prisons.

Gilbert Smith: Formerly Reader in the Department of Social Administration and Social Work at Glasgow University, he has recently been appointed Professor of Social Administration at the University of Hull. He is the author of *Social Work and the Sociology of Organisations* (2nd Edition 1979) and *Social Need: Policy, Practice and Research* (1980), and various articles on sociology and social policy.

David Watson: Lecturer in the School of Applied Social Studies, University of Bristol. His publications include *Talking about Welfare* (1976), *Philosophy and Social Work* (1978) (both co-edited with N. Timms) and *Caring for Strangers* (1980).

J. T. Winkler: Lecturer in Sociology in the Social Policy Unit at the Cranfield Institute of Technology. He has published major articles on corporatism in the *European Journal of Sociology* and the *British Journal of Law and Society*.

Ken Young: Senior Research Fellow at the Policy Studies Institute, London. His publications include *Local Policies and the Rise of Party* (1975), *Essays on the Study of Urban Politics* (1975) and (with John Kramer) *Strategy and Conflict in Metropolitan Housing* (1978).

Notes

Introduction

1. A report on the workshops (Adler and Asquith 1979) and copies of each of the papers that were discussed is available from the Social Science Research Council, 1 Temple Avenue, London EC4Y 0BD. The report itself is in three parts: in the first part we summarise each of the papers that were discussed; in the second part we identify the major themes which emerged from the papers and the discussions which they provoked, and discuss their implications for future research; while in the third part we put forward a research agenda and indicate, where appropriate, those methodological and theoretical approaches which seem to us to be most promising.

Chapter 4

1. This study was undertaken with the financial assistance of the DHSS, although responsibility for its form and content is entirely our own. Those interested in a more detailed analysis of our findings should see Giller and Morris (1981).
2. Our findings have been presented to the social workers concerned, and they have acknowledged them as a valid representation of the processes involved.
3. In a further fourteen cases the social workers responsible said they would have made a positive recommendation for a care order had they not been on strike.
4. We do not wish to imply that these decisions once made are fixed for all time. Social workers' assessment of moral character only holds until further notice. Our research suggests that such assessments can change, particularly after residential assessment or further delinquency. We have not discussed this issue in this paper but it is discussed in Giller and Morris (1981).

Chapter 6

1. Jimmy Martin was a limbless boy who was successively refused the higher and lower rate attendance allowance and whose case received considerable attention in Parliament and the press.

Chapter 8

1. Approximately 30 per cent of all associations registered in the West Midlands were in breach of this criterion. (See note 2 for details of study.)
2. Research conducted from 1976 to 1979 in the West Midlands covering a sample of housing associations (eighty) operating in that area. Full report available as *Imperfect Implementation: A Study of the Housing Corporation Administration of the 1974 Housing Act*, Centre for Urban and Regional Studies, University of Birmingham, 1980.

Chapter 11

1. The system of Children's Hearings is I think based upon a consensual model,
   which may be inapplicable to our society. Even so, participation, in this area of
   social regulation or any other, may help develop consensus, even where the
   decision is legally enforceable.

References

Abel, R. (1973), 'Law Books and Books about Law', *Stanford Law Review* **26,** pp. 175–228.

Abler, R., Adams, J. S. and Gould, P. (1977), *Spatial Organisation*, London, Prentice Hall.

Adler, M. and Asquith, S. (1979), Workshops on Discretionary Decision-making in Law and Social Policy: final report, London, SSRC.

Albrow, M. (1970), *Bureaucracy*, London, Macmillan.

Alderson, J. (1977), 'From Resources to Ideas', *Ditchley Conference Papers on Preventive Policing*.

Althoff, P. and Rush, M. (1972), *An Introduction to Political Sociology*, Indianapolis, Bobbs-Merrill.

Arrow, K. J. (1972), 'Gifts and Exchanges', *Philosophy and Public Affairs* **1,** (4), pp. 343–62.

Asquith, S. (1977), 'Relevance and Lay Participation in Juvenile Justice', *British Journal of Law and Society* 4 (1), pp. 61–76.

Asquith, S. (1979a), 'Legality and the Hidden Politics of Delinquency', in P. Brown and T. Bloomfield (eds.), *Legality and Community: the Politics of Juvenile Justice in Scotland*, Aberdeen People's Press.

Asquith, S. (1979b), 'Legal and Welfare Modes of Thought in Juvenile Justice', in J. Selosse (ed.), *Le Travail avec les Familles de Jeunes Marginaux*, Annales de Vaucresson.

Aubert, V. (1978), 'On Sanctions', in B. M. Blegvad, C. M. Campbell and C. J. Schuyt (eds.), *European Yearbook of Law and Sociology*, The Hague, Martinus Nijhoff.

Backett, M. (1977), 'Consumer Detriment in Health' in F. Williams (ed.) *Why the Poor Pay More*, London, National Consumer Council.

Bachrach, P., and Baratz, M. S. (1970), *Power and Poverty*, New York, Oxford University Press.

Baldwin, J. D. and Baldwin, J. I. (1978), 'Behaviorism on *verstehen* and *erklären*', *American Sociological Review* **43** (June), pp. 335–47.

Baldwin, J. and Bottomley, A. K. (1978), *Criminal Justice: selected readings*, London, Martin Robertson.

Balint, E. and Norel, J. S. (eds.) (1973), *Six Minutes for the Patient*, London, Tavistock.

Bankowski, Z. (1979), 'The Social Context of Juvenile Justice in Scotland', in P. Brown and T. Bloomfield (eds.), *Legality and Community: the Politics of Juvenile Justice in Scotland*, Aberdeen People's Press.

Bankowski, Z. and Mungham, G. (1978), 'Law and Lay Participation', in B. M. Blegvad, C. M. Campbell and C. J. Schuyt (eds.), *European Yearbook of Law and Sociology*, The Hague, Martinus Nijhoff.

Barry, B. (1970), *Sociologists, Economists and Democracy*, London, Collier-Macmillan.

Bateson, G. (1944), 'Cultural Determinants of Personality' in J. Hunt (ed.), *Personality and the Behavior Disorders*, New York, Ronald Press.

Becker, H. (1968), *Through Values to Social Interpretation*, New York, Greenwood Press.

Benn, A. (1973), 'Heath's Spadework for Socialism', *Sunday Times*, 25 March.

Benson, J. (1976), 'The Concept of Community' in N. Timms and D. Watson (eds.), *Talking about Welfare*, London, Routledge and Kegan Paul.

Berger, P. and Luckman, T. (1966), *The Social Construction of Reality*, London, Allen Lane.

Berlant, J. L. (1975), *Profession and Monopoly*, Berkeley, University of California Press.

Bittner, E. (1967), 'The Police on Skid-row', *American Sociological Review* **32,** (5), pp. 699–715.

Bittner, E. (1973), 'The Concept of Organization', in G. Salaman and K. Thompson (eds.), *People and Organizations*, London, Longman for the Open University Press.

Black, D. (1972), 'The Boundaries of Legal Sociology', *Yale Law Journal* **81,** pp. 1086–1100.

Black, D. (1976), *The Behaviour of Law*, London, Academic Press.

Blau, P. M. (1966), 'Orientation towards Clients in a Public Welfare Agency', *Administrative Science Quarterly* **5,** pp. 341–61.

Blau, P. M. (1963), *The Dynamics of Bureaucracy*, revised edn., Chicago, Chicago University Press.

Blaxter, M. (1976), *The Meaning of Disability: a sociological study of impairment*, London, Heinemann.

Bloor, M. J. and Horobin, G. W. (1975), 'Conflict and Conflict Resolution in Doctor-patient Interaction', in C. Cox and A. Mead (eds.), *A Sociology of Medical Practice*, London, Collier-Macmillan.

Blumberg, A. S. (1967), *Criminal Justice*, Chicago, Quadrangle Books.

Booth, A. F. (1978), 'An Administrative Experiment in Unemployment Policy in the Thirties', *Public Administration* **56** (Summer), pp. 139–57.

Bottomley, A. K. (1973), *Decisions in the Penal Process*, London, Martin Robertson.

Bottomore, T. (1979), *Political Sociology*, London, Hutchinson.

Bottoms, A. E. (1974), 'On the De-criminalization of the English Juvenile Court', in R. Hood (ed.), *Crime, Criminology and Public Policy*, London, Heinemann.

Bottoms, A. E. and Preston, E. H. (1980), *The Coming Penal Crisis*, Edinburgh, Scottish Academic Press.

Boulding, K. E. (1956), *The Image*, Ann Arbor, University of Michigan Press.

Boulding, K. E. (1967), 'The Boundaries of Social Policy', *Social Work* (USA) **12** (1), pp. 3–11.

Bradshaw, J. (1975), 'The Family Fund', in N. Newman (ed.), *In Cash or Kind*, Department of Social Administration, University of Edinburgh.

Briggs, E. and Deacon, A. (1973), 'The Creation of the Unemployment Assistance Board', *Policy and Politics* **2** (1), pp. 43–62.

Brittan, S. (1975), 'The Economic Contradictions of Democracy', *British Journal of Political Science* **5** (2), pp. 129–160.

Brody, S. R. (1976), *The Effectiveness of Sentencing: a review of the literature*, Home Office Research Study no. 35.

Brotherston, J. (1971), 'The Evolution of Medical Practice', in G. McLachlan and T. McKeown (eds.), *Medical History and Medical Care: a symposium*, London, Academic Press.

Brotherston, J. (1977), 'Inequality: is it inevitable?', in C. Carter and J. Peel (eds.), *Equalities and Inequalities in Health*, London, Academic Press.

Brown, P. D. and Bloomfield, T. (eds.) (1979), *Legality and Community: the Politics of Juvenile Justice in Scotland*, Aberdeen People's Press.

Brown, W. and Sissons, K. (1976), *A Positive Incomes Policy*, Fabian Tract 442.

Browne, E. (1978), 'Social Work Activities' in O. Stevenson and P. Parsloe (eds.) *Social Service Teams: the practitioner's view*, London, HMSO.

Bull, D. (1979), 'The Limited Language of Discretion', Paper for the Social Science Research Council Workshop on Discretionary Decision-making in Law and Social Policy.

Bull, D. (1980), 'Open Government and the Review of Supplementary Benefits', in M. Brown and S. Baldwin (eds.), *The Yearbook of Social Policy in Britain*, London, Routledge and Kegan Paul.

Burns, T. and Stalker, G. (1966), *The Management of Innovation*, London, Tavistock.

Buxton, M. J. and Klein, R. E. (1975), 'Distribution of Hospital Provision: Policy Themes and Resource Variations', *British Medical Journal*, 8 February, pp. 345–49.

Cargill, D. (1967), 'Self-treatment as an Alternative to Rationing Medical Care', *Lancet* 1, pp. 1377–8.

Carmichael, C. (1969), 'Developments in Scottish Social Work: changes in the law and implications for the future, *Applied Social Studies* **1** (1), pp. 35–42.

Carmichael, C. (1977), 'Switch on the Light', *New Society*, 20 January.

Castles, F. G., Murray, D. J. and Potter, D. C. (eds.) (1971), *Decisions, Organizations and Society*, Harmondsworth, Penguin and The Open University Press.

Chambliss, W. and Seidman, R. (1971), *Law, Order and Power*, Baton Rouge, Addison-Wesley.

Chapman, L. (1978), *Your Disobedient Servant*, London, Chatto and Windus.

Christie, N. (1977), 'Conflict as Property', *British Journal of Criminology* **17** (1), pp. 1–15.

Cicourel, A. (1977), *The Social Organization of Juvenile Justice*, 2nd edn., London, Heinemann.

Cicourel, A. and Kitsuse, J. J. (1963), *The Educational Decision-makers*, Indianapolis and New York, Bobbs-Merrill.

Clarke, J. (1980), 'Social Democratic Delinquents and Fabian Families', in National Deviancy Conference (ed.), *Permissiveness and Control*, London, Macmillan.

Cohen, S. (1974), 'Criminology and the Sociology of Deviance in Britain', in P. Rock and M. McIntosh (eds.), *Deviance and Social Control*, London, Tavistock.

Cohen, S. (1979), 'Crime and Punishment: some thoughts on theories and policies', *New Society*, 1 March.

Coleman, V. (1977), *The Medicine Men*, London, Arrow.

Cooper, M. H. (1975), *Rationing Health Care*, London, Croom-Helm.

Cornford, J. (ed.) (1975), *The Failure of the State*, London, Croom-Helm.

Corrigan, P. and Leonard, P. (1978), *Social Work Practice under Capitalism*, London, Macmillan.

Coser, L. (1956), *The Functions of Social Conflict*, London, Routledge and Kegan Paul.

Council of Europe (1980a), 13th Criminological Research Conference, *Public Opinion in relation to Crime and Criminal Justice*, Strasbourg.

Council of Europe (1980b), *De-criminalisation*, Strasbourg.

Cousins, P. (1976), 'Voluntary Organisations and Local Government in three South London Boroughs', *Public Administration* **54** (Spring), pp. 63–81.

Cox, T. (1978), *Stress*, London, Macmillan.

Crozier, M. (1964), *The Bureaucratic Phenomenon*, London, Tavistock.

Daintith, T. (1971), 'Some Characteristics of Economic Law in the United Kingdom', in G. Rinck (ed.), *Begriff und Prinzipien des Wirtschaftsrechts*, Frankfurt, Metzner.

Daintith, T. (1974), 'Public Law and Economic Policy', *Journal of Business Law*, pp. 9–22.

Daintith, T. (1976a), 'Regulation by Contract: the new prerogative', *Current Legal Problems* **32**, pp. 41–64.

Daintith, T. (1976b), 'The Functions of Law in the Field of Short-term Economic Policy', *Law Quarterly Review*, January, pp. 62–78.

Daintith, T. (1979), 'Recent Trends in the Implementation of Economic Policy and their Constitutional Consequences', paper presented at IALS legal workshop.

Dalglish, C. (1979), 'Illiteracy and the Offender', M.Sc. thesis, Cranfield Institute of Technology.

Dallmayer, F. R. and McCarthy, T. A. (eds.) (1977), *Understanding and Social Inquiry*, Notre Dame, University of Indiana Press.

Davies, B. (1968), *Social Needs and Resources in Local Services*, London, Michael Joseph.

Davies, B., Barton, A., McMillan, I. and Williamson, V. (1971), *Variations in Services for the Aged: a causal analysis*, London, Bell.

Davis, A. and Strong, P. C. (1976), 'The Management of a Therapeutic Encounter', in M. J. Wadsworth and D. Robinson (eds.), *Studies in Everyday Medical Life*, London, Martin Robertson.

Davis, K. C. (1971), *Discretionary Justice: a preliminary inquiry*, Urbana, University of Illinois Press.

Denzin, N. K. (1978), *The Research Act: a theoretical introduction to sociological methods*, 2nd edn., New York, McGraw-Hill.

Donnison, D. (1977a), 'Against Discretion', *New Society*, 15 September.

Donnison, D. (1977b), 'How Much Discretion', *Supplementary Benefits Commission Notes and News*.

Donnison, D. (1978a), 'Review of the Supplementary Benefits scheme', *Social Work Today* **10** (4), 19 September.

Donnison, D. (1978b), 'The Economic and Political Context', in J. Barnes and N. Connelly (eds.), *Social Care Research*, London, Bedford Square Press.

Donnison, D., Chapman, V., Meacher, M., Sears, A. and Unwin, K. (1975), *Social Policy and Administration Revisited*, London, Allen and Unwin.

Downes, D. and Rock, P. (eds.) (1979), *Deviant Interpretations*, London, Martin Robertson.

Dubos, R. (1960), *The Mirage of Health*, London, Allen and Unwin.

Dunlop, D. (1973), *Medicines in our Time*, London, Nuffield Provincial Hospitals Trust.

Dunsire, A. (1978), *Implementation in a Bureaucracy: Vol. I: the executive process*, London, Martin Robertson.

Dworkin, R. (1977), *Taking Rights Seriously*, London, Duckworth.

Easton, D. (1965), *A Framework for Political Analysis*, Englewood Cliffs, N.J., Prentice Hall.

Elston, M. A. (1977), 'Medical Autonomy: challenge and response', in K. Barnard and K. Lee (eds.), *Conflicts in the National Health Service*, London, Croom-Helm.

Emerson, R. (1969), *Judging Delinquents*, Chicago, Aldine.

Ennals, D. (1976), DHSS press release, 23 June.

Ermath, M. (1978), *Wilhelm Dilthey: the critique of historical reason*, Chicago, University of Chicago Press.

Fine, B., Kinsey, R., Lee, J., Picciotto, S. and Young, J. (eds.) (1979), *Capitalism and the Rule of Law: from deviancy theory to Marxism*, London, Hutchinson.

Fishbein, M. (1967), 'Attitudes and the Prediction of Behavior', in M. Fishbein (ed.), *Readings in Attitude Theory and Measurement*, New York, Wiley.

Forrester, J. W. (1969), *Urban Dynamics*, Cambridge, Mass., MIT Press.

Foster, P. (1979), 'The Informal Rationing of Primary Medical Care', *Journal of Social Policy* **8** (4), pp. 489–509.

Foucault, M. (1977), *Discipline and Punish: the birth of the prison*, London, Allen and Unwin.

Freidson, E. (1970a), *Profession of Medicine: a study of the sociology of applied knowledge*, New York, Dodd, Mead and Co.

Freidson, E. (1970b), *Professional Dominance*, Chicago, Aldine.

Freidson, E. and Rhea, B. (1963), 'Processes of Control in a Company of Equals', *Social Problems* **11** (Fall), pp. 119–31.

Friedman, L. and Macaulay, S. (eds.) (1977), *Law and the Behavioural Sciences*, 2nd edn., Indianapolis, Bobbs-Merrill.

Fuller, L. (1969), *The Morality of Law*, New Haven, Yale University Press.

Galanter, M. (1977), 'Notes on the Future of Social Research in Law', in L. M. Friedman and S. Macaulay (eds.), *Law and the Behavioural Sciences*, Indianapolis, Bobbs-Merrill.

Ganz, G. (1967), 'The Control of Industry by Administrative Process', *Public Law*, Summer, pp. 93–106.

Ganz, G. (1972), 'Allocation of Decision-making Functions' (Part II), *Public Law*, (Winter), pp. 229–308.

Ganz, G. (1974), *Administrative Procedures*, London, Sweet and Maxwell.

Garrison, F. H. (1929), *History of Medicine*, Philadelphia, W. B. Saunders & Co.

Geertz, C. (1973), 'Ideology as a Cultural System', in C. Geertz, *The interpretation of cultures*, New York, Basic Books.

Gellman, D. D., Lachaine, R. and Law, M. M. (1977), 'The Canadian Approach to Health Policies and Programs', *Preventive Medicine* **6,** pp. 265–75.

George, V. and Wilding, P. (1976), *Ideology and Social Welfare*, London, Routledge and Kegan Paul.

Giddens, A. (1976), *New Rules of Sociological Method*, London, Hutchinson.

Giddens, A. (1979), *Central Problems in Sociological Theory*, Berkeley, University of California Press.

Giller, H. and Morris, A. (1981), *Care and Discretion*, London, Burnett Books.

Gillis, J. R. (1973), *Youth and History*, London, Academic Press.

Gordon, I., Lewis, J. and Young, K. (1977), 'Perspectives on Policy Analysis', *Public Administration Bulletin* **25**, pp. 26–35.

Goss, M. (1963), 'Patterns of Bureaucracy among Hospital Staff Physicians', in E. Freidson (ed.), *The Hospital in Modern Society*, New York, Free Press.

Gough, I. (1975), 'State Expenditure in Advanced Capitalism', *New Left Review* **92**, pp. 53–92.

Gough, I. (1979), *Political Economy of the Welfare State*, London, Macmillan.

Gould, F. and Roweth, B. (1978), 'Politics and Public Spending', *Political Quarterly* **49** (2), pp. 222–7.

Gould, F. and Roweth, B. (1980), 'Public Spending and Social Policy – UK, 1950–1977', *Journal of Social Policy* **9** (3), pp. 337–58.

Gouldner, A. V. (1968), 'The Sociologist as Partisan: Sociology and the Welfare State', *American Sociologist* **3** (May) pp. 103–116.

Grace, C. and Wilkinson, P. (1978), *Negotiating the Law*, London, Routledge and Kegan Paul.

Haagensen, C. D. and Lloyd, W. (1943), *A Hundred Years of Medicine*, New York, Sheridan House.

Habermas, J. (1976a), 'Problems of Legitimation in Late Capitalism', in P. Connerton (ed.), *Critical Sociology*, Harmondsworth, Penguin Books.

Habermas, J. (1976b), *Legitimation Crisis*, London, Heinemann.

Hague, D., Mackenzie, W. and Barker, T. (1975), *Public Policy and Private Interests: the institutions of compromise*, London, Macmillan.

Hall, A. S. (1974), *The Point of Entry: a study of client reception in the social services*, London, Allen and Unwin.

Hall, P., Land, H., Parker, R. and Webb, A. (1975), *Change, Choice and Conflict in Social Policy*, London, Heinemann.

Hall, S., Critcher, C., Jefferson, T., Clarke, J. and Roberts, B. (eds.) (1978), *Policing the Crisis: mugging, the state, and law and order*, London, Macmillan.

Handler, J. (1966), 'Controlling Official Behaviour in Welfare Administration', in J. tenBroek (ed.), *The Law of the Poor*, Scranton, Pennsylvania, Chandler Publishing Co., pp. 155–86.

Hardiker, P. (1977), 'Social Work Ideologies in the Probation Service', *British Journal of Social Work* **7** (2), pp. 131–54.

Hardiker, P. and Webb, D. (1979), 'Explaining Deviant Behaviour: the social context of "action" and "infraction" accounts in the probation service', *Sociology* **17**, pp. 1–17.

Harris, J. (1979), 'What Happened after Beveridge?', *New Society*, 25 January.

Hart, H. L. A. (1961), *The Concept of Law*, Oxford, Clarendon Press.

Haug, M. (1976), 'The Erosion of Professional Authority: a cross-cultural inquiry in the case of the physician', *Health and Society* **54**, pp. 83–106.

Hegel, G. (1976), *The Philosophy of Right*, Oxford, Clarendon Press.

Hennock, E. (1968), 'The Poor Law Era', *New Society*, 29 February.

Henry, S. (1978), 'The Dangers of Self-help Groups', *New Society*, 22 June.

Herman, M. (1972), *Administrative Justice and Supplementary Benefits*, London, Bell.

Hill, M. J. (1972), *The Sociology of Public Administration*, London, Weidenfeld and Nicolson.

Hill, M. J. (1979), 'Implementation and the Central–local Relationship', in *Central–local Government Relationships*, London, SSRC.

Hodge, H. (1975), 'Discretion in Reality', in M. Adler and A. Bradley (eds.), *Justice, Discretion and Poverty*, London, Professional Books.

Hogarth, J. (1971), *Sentencing as a Human Process*, Toronto, University of Toronto Press.

Hood, C. C. (1974), 'Keeping the Centre Small', *Political Studies* **26** (1), pp. 30–46.

Hood, C. C. (1976), *The Limits of Administration*, London, Wiley.

Hood, C. C. and Bradshaw, J. R. (1977), 'Implications of an Unorthodox Agency', *Public Administration* **55** (Winter), pp. 447–64.

Hood, R. (1962), *Sentencing in Magistrates' Courts*, London, Stevens.

Howe, G. H. (1970), *A National Atlas of Disease Mortality in the United Kingdom*, London, Thomas Nelson and Sons.

Hulsman, L. H. C. (1978), *Alternatives to Criminal Justice*, address to Howard League for Scotland (unpublished).

Illich, I. (1971), *De-schooling Society*, London, Calder and Boyars.

Illich, I. (1975), *Medical Nemesis*, London, Calder and Boyars.

Illich, I. (1977), *Disabling Professions*, London, Marion Boyars.

Jackson, M. B. and Valencia, B. M. (1979), *Financial Aid through Social Work*, London, Routledge and Kegan Paul.

Jacob, P. E. and Flink, J. J. (1962), 'Values and their Function in Decision-making', *American Behavioral Scientist* (Special Supplement), May.

Jewson, N. (1974), 'Medical Knowledge and the Patronage System in 18th century England', *Sociology* **8**, pp. 369–85.

Johnson, T. (1972), *Professions and Power*, London, Macmillan.

Jones, K., Brown, J. and Bradshaw, J. (1978), *Issues in Social Policy*, London, Routledge and Kegan Paul.

Jowell, J. L. (1975), *Law and Bureaucracy: administrative discretion and the limits of legal action*, Port Washington, Dunellen.

Jowell, J. L. (1979), 'Official Discretion: problems, trends and influences', paper for the SSRC Seminar on discretionary decision-making in law and social policy.

Kagan, R. A. (1978), *Regulatory Justice*, New York, Russell Sage.

Kincaid, J. (1978), 'Plea for SB Control', *Social Work Today*, 20 July.

King, A. (1975), '"Overload": problems of governing in the 1970s', *Political Studies* **23** (2 and 3), pp. 284–96.

Klein, R. (ed.) (1975), *Social Policy and Public Expenditure 1975: inflation and priorities*, London, Centre for Studies in Social Policy.

Kluckhohn, C. (1951), 'Value Orientations in the Theory of Action', in T. Parsons and E. Shils (eds.), *Towards a General Theory of Action*, Cambridge, Harvard University Press.

Kluckhohn, F. R. and Strodtbeck, F. L. (1961), *Variations in Value Orientations*, Evanston Row, Peterson.

Labour Research (1980), *Dismantling the Welfare State*, May.

Lalonde, M. (1975), *A New Perspective on the Health of Canadians: a working document*, Ottawa, Information Canada.

Lambert, J., Blackaby, B. and Paris, C. (1978), *Housing Policy and the State: allocation, access and control*, London, Macmillan.

Lane, R. E. (1972), *Political Man*, New York, Free Press.

Lane, R. E. (1973), 'Patterns of Political Belief', in J. N. Knutson (ed.), *Handbook of Political Psychology*, San Francisco, Jossey-Bass.

La Porte, T. (1975), *Organised Social Complexity*, Princeton N.J., Princeton University Press.

Lasswell, H. and Kaplan, A. (1952), *Power and Society*, London, Routledge and Kegan Paul.

Lawson, A. (1979), 'Taking the Decision to Remove the Child from the Family', Unpublished paper presented at the Annual Conference of the British Sociological Association, University of Warwick, 9–12 April.

Lemert, E. (1967), 'Juvenile Court – Quest and Realities', *President's commission on law enforcement and the administration of justice.*

Lemon, N. (1974), 'Training, Personality and Attitude as Determinants of Magistrates' Sentencing', *British Journal of Criminology* **14** (1), pp. 34–48.

Levitt, R. (1976), *The Reorganised National Health Service*, London, Croom-Helm.

Lewin, K. (1948), *Resolving Social Conflicts*, New York, Harper and Row.

Lewin, K. (1952), *Field Theory in Social Science*, New York, Harper and Row.

Lewis, J. and Flynn, R. (1979), 'The Implementation of Urban and Regional Planning Policies', *Policy and Politics* **7** (2), pp. 123–44.

Lewis, N. (1976), 'Council Housing Allocation: problems of discretion and control', *Public Administration* **54** (Summer), pp. 147–60.

Lipsky, M. (1976), 'Toward a Theory of Street Level Bureaucracy', in W. D. Hawley and M. Lipsky (eds.), *Theoretical Perspectives on Urban Politics*, Englewood Cliffs, Prentice Hall.

Lister, R. (1975), *Justice for the Claimant* (Poverty Research Series 4), London, Child Poverty Action Group.

Lister, R. (1979a), *The No-cost No-benefit Review*, London, Child Poverty Action Group.

Lister, R. (1979b), 'Social Assistance: a civil servant's review', *Journal of Social Welfare Law*, March, pp. 133–46.

Low, C. M. (1978), 'The Sociology of Criminal Justice: progress and prospects', in J. Baldwin and A. K. Bottomley (eds.), *Criminal Justice*, London, Martin Robertson.

Lukes, S. (1974), *Power: a radical view*, London, Macmillan.

Lukes, S. (1977), 'The New Democracy', in *Essays in Social Theory*, London, Macmillan.

Lynes, T. (1975), 'Unemployment Assistance Tribunals in the 1930s' in M. Adler and A. Bradley (eds.), *Justice, Discretion and Poverty*, London, Professional Books.

Lynes, T. (1977), 'The Making of the Unemployment Assistance Scale', printed as appendix 1 of *Low Incomes*, Supplementary Benefits Administration Paper 6, London, HMSO.

MacCormick, D. N. (1978), *Legal Reasoning and Legal Theory*, Oxford, Clarendon Press.

Macintyre, S. (1978), 'Some Notes on Record Taking and Making in an Antenatal Clinic', *Sociological Review* **26** (3), pp. 595–611.

Macpherson, C. B. (1975), 'Capitalism and the Changing Concept of Property', in E. Kamenka and R. Neale (eds.), *Feudalism, Capitalism and Beyond*, London, Edward Arnold.

Marshall, T. H. (1963), 'Citizenship and Social Class', in *Sociology at the Crossroads*, London, Heinemann.

Martin, F. and Murray, K. (1976), *Children's Hearings*, Edinburgh, Scottish Academic Press.

Matza, D. (1964), *Delinquency and Drift*, New York, Wiley.

Mayer, J. and Timms, N. (1970), *The Client Speaks*, London, Routledge and Kegan Paul.

McBarnett, D. (1978), 'False Dichotomies in Criminal Justice Research', in J. Baldwin and A. K. Bottomley (eds.), *Criminal Justice*, London, Martin Robertson.

McHugh, P. (1968), *Defining the Situation*, New York, Bobbs-Merrill.

McKeown, T. (1965), *Medicine in Modern Society*, London, Allen and Unwin.

McKeown, T. (1975), 'Health and Humanism', in G. McLachlan (ed.), *Problems and Progress in Medical Care*, 5th series, London, Nuffield Provincial Hospital Trust.

McKeown, T. (1976), *The Role of Medicine; dream, mirage or nemesis?* London, Nuffield Provincial Hospital Trust.

McKeown, T. and Record, R. G. (1962), 'Reasons for the Decline in Infant Mortality in England and Wales during the Nineteenth Century', *Population Studies* **16** (2), pp. 94–122.

Mechanic, D. (1977), 'The Growth of Mechanical Technology and Bureaucracy: implications for medical care', *Health and Society* **55** (Winter), pp. 61–78.

Mey, H. (1972), *Field Theory: a study of its application in the social sciences*, London, Routledge and Kegan Paul.

Miller, G. A., Galanter, E. and Pribram, K. H. (1960), *Plans and the Structure of Behavior*, New York, Holt, Rinehart and Winston.

Millett, J. D. (1940), *The Unemployment Assistance Board: a case study in administrative autonomy*, London, Allen and Unwin.

Moore, P. (1980), 'Counter-culture in a Social Security Office', *New Society*, 10 July.

Morris, A. and Giller, H. (1977), 'The Juvenile Court: the client's perspective', *Criminal Law Review*, April, pp. 198–205.

Morris, A. and Giller, H. (1979), 'Juvenile Justice and Social Work in Britain', in H. Parker (ed.), *Social Work and the Courts*, London, Edward Arnold.

Morris, J. N. (1967), *The Uses of Epidemiology*, Edinburgh, Livingstone.

Morris, N. and Hawkins, G. (1970), *The Honest Politician's Guide to Crime Control*, Chicago, University of Chicago Press.

Murphy, A. E. (1965), *The Theory of Practical Reason* (ed. A. I. Melden), La Salle, Ill., Open Court Publications.

National Council for Social Service (1980a), *Local Voluntary Organisations and Cuts in Public Expenditure 1979–80/1980–81*, Information Sheet No. 10, January.

National Council for Social Service (1980b), *Advice Centres in Crisis*, Briefing, January.

Neisser, U. (1967), *Cognitive Psychology*, New York, Prentice Hall.

Nelken, D. (1976), 'Extending the Use of Police Cautions: a critical appraisal', *Criminal Law Review*, June, pp. 360–74.

Nelken, D. (1980a), 'Review Article: from deviancy theory to Marxism?', *International Journal for the Sociology of Law* **8**, pp. 193–212.

Nelken, D. (1980b), 'Is there a Crisis in Law and Legal Ideology?', paper delivered at International Sociological Association Conference, Madison-Wisconsin, USA.

Nelken, D. (1981), *Landlords, Law and Crime*, London, Academic Press.

Neumann, F. (1957), *The Democratic and Authoritarian State*, Glencoe, Free Press.

Niner, P. (1979), 'Associations Match Council Selection', *Roof* **4** (4), pp. 125–6.

Nonet, P. (1969), *Administrative Justice: advocacy and change in a government agency*, New York, Russell Sage.

Nonet, P. and Selznick, P. (1978) *Law and Society in Transition: toward responsive law*, New York, Octagon Books.

Nove, A. (1969), *The Soviet Economy*, London, Allen and Unwin.

Observer (1980), 'Anti-fraud Drive "Millions Short"', 3 August.

Offe, C. (1976), 'Political Authority and Class Structures', in P. Connerton (ed.), *Critical Sociology*, Harmondsworth, Penguin Books.

O'Higgins, M. (1980), *Measuring the Hidden Economy*, London, Outer Circle Policy Unit.

Oldham, J., Pickering, G., Roberts, J. A. and Sowry, G. S. (1960), 'The Nature of Essential Hypertension', *Lancet* **1**, pp. 1085–93.

Packman, J. (1975), *The Child's Generation*, Oxford and London, Basil Blackwell and Martin Robertson.

Parkes, C. M. (1971), 'Psycho-social Transitions: a field of study', *Social Science and Medicine* **5**, pp. 101–15.

Parry, M. (1977), 'Health Care' in R. Underwood (ed.), *The Future of Scotland*, London, Croom-Helm.

Parry, N. and Parry, J. (1976), *The Rise of the Medical Profession*, London, Croom-Helm.

Parsloe, P. and Hill, M. J. (1978), 'Supervision and Accountability' in O. Stevenson and P. Parsloe (eds.), *Social Service Teams: the practitioners' view*, London, HMSO.

Parsons, T. (1949), 'The Professions and Social Structure', in *Essays in Sociological Theory*, New York, The Free Press of Glencoe.

Parsons, T. (1952), 'Social Structure and Dynamic Process: the case of modern medical practice', in *The social system*, London, Routledge and Kegan Paul.

Parsons, T. (1964), *Social Structure and Personality*, New York, The Free Press of Glencoe.

Pearson, G. (1975), *The Deviant Imagination*, London, Macmillan.

Perrow, C. (1965), 'Hospitals: Technology, Structure and Goals', in J. March (ed.), *Handbook of Organizations*, Chicago, Rand-McNally.

Petch, A. (1977), *Consumer Reaction in the Social Services*, Diploma Dissertation, University of Stirling.

Peters, R. S. (1958), *The Concept of Motivation*, London, Routledge and Kegan Paul.

Pinker, R. (1971), *Social Theory and Social Policy*, London, Heinemann.

Platt, A. (1975), 'Prospects for a Radical Criminology in the USA', in I. Taylor, P. Walton and J. Young (eds.), *Critical Criminology*, London, Routledge and Kegan Paul.

Powles, J. (1973), 'On the Limitations of Modern Medicine', *Science, Medicine and Man* **1**, pp. 1–30.

Pressman, J. and Wildavsky, A. (1973), *Implementation*, Berkeley, University of California Press.

Prosser, T. (1977), 'Poverty, Ideology and Legality: supplementary benefit appeal tribunals and their predecessors', *British Journal of Law and Society* **4** (1), pp. 39–60.

Prosser, T. (1979), 'Politics and Judicial Review', *Public Law*, Spring, pp. 59–83.

Rabkin, J. and Struening, E. (1976), 'Life Events, Stress and Illness', *Science* **194**, pp. 1013–20.

Radzinowicz, L. and Hood, R. (1979), 'Judicial Discretion and Sentencing Standards: Victorian attempts to solve a perennial problem', *University of Pennsylvania Law Review* **127**, pp. 1288–1349.

Raffel, S. (1979), *Matters of Fact*, London, Routledge and Kegan Paul.

Rahe, R. H., Flóistad, I., Bergan, T., Ringdal, R., Gerhardt, R., Gunderson, E. and Arthur, R. (1974), 'A Model for Life Changes and Illness Research', *Archives of General Psychiatry* **31**, pp. 172–7.

Randall, R. (1973), 'Influence of Environmental Support and Policy Space on Organisational Behavior', *Administrative Science Quarterly* **18**, pp. 236–47.

Rees, A. M. (1972), 'Access to the Personal Health and Welfare Services', *Social and Economic Administration* **6**, pp. 34–43.

Rees, S. (1978), *Social Work Face to Face*, London, Edward Arnold.

Reich, C. A. (1963), 'The New Property', *Yale Law Journal* **73** (5), pp. 733–87.

Reich, C. A. (1964), 'Individual Rights and Social Welfare: the emerging legal issues', *Yale Law Journal* **74** (7), pp. 1245–57.

Reich, C. A. (1965), 'Law of the Planned Society', *Yale Law Journal* **75** (8), pp. 1227–70.

Rendel, M. (1970), *The Administrative Functions of the French Conseil d'etat*, London, Weidenfeld and Nicolson.

Ringen, K. (1979), 'The "New Element" in National Health Policies: the care of Norway's nutrition and food policy', *Social Science and Medicine*, 13C (1), pp. 33–41.

Rose, H. (1973), 'Who Can Re-label the Claimant', *Social Work Today*, 20 September.

Rose, R. (1979), 'Overloaded Governments: is there fire behind the smoke', *Political Studies* **27**, pp. 351–70.

Routh, G. (1980), *Occupation and Pay in Great Britain, 1906–79*, London, Macmillan.

Rowbottom, R. (1973), *Hospital Organisation*, London, Heinemann.

Sainsbury, E. (1975), *Social Work with Families*, London, Routledge and Kegan Paul.

Salaman, G. and Thompson, K. (1973), *People and Organizations*, London, Longman for the Open University Press.

Scheingold, S. A. (1974), *The Politics of Rights: lawyers, public policy and political change*, New Haven, Yale University Press.

Schmitthoff, C. (1966), 'The Concept of Economic Law', *Journal of Business Law*, October, pp. 309–19.

Schreiner, P. (1978), 'Social policy in the 1980s', Government Secretariat for Long Term Planning and Co-ordination, Oslo.

Schur, E. M. (1973), *Radical Non-intervention: rethinking the delinquency problem*, Englewood Cliffs, Prentice-Hall.

Schutz, A. (1967), 'Concept and Theory Formation in the Social Sciences', in *Collected Papers, Vol. I: the problem of social reality*, The Hague, Martinus Nijhoff.

Schutz, A. (1971), *On Phenomenology and Social Relations*, (ed. H. Wagner), Chicago, University of Chicago Press.

Scott, R. (1968), *The Making of Blind Men*, New York, Russell Sage.

Sellin, T. and Wolfgang, M. E. (1964), *The Measurement of Delinquency*, New York, Wiley.

Sharpe, T. (1978), 'Unfair Competition between Public Supported and Private Enterprises and Non-supported Enterprises', paper delivered to Tenth International Congress of Comparative Law.

Sharpe, T. (1979), 'Discretion in Economic Policy', paper for the SSRC Workshop on discretionary decision-making in law and social policy.

Sheehan, A. (1975), *Criminal Procedure in Scotland and France*, Edinburgh, HMSO.

Shonfield, A. (1965), *Modern Capitalism*, London, Oxford University Press.

Simpson, A. W. B. (1973), 'Common Law and Legal Theory', in A. W. B. Simpson (ed.), *Oxford Essays in Jurisprudence* (2nd series), Oxford, Clarendon Press.

Singer, C. and Underwood, E. A. (1962), *A Short History of Medicine*, Oxford, Clarendon Press.

Singer, P. (1973), 'Altruism and Commerce: a defense of Titmuss against Arrow', *Philosophy and Public Affairs* **2** (3), pp. 312–20.

Smith, F. B. (1979), *The People's Health, 1830–1910*, London, Croom-Helm.

Smith, G. (1977), 'The Place of "Professional Ideology" in the Analysis of "Social Policy"', *Sociological Review* **25** (4), pp. 843–65.

Smith, G. (1980), *Social Need*, London, Routledge and Kegan Paul.

Smith, G. and Harris, R. (1972), 'Ideologies and Need and the Organization of Social Work Departments', *British Journal of Social Work* **2** (1), pp. 27–45.

Stevenson, O. (1973), *Claimant or Client?*, London, Allen and Unwin.

Stevenson, O. and Parsloe, P. (1978), *Social Service Teams: the practitioner's view*, London, HMSO.

Strauss, A., Schatzman, L., Bucher, B., Ehrlich, D. and Sabshin, M. (1964), *Psychiatric Ideologies and Institutions*, London, Collier-Macmillan.

Szasz, T. and Hollender, M. (1956), 'A contribution to the Philosophy of Medicine: the basic models of the doctor–patient relationship', *Archives of Internal Medicine* **97**, pp. 585–93.

Tay, A. E. and Kamenka, E. (1975), 'Beyond Bourgeois Individualism: the contemporary crisis in law and legal ideology', in E. Kamenka and R. S. Neale (eds.), *Feudalism, Capitalism and Beyond*, London, Edward Arnold.

Tay, A. E., Kamenka, E. and Brown, R. (eds.) (1978), *The Law and Society*, London, Edward Arnold.

Taylor, I., Walton, P. and Young, J. (1973), *The New Criminology*, London, Routledge and Kegan Paul.

Taylor, I., Walton, P. and Young, J. (eds.) (1975), *Critical Criminology*, London, Routledge and Kegan Paul.

Thomas, D. (1974), 'The Control of Discretion', in R. Hood (ed.), *Crime, Criminology and Public Policy*, London, Heinemann.

Thomas, D. (ed.) (1979), *The Future of Sentencing*, Cambridge, Institute of Criminology.

Thompson, J. (1967), *Organisations in Action*, New York, McGraw-Hill.

Titmuss, R. (1958), 'The Social Division of Welfare', in *Essays on 'the Welfare State'*, London, Allen and Unwin.

Titmuss, R. M. (1968), *Commitment to Welfare*, London, Allen and Unwin.

Titmuss, R. M. (1970), *The Gift Relationship*, London, Allen and Unwin.

Titmuss, R. M. (1971), 'Welfare "Rights", Law and Discretion', *Political Quarterly* **42** (2), pp. 113–32.

Tittle, C. R. and Hill, R. J. (1967), 'Attitude Measurement and Prediction of Behavior: an evaluation of conditions and measurement techniques', *Sociometry* **30** (2), pp. 199–213.

Townsend, P. (1974), 'Inequality and the Health Service', *Lancet* **1**, pp. 1179–90.

Townsend, P. (1979), 'Social Policy in Conditions of Scarcity', *New Society*, 10 May.

Tudor-Hart, J. (1975), 'The Inverse Care Law', in C. Cox and A. Mead (eds.), *A Sociology of Medical Practice*, London, Collier-MacMillan.

Turner, H. and Wilkinson, F. (1975), 'The Seventh Pay Policy', *New Society*, 17 July.

Twining, W. and Miers, D. (1976), *How to Do Things with Rules*, London, Weidenfeld and Nicolson.

Unger, R. M. (1976), *Law in Modern Society*, New York, The Free Press.

United Nations Secretariat (1975), *United Nations, Criminal Legislation, Judicial Procedures and other forms of Social Control in the Prevention of Crime*, A/CONF. 56/7, New York.

van Meter, D. S. and van Horn, C. E. (1975), 'The Policy Implementation Process: a conceptual framework', *Administration and Society* **6** (4), pp. 445–88.

Vickers, Sir G. (1965), *The Art of Judgment*, London, Chapman and Hall.

Vickers, Sir G. (1968), *Value Systems and Social Processes*, London, Tavistock.

Vosey, M. (1975), *A Constant Burden: the reconstruction of family life*, London, Routledge and Kegan Paul.

Wadsworth, M., Butterfield, W. and Blaney R. (1971), *Health and Sickness: the choice of treatment*, London, Tavistock.

Wadsworth, M. and Robinson, D. (eds.) (1976), *Studies in Everyday Medical Life*, London, Martin Robertson.

Walker, N. (1974), 'Some Thoughts on the Penal Involvement Rate', in L. Blom-Cooper (ed.), *Progress in Penal Reform*, Oxford, Clarendon Press.

Watson, D. (1977), 'The Layman's Part', unpublished paper given to Scottish Jurisprudence Group, Stirling.

Watson, D. (1980), *Caring for Strangers*, London, Routledge and Kegan Paul.

Weir, S. and Simpson, R. (1980), 'Are the Local Authority Social Services being Bled Dry', *New Society*, 10 July.

West, P. (1976), 'The Physician and the Management of Childhood Epilepsy', in M. Wadsworth and D. Robinson (eds.), *Studies in Everyday Medical Life*, London, Martin Robertson.

Wilensky, H. (1976), *The New Corporatism: centralisation and the welfare state*, New York, Russell Sage.

Williams, B. (1973), 'Egoism and Altruism', in *Problems of the Self*, Cambridge, Cambridge University Press.

Williams, D. G. T. (1974), 'Prosecution, Discretion and the Accountability of the Police', in R. Hood (ed.), *Crime, Criminology and Public Policy*, London, Heinemann.

Wilson, J. G. (1975), *Thinking about Crime*, New York, Basic Books.

Winch, P. (1958), *The Idea of a Social Science*, London, Routledge and Kegan Paul.

Winch, P. (1972), 'Nature and Convention', in *Ethics and Action*, London, Routledge and Kegan Paul.

Winkler, J. (1975), 'Law, State and Economy: the Industry Act 1975 in context', *British Journal of Law and Society* **2** (2), pp. 103–28.

Winkler, J. (1976), 'Corporatism', *European Journal of Sociology* **17** (1), pp. 100–36.

Wittgenstein, L. (1958), *Philosophical Investigations*, (trans. G. E. M. Anscombe), Oxford, Basil Blackwell.

Wolfe, A. (1978), 'Analysing the Welfare State', *Theory and Society* **6** (20), pp. 293–9.

Wolfenden Committee, The (1978), *The Future of Voluntary Organisations*, London, Croom-Helm.

Young, K. (1977), '"Values" in the policy process', *Policy and Politics* **5** (3), pp. 1–22.

Young, K. (1979), 'Intervention as a Stress Response', Project Working Paper no. 6, School for Advanced Urban Studies, University of Bristol.

Young, K., Mason, C. and Mills, L. (1980), *Urban Governments and Economic Change*, London, SSRC.

Young, K. and Mills, L. (1980), *Public Policy Research: a review of qualitative methods*, London, SSRC.

Young, K. and Mills, L. (1981), *Managing the Post-industrial City*, London, Heinemann.

Young, P. J. (1980), 'Punishment and Social Organisation', in Z. Bankowski and G. Mungham (eds.), *Essays in Law and Society*, London, Routledge and Kegan Paul.

Youngson, A. J. (1979), *The Scientific Revolution in Victorian Medicine*, London, Croom-Helm.

Zimmerman, D. H. (1969a), 'Tasks and Troubles: the practical bases of work activities in a public assistance organization', in D. Hansen (ed.), *Explorations in Sociology and Counselling*, Boston, Houghton Mifflin.

Zimmerman, D. H. (1969b), 'Record-keeping and the Intake Process in a Public Welfare Agency', in S. Wheeler (ed.), *On Record: files and dossiers in American life*, New York, Russell Sage.

Zimmerman, D. H. (1971), 'The Practicalities of Rule Use', in J. D. Douglas (ed.), *Understanding Everyday Life*, London, Routledge and Kegan Paul.

Zola, E. and Miller, M. (1975), 'The Erosion of Medicine from Within', in E. Freidson (ed.), *The Professions and their Futures*, New York, Free Press.

Official Publications

Central Policy Review Staff (1977), *Population and the Social Services*, HMSO.

Children's Hearings (Scotland) Rules 1971, HMSO, no. 492 (S60).

Department of Health and Social Security (1976a), *Prevention and Health, Everybody's Business: a reassessment of public and personal health*, HMSO.

Department of Health and Social Security (1976b), *Sharing Resources for Health in England*, Report of the Resources Allocation Working Party, HMSO.

Department of Health and Social Security (1977a), *Priorities in the Health and Social Services: the way ahead*, HMSO.

Department of Health and Social Security (1977b), *Supplementary Benefits Handbook* (revised ed.), Supplementary Benefits Administration Paper 2, HMSO.

Department of Health and Social Security (1978), *Social Assistance: a review of the supplementary benefits scheme in Great Britain*, DHSS.

Department of Health and Social Security (1979), *Response of the Supplementary Benefits Commission to 'Social Assistance'*, Supplementary Benefits Administration Paper 9, HMSO.

Hansard (1935a), *House of Commons Parliamentary Debates*, 17 December 1934, Vol. 296.

Hansard (1935b), *House of Commons Parliamentary Debates*, 28 January 1935, Vol. 297.

Hansard (1935c), *House of Lords Parliamentary Debates*, 14 February 1935, Vol. 95.

Hansard (1972), *House of Commons Parliamentary Debates*, 29 November 1972, Vol. 847.

Hansard (1974), *House of Commons Parliamentary Debates*, 6 May 1974, Vol. 873.

Hansard (1975), *House of Commons Parliamentary Debates*, 2 February 1976, Vol. 904.

House of Commons (1978/79), *Report of the Committee on Public Accounts*, HC 327, HMSO.

Housing Corporation (1974), *Annual Report*.

Housing Corporation (1976), *Board Agenda Paper* HC/9/76.

Housing Corporation (1978), *Circular 3/78* 'In the Public Eye'.

Memorandum on the draft Unemployment Assistance (Determination of need and assessment of needs) Regulations (1934), Cmd 4791, HMSO.

Memorandum of the draft Unemployment Assistance (Determination of need and assessment of needs) Regulations (1936), Cmd 5229, HMSO.

Mortality statistics (Area) (1976) (1978), HMSO.

Public expenditure 1979–80 (1976) (White Paper), Cmnd 6393, HMSO.

Reform of the Supplementary Benefits Scheme (1979), (White Paper), Cmnd 7773, HMSO.

Report on the Committee on National Expenditure (Chairman: Sir George May) (1931), Cmd 3920, HMSO.

Report of the Committee on the Preparation of Legislation (Chairman: D. Renton) (1975), Cmnd 6053, HMSO.

Report of the Royal Commission on Unemployment Insurance (Chairman: Holman Gregory) (1932), Cmd 4185, HMSO.

Report of the Unemployment Assistance Board for 1935 (1935/36), Cmd 5177, HMSO.

Report of the Unemployment Assistance Board for 1937 (1937/38), Cmd 5752, HMSO.

Report of the Royal Commission on Medical Education (Chairman: Lord Todd) (1968), Cmnd 3569, HMSO.

Report of the Royal Commission on the National Health Service (Chairman: A. Merrison) (1979), Cmnd 7615, HMSO.

Report of the Supplementary Benefits Commission for 1976 (1977), Cmnd 6910, HMSO.

Report of the Supplementary Benefits Commission for 1977 (1978), Cmnd 7392, HMSO.

Report of the Supplementary Benefits Commission for 1978 (1979), Cmnd 7725, HMSO.

Royal Commission on the National Health Service (1978), *Allocating Health Resources: a commentary on the report of the Resource Allocation Working Party*, Research paper number 3, HMSO.

Social Work (Scotland) Act 1968, HMSO, Chapter 49.

The General Household Survey – 1976 (1977), HMSO.

The Government and the Voluntary Sector: a consultative document (1978), Home Office.

The Unemployment Assistance (Determination of Need and Assessment of Needs) Regulations 1934 (1934), SRO 1424.

The Unemployment Assistance (Determination of Need and Assessment of Needs) Regulations 1936 (1936), SRO 776.

Index